The reagan revolution and the developing
countries (80-90) a seminal decade for predicting
the world economic future

The reagan revolution and the developing countries (80-90) a seminal decade for predicting the world economic future

Together with a long term historical perspective with implications for predicting the world economic future

LAWRENCE FEINER AND
RICHARD MELSON

iUniverse, Inc.
Bloomington

The Reagan Revolution And The Developing
Countries (80-90) A Seminal Decade For
Predicting The World Economic Future

Together With A Long Term Historical Perspective With
Implications For Predicting The World Economic Future

iUniverse books may be ordered through booksellers or by contacting:

iUniverse
1663 Liberty Drive
Bloomington, IN 47403
www.iuniverse.com
1-800-Authors (1-800-288-4677)

ISBN: 978-1-4620-6189-1 (sc)
ISBN: 978-1-4620-6190-7 (ebk)

Printed in the United States of America

iUniverse rev. date: 10/27/2011

CONTENTS

CHAPTER 1

HOW TO THINK ABOUT THE FUTURE

On June 4, 1992, a conference entitled *Scanning the Future*:

Perspectives for the World Economy up to 2015 took place in The Hague.

A Japanese participant, Chikashi Moriguchi, Director of the Osaka Institute of Social and Economic Research, prefaced his speech by saying, "Scanning the Future is one of the most interesting topics for us Japanese, whose national hobby is forecasting. Jesus Christ said 'Don't worry about tomorrow', and western civilization seems to be observing his teaching; a mass society is preoccupied with enjoying the present. Meanwhile oriental wisdom teaches us (as Japanese) to 'worry about tomorrow'."

On the other hand, an American participant, the American economist, Rudiger Dornbusch of MIT said, "I think anyone who is right on a 25 year outlook either is a lunatic or else is unbearably lucky."

Indeed, the idea of a future that was, in any sense, predictable has often seemed strange to the western mind.[1] After all, the British economist Lord Keynes said, "In the long run, we're all dead" and the classical Greek playwrite Aeschylus said, "You'll know the future when it happens. Until then don't think about it."

Nonetheless, within the last several years, American anxieties about the long term future have begun to mount. More and more American books have appeared which attempt to analyze the long term future. Few of these books, in our opinion, have adequately conceptualized how to do such an analysis. This is not surprising. The last 100 years of American experience make it very difficult to know how to think about the long term future. After all, within the last century, the lives of each new generation of Americans have been totally transformed by radically new technologies, technologies whose existence was unknown to previous generations. Who, in the 19th century, for example, could have predicted television or nuclear weapons? Who, in 1930, could have predicted the transistor? And who, as recently as 1984, could have predicted the existence of high temperature superconductivity? Surely, the future will be heavily influenced, if not determined, by radically new technologies the physics and chemistry of which is unknown today[i]. And, if the natural science of these new technologies is as yet unknown, then, surely, the social and economic implications of these technologics must be equally unknown. In fact, it's almost laughably easy to construct technological scenarios that so change everything as to render forecasting impossible. For example, In The Great Reckoning, 1992, J. D. Davidson and Lord W. Rees-mogg construct the following scenario:

"As unlikely as it may seem, a supercomputer could be possible in a form so tiny that it would fit comfortably in a single human cell. Such molecular computers would make possible the construction of numerically controlled assemblers for manipulating matter at the atomic level—which is known as nanotechnology . . . Human control over nature at the molecular level implies a new, post-industrial strength magic. Scientists who study nanotechnology believe that within decades self-replicating molecular 'machines' will be able to construct practically any product the heart desires—almost without assistance from human labor. Inanimate objects—from an automobile to a baked Alaska—could be programmed for assembly in much the same way that living organisms are programmed by genetic coding, built cell by cell, or molecule by molecule, from a soup of raw ingredients. Think what that might mean . . . Those who design nanotechnology will be able to totally control oven physically alter other human beings. Invisible machines, programmed through Artificial Intelligence, could literally force anyone to behave in any way the . . . programmer wished. It would no longer be necessary to put a gun to someone's head to force obedience."

The authors use this technological development to forecast "a new feudalism". Their analysis goes like this. In the same way that stirrups and mounted armor allowed landed barons and their knights to "privatize" political and power, so, according to The Great Reckoning, will nanotechnology allow its owners to privatize political power.

A striking scenario, to be sure, but, realistically, how could one even begin to determine when, if ever, such technology will become viable, and what its impact will be when it does? A development like this would foil all previous attempts at prediction. And, of course, one could extend such "techno-fantasizing" forever. One could, for example, postulate an artifical virus that turns all living matter into polystyrene, or a defective "cold fusion" car that blows up the planet when you step on the accelerator, and so on[ii]. The basic point is that, if, the future = the present + technological surprises which change everything then, the future is inherently unknowable, since radically new technologies are inherently unknowable. After all, a known + an unknown is also an unknown.

Environmental Unknowns

Another factor that might have enormous and potentially unpredictable effects on all aspects of human life is global environmental change. For example, in the early 20th century, scientists such as Svante Arrhenius, and others, predicted that increases in the atmospheric concentration of carbon dioxide, caused by the industrial revolution, could eventually bring about large changes in the global climate. In the early 1970's, predictions were made that chlorofluorcarbons from spray cans and exhaust from stratospheric passenger jets could eventually cause a reduction in stratospheric ozone and a consequent increase in ultraviolet radiation with damaging health effects. However, up until the mid 1980's, it was assumed that fundamental global environmental change would, if it took place at all, take place gradually, over the course of centuries, or perhaps over the course of generations at worst. This assumption was shattered in 1985 when an enormous hole in the stratospheric ozone layer was discovered over the antarctic. In the next two years it was demonstrated that this hole in the ozone layer was almost certainly due to chloroflurocarbon pollution. Worldwide observations over the next several years showed that the global stratospheric ozone layer worldwide was being depleted at a rate faster than anyone had anticipated, with consequences that have yet to be determined.

In other words, global environmental change, possibly very destructive global environmental change, need not take place gradually, but could come on suddenly and in a totally unexpected way. Therefore, one can never rule out the possibility of a "global environmental surprise" whose repercussions will foil all previous attempts at prediction. And, of course, if one is in a "doomsday mood", it's all to easy to concoct such "world altering" environmental scenarios. Here's an example from The End of Nature, by Bill McKibben:

"Some of the potential feedbacks (of global warming) are so large that they might make us forget someday what caused the original warming. We have already looked at one: the potential release of methane trapped in the tundra and the mud of the sea that would enormously add to the warming blanket around the earth. But methane is a little hard to imagine. It's easier and—and more troubling to me to think about the forest—All told forests, plants and soil (which gives up its carbon more rapidly as trees die) contain something more than 2 trillion tons of carbon, probably more than a third of it in the middle and high latitudes. 'We're working with maybe a million tons that could be mobilized,' says George Woodwell, an ecologist and director of the Woods Hole Research Center. By contrast the atmosphere now contains only 750 billion tons. So even a fairly small change in the forests could substantially increase the amount of carbon in the atmosphere, exacerbating the warming. There are signs—frightening signs—that some of these feedback loops are starting to kick in, that the warm years of the 1980's may be triggering an endless cycle."

One could concoct many examples of such "downward spirals". For example, melting of the polar ice caps could increase the amount of heat absorbed by the earth and thus increase the global warming. A hotter climate could lead to more forest fires which could release more carbon dioxide and thus could increase global warming. Increased ultraviolet radiation from ozone depletion could destroy marine organisms that take down carbon dioxide from the atmosphere and thus could increase global warming, and so on. In fact, anything could happen. (And does happen in the popular environmental literature.) Therefore, the future = the present + technological surprises which change everything + global environmental surprises which change everything

A known plus two unknowns equals an unknown. The long term future is doubly unpredictable. Worrying about it becomes like worrying about the afterlife. Not the kind of worrying that can form the basis of a rational business plan.

Into an Endless Labyrinth

One attempt to get around this dilemma is to use the scenario approach, in which one asks conditional questions, questions such as: "What will the effect of a longer growing season be on Russian agriculture, assuming that there is a longer growing season?", or "What will the effect of robots with human levels of intelligence on employment be, assuming that such robots are ever developed." One answers these questions with conditional predictions, predictions such as:, "If the average global temperature rise is such and such over the next 50 years, then the economic consequences will be so and so" or "If cheap room temperature superconducting wires become feasible, then the effect on the energy industry will be thus and so", etc.

While the scenario approach might seem like a logical way to analyze the future, in fact it's not. This is because it leads to so many combinations, permutations, and bifurcations, that it ultimately defeats all attempts at analysis.

To illustrate this point, let's look at Prof. Paul Kennedy's book, *Preparing for the 21th Century*. This book compares the current global situation to the situation in 18th Europe. At that time, Europe was experiencing a population explosion. There were predictions that continued growth of population would eventually result in a "demographic catastrophe" (famines, upheavals, wars, etc.) In fact, this demographic catastrophe was averted by the industrial and agricultural revolutions, which, by vastly increasing economic output, allowed the increased population to be fed and housed. Today, the world as a whole is experiencing a far larger population explosion. In addition (according to Prof. Kennedy) the world is also experiencing two new revolutions; a "new industrial revolution" and a "new agricultural revolution". The new industrial revolution is the use of robotics in manufacturing, and the new agricultural revolution is the use of biotechnology in plant breeding. Will these two revolutions, allow a future "demographic catastrophe" to be avoided? Will they allow a future environmental catastrophe to be avoided?

Prof. Kennedy proceeds by trying to "cover all the bases". What will happen, he asks, if agriculture is replaced by factory production of food? What will happen if manufacturing becomes 100% automated? What will happen to Asia if global warming drastically reduces rice yields? What will happen to Asian rubber growers if in vitro production of rubber becomes a reality? What will happen if the Russian permafrost melts? And so on. The problem with this approach is that it's like trying to play chess by analyzing all possible sequences of chess board configurations. The task it attempts, isn't humanly possible. What then can one expect from the attempt? Obviously this.

"It could be that richer nations with food deficits will embrace the biotech revolution to save foreign exchange on imported agricultural goods, whereas food-surplus countries will restrict the technology out of deference to their farming constituencies. Here, of course, the contrast between Japan's position and that of the United States and Europe could not be more marked. Japan's difficult geography is exactly the sort of terrain that crop biotechnology is designed to enhance, while animal growth hormones would benefit Japan's consumers—now moving towards a meat diet—and contribute to national self sufficiency in food . . . Such a differentiated response could lead to further tensions over agricultural trade, as food exporting countries like Australia and the United States find that their produce, while needed by developing countries unable to pay for it, is not required by richer nations increasingly able to create their own biotech substitutes at home. Japanese-American relations, already soured by other commercial quarrels, would only worsen if Japan were no longer a major market for American farm exports."

This is an example of what we call the scenario approach. It makes a complicated series of assumptions. It assumes that Japan replaces American farm exports with biotechnology. It assumes that no compensating markets appear in the developing world. It assumes that the Japanese biotechnology industry requires no imports of American goods or services. It assumes that American businesses makes no breakthroughs in biotechnology (as they have in computer technology) which give them an advantage in the Japanese market. And it assumes that no other events materialize to improve Japanese-American relations despite the drop American-Japanese agricultural trade. If you take away the assumptions, you are left with the not very informative statement that, if biotechnology comes to have a significant effect on the composition of Japanese-American trade, it will also have a significant effect on Japanese-American trade relations. Which illustrates another problem with the scenario approach to analyzing the future. The scenario approach tends to lead to a kind of analysis that we call a "reverse anachronism". A "reverse anachronism" is an analysis which projects a complex chain of causes and effects forward into the future, while tacitly assuming that everything else remains constant. The problem, however, is that everything else never remains constant. This is because human history evolves as a totality. There is very little that can be "left to one side".

To illustrate this point further, let's look at another example of a "reverse anachronism":

"Companies in the developed world are investing in new technologies which could greatly harm poor societies, by providing substitutes for millions of jobs in agriculture and industry . . . If the biotech revolution can make redundant certain forms of farming, the robotics revolution could eliminate many type of assembly and manufacturing jobs . . . Marvelous though the technologies may be, they neither offer solutions to the global demographic crisis nor bridge the gap between North and South." P. Kennedy, 1993.

In other words, while biotechnology and robotics might have the potential to feed the world's expanding population, they will not actually accomplish this task, because they will make most of the world's people redundant? This statement assumes that people not needed for manufacturing, or for certain types of farming, will, in the future, not be needed for anything. In fact, whatever happens in the future, it's hard to imagine that the task of global economic development for the billions of people in the world, including the production and distribution of goods and services, the construction of infrastructure and housing, the provision of health care services including birth control services, the recycling and disposal of waste, and the restoration of the environment to the extent that it should be necessary, could possibly be accomplished without the efforts of billions of people, even if manufacturing is done by robots, and even if food is produced in factories. It's not going to be carried out by someone sitting at a console. Of course, whether, and to what extent, such global development actually takes place, in what regions of the world, in what manner, and with what effects on the people involved, is more or less the history of the next century, and will be affected by so many factors that one could spend a lifetime just listing them.

This brings us back to our basic dilemma, which is; How does one think about the future, when there are so many variables, and so many interconnections, that any attempt to "reason our way forward" immediately leads us into an endless maze?

In economics, this dilemma is gotten around by means of a device known as a general equilibrium model. A general equilibrium model is a system of mathematical equations which expresses all the interconnections between the relevant variables. What we would really like to have is a general equilibrium model for all of human history. Unfortunately, such a device is about as likely as the prospect of Bill Clinton "growing" the entire world economy by sitting at a console and creating nanotechnological microbes.

History and Prophecy

So where does that leave us? First of all, it leaves us in a position where we just have to accept the fact that, in the future, a technological, or environmental development could emerge that renders all previous predictions pointless. Now, while this state of affairs might seem to make our dilemma insoluble, it actually points the way to a partial solution. The solution we have in mind is this: We will look for as many trends as possible which are as invariant as possible to as wide a range of environmental scenarios as possible and to as wide range of technological scenarios as possible. This will give us a "stable platform" from which to analyze current developments and predict future trends. Our primary goal in this effort, by the way, is not simply to extrapolate from current tendencies, but rather to "see around corners" and to predict future "surprises". We have found, over the past 20 years, that this "stable platform" approach has enabled us to make predictions that are more right than wrong most of the time, and which anticipated many things that people called "surprises".

To begin with, here is an example of a trend that is invariant to a wide range of technological scenarios and wide range of environmental scenarios. It is taken from the *World Bank Development Report* of 1991:

"No matter what the outlook in the industrial countries, the world's long-term prosperity and security—by sheer force of numbers—depends on LDC development."

Now this statement might sound like a pious platitude, the kind of pious platitude that is always showing up in World Bank Development Reports, too vague to be of any use in making predictions. On the other hand, it is amazing how many predictions, over the past 20 years, have gone astray precisely on this point. In fact, we can say that the main driving force for change, in the next century, will be the relations between the rich countries and poor countries; the main driving force for change, at present, is the relations between the rich countries and poor countries; and the main driving force for change, over the past 30 years, has been the relations between the rich countries and poor countries.

Now this statement might sound too extreme. However, we will show, in this book, that, not only is this statement true, but that it is also very useful for making predictions. To elucidate a bit, let's quote from our own book, Toward the 21th Century, published in Japan in 1985:

"Here's a helpful way of thinking about the long term future, Suppose you are walking down a path and you want to see into the distance. What can you do? Well, you can go up. You can climb to the top of a tree, say, or go upward in a balloon or helicopter. The further up you are, the further ahead you are able to see. Suppose, now, that we could look at human society in a glance as though it were a landscape. Suppose that we were to get into an imaginary spaceship and go upward ten to twenty thousand miles from the earth and then look at human society as it distributes itself over the surface of the earth. What would we see? We would see islands of overdevelopment surrounded by a sea of underdevelopment! We would see a small minority of the earth's population living in developed, industrial societies, with mechanical means of production, mechanical means of transportation, electronic and mechanical means of communication, with a relatively high standard of living, a long life expectancy and a low infant mortality rate. And then we would see the majority of human beings on the planet living in societies that we would call underdeveloped, societies with high infant mortality rates, with an enormous amount of poverty and in some cases with outright famine and starvation. In fact, if one looks at human society as a whole from a global point of view, one comes to the conclusions that human society as a whole is in a chronic state of underdevelopment.

Now in fact this image of human society from outer space gives one a great deal of information about the long term future. It gives one a great deal of information about what future economic problems and opportunities are going to be like. It gives one a great deal of information about future trends not only in economics finance and politics but also in art, fashion and culture. In other words, we will show that this mental image of human society as seen from outer space is a good place to start in evaluating the future.

For the moment, let's address the present. Certainly this image of the planet as islands of overdevelopment in a sea of underdevelopment, this image of the planet as composed of a developed section and an underdeveloped section, a rich section and a poor section, might seem rather remote from the mind of the average middle class American.

Not so! On a subconscious level, the average American is intensely aware of this mental image and is in fact intensely disturbed by it. In fact, over the course of the last decade, this sub-conscious image in the American psyche of the gap between the rich and poor sections of the planet has been the driving force behind most of the political developments that have taken place in the United States. In this book, we will show many of the issues and fashions in the United States over the past ten years such as neo-conservatism, supply side economics, Reaganism, protectionism, the so-called 'Black/Jewish' conflict, Christian fundamentalism, yuppy-ism, drugs, terrorism, all of these disparate issues are at root nothing other than the so-called 'North/South' problem in disguise.

More generally, looking at the details of any particular political trend or movement gives one a lot of information about the overall structure of human society and, conversely, looking at the overall structure of human society gives one a great deal of new perspective on the details of any particular political trend or movement.

Let's take an example of this from American political life. Certainly everyone is aware of the enormous and voluminous press coverage given to the Arab/Israeli dispute. And certainly almost everybody has wondered why a dispute between the Israelis and the Palestinians, who together comprise a very small percentage of the world's population, should command so much of the world's attention.

Of course, the obvious explanation is that the holy land, Palestine/Israel was the origin of the West's Judeo-Christian heritage and thus would always command the world's attention for symbolic reasons. This explanation, while not false, does not in fact really explain the phenomenon. It does not, for example, explain why the Japanese and Asians are so concerned with this issue, or why this issue is so much more continuously 'on people's minds' than it was in the past. Our mental image of human society gives us the explanation.

The reason why the Arab/Israel dispute has such emotional and symbolic resonance is that it represents in microcosm the cleavage between the developed and underdeveloped areas of the world, the so-called 'North/South gap'. Since 1967, in particular, the Palestinians have become symbolic of Third World aspirations as a whole and the Jews and Israelis have become symbolic of the aspirations of the West as a whole.

When the Palestinian cause is seen to be gaining favor, this is seen as an 'omen' or 'portent' that the Third World as a whole is gaining in status and importance, and that the concerns of its populations will have a greater importance in the future.

Conversely, when the Israeli cause seems to be gaining favor (as after the Achille Lauro incident in '85) this is seen as an 'omen' that the population of the Third World are marginal to the West's long term future.

Thus, the Arab/Israeli dispute is followed anxiously and nervously by many people all over the world because it represents 'portent' of 'where the world is headed'.

So, to reiterate what we are saying, an intense, possibly subconscious, awareness of the North-South divide lies at the root of most of the issues, trends and fashions in American public life today. Many examples of this fact can be given. Let's take one such example and look at Christian Fundamentalism from this perspective.

A while ago there was a lady on *the MacNeil/Lehrer* show who was objecting to 'secular humanist' books in school libraries. Her basic objection to secular humanism was that if 'Buddha, Mohammed, Christ and Moses were all just religious leaders and all the same' then 'wouldn't those people out there want to come here and take what we have?' In other words, if you accept secular humanism, then how do you justify the gap between 'them' and 'us'. To continue with this example, back in 1984, after Reagan gave a (for him) pro-UN speech advocating more funding for Third World loans, the TV fundamentalist preacher Jimmy Swaggart gave a sermon in which he said, 'The Devil has entered the White House'.

Many other examples will be given in future chapters of disparate issues such as drugs, trade, population, the environment, contras and others in which the underlying issues is the relations between the rich and poor areas of the planet.

Let's go back to our overall mental image of human society as islands of overdevelopment in a sea of underdevelopment. Let's add on another dimension, the time dimension.

What is the time dimension of human society as seen from a great distance? To get this time dimension, let's go back not just ten or twenty years, but two hundred years to the beginnings of industrial capitalism in England. Industrial capitalism had its origins in the textile industry in England. It then spread to other sectors of the economy such as mining, metals, railroads and agriculture. It then spread from beyond its origins in England to other areas of the world. It spread to Europe. It spread to the United States. It spread to Australia. It spread to some regions and sectors of the less developed countries.

So, to oversimplify enormously, the time dimension of our mental image of human society is the spread of industrial capitalism from its origins in the textile industry in England into more and more geographical areas of the earth and into more and more sectors of human activity.

Now let's put the space dimension and the time dimension together to complete our mental image of human society. To do this, pretend that we get into our mental spaceship and go ten thousand miles from earth to look at human society from a great distance. Pretend, furthermore, that an alien astronaut approaches us, points to the earth and says, 'Tell me what's going on down there. What are those billions of human beings doing? And be brief. Tell me in one page.' Here's what our answer would sound like:

The global system of industrial capitalism is trying to expand from its base in the developed economies into the less developed areas of the world. For the past 20 years, the capitalist world economy has been trying to expand into the LDC's and has been constantly running against two barriers to this expansion, namely agricultural and social backwardness in the LDC's and anti-Third World sentiment in the developed economies. The various crises and difficulties of the past 20 years, the oil shock, the LDC debt crisis, the Iranian upheaval, the problems in the Middle East are all due to the shock waves generated by the turbulent expansion of the capitalist system into the less developed areas of the world.

In other words, the various blockages to sustainable development which have historically afflicted the 'peripheral' less developed economies are afflicting the world economy as a whole, creating a global economic crisis of stagnation whose main effects are in the less developed areas of the world, but which none the less has important repercussions in the developed economies as well."

We will discuss these issues in more detail in later chapters. In this chapter, however, we will continue to play "the devil's advocate" and will stress the difficulties involved in predicting future trends. Take, for example, the problem of analyzing the future of a poor, underdeveloped country. Of course, it's easy enough to say that poverty and discontent can lead to violence and upheaval. On the other hand, poverty and discontent can also lead to ingenuity and resourcefulness. Ingenuity and resourcefulness, under the right circumstances, can lead to economic development; and economic development, after all, consists of millions of individual decisions, many of them ingenious and many of them inspired, arrived at by millions of individual people, decisions which cannot possibly be second guessed in advance. And, if we cannot predict human resourcefulness in advance, then how can we possibly predict economic development in advance? And if things are complicated in a single country, then how can they be anything less than a thousand times more complicated for the world as a whole, where we have to take into account all the ideas and inspirations that can come from billions of minds?

And, if this isn't bad enough, what about the role of chance and accident in shaping the future? The Islamic Fundamentalists, for example, believe that chance was the most important factor in human history.

"The (Ummayad) coup d' etat which changed the nature of power (from Islamic to non-Islamic) was the result of an unfortunate chance, if (the Caliph) Ali had arrived sooner all of history would have been different." S. Qutb, 1949.

While this is not the place to get into a long metaphysical discussion on the role of chance in human affairs, it is certainly reasonable to assume that chance and accident do play an important role in shaping history, and, furthermore, they play a role which is potentially decisive, a role not confined merely to random deviations from some sort of a trend. For example, in the spring of 1993, The National Interest devoted a special edition to the death of communism. The main question addressed in this edition was why, with all the scholarly effort devoted to the Soviet Union and communism since the beginning of the cold war, did no one even come close to predicting that communism and the Soviet Union would utterly collapse within a period of three years. The main conclusion reached by many of the authors was that there was a large element of chance in the collapse of the Soviet Union. Specifically, had someone other than Gorbachev succeeded to Chernenko as leader of the Soviet Union in 1985, the Soviet Union could have survived for decades, or possibly for a good deal longer.

"As chance would have it, the 1985 succession brought to office an aberrant figure whose course toward revolution . . . was not forced on him by an aroused society or by compelling circumstances; it stemmed from his highly individual perceptions and experimental bent, his openness to the ideas of intellectuals . . . and the erosion of his commitment to Marxist-Leninist ideology and the Stalinist institutions to which it had given rise. The Soviet system of cadres selection was designed to prevent leaders with such political characteristics from advancing in it. That Gorbachev nevertheless rose to its summit, winning the office that enabled him to command the Party's vast personnel and resources, was due to a series of fortunate events that borders on the providential." M. Rush, 1993

The historic events now taking place in the eastern bloc countries, the dramatic shift in the global balance of power, the opening of a vast new region to outside investment, the change in the global nuclear threat, the sudden fragmentation in political authority and the radical economic changes in over one sixth of the earth's land area, all these things are having an enormous effect on world politica as a whole. The Gulf war, the war in the Balkans, the European monetary crisis, the conflict between the US and Israel over the settlements, the ending of 12 years of Republican Presidential rule are all related, in some way, to the collapse of communism and the ending of the cold war. Since many of these events were surprising when they took place, a general impression seems to have arisen that world politics as a whole is "chaotic" and unpredictable. This has led to a new "world view", expressed by such books as Out of Control by Zbigniew Brzezinski, and Pandemonium by Senator Daniel Patrick Moynihan, that chaos, chance and political fragmentation are now the order of the day.

This alone would seem to pose insuperable difficulties for prediction.

Nonetheless, we still maintain (and will demonstrate in this book) that these difficulties can be partially overcome. We say this because, despite the inherent unpredictability of human behavior, historical tendencies and processes do exist which have a great deal of "historical inertia". Structural patterns in global society do exist which persist over very long periods of time.

Although E. L. Jones (1994) (in our opinion) overstates the case when he conjectures that "world affairs behave as if propelled by a mixture of deterministic processes, to which we may find some clues by careful analysis, and stochastic (random) ones that are likely to wrench the entire system off course from time to time", nonetheless, we agree that it can be useful to act as though this were true, because it is the search for such historical "deterministic processes" that will enable us to build a "stable conceptual platform", from which to analyze the future for a span of 10 years to 40 years forward.

Our goal in short is to use historical "deterministic processes" in order to predict and analyze future "surprises". Now this might seem like a confusing and contradictory metaphor, so let's explain it.

Historical processes are usually discussed with reference to:

(1) linear trends, i.e. as time passes, technological capabilities and scientific knowledge advance, economic output increases, etc.;
(2) cyclical patterns of a repeating nature, i.e. the rise and fall of dynasties, the "swing of the pendulum" from conservative to liberal, liberal to conservative, and so on; and
(3) turning points and surprises of the "this changes everything" variety; i.e. the OPEC price rises of the 70's and the fall of communism in 1989-1991.

Historical analyses have been used to extrapolate linear trends in order to provide future prognoses. For example: "technological advances have propelled economic growth in the West for the last 200 years and so they will for the next 200 years." Analyses of cyclical patterns in history have been used to provide "lessons of history" which supposedly shed light on current conditions. For example: "Spain declined when it spent too much on the military, and England declined when it spent too much on the military, and now it's America's turn to decline because it spent too much on the military." or "hyperinflation in the Weimar republic led to a fascist takeover and so it will in Russia."

However, in analyzing an extreme "discontinuity", such as, for example, the fall of communism, there is a tendency to assume that historical reasoning is of little use, that the effect of the past has been overwhelmed. After the end of the cold war in 1989, for example, there was even talk of the "end of history" (F. Fukuyama, 1989). The point that we want to stress, however, is that it is precisely when such a historical "discontinuity" occurs that historical analysis is most useful in projecting future trends. This is because the same historical "equations of motion" which, at certain times, can produce gradual linear change, can also, at other times, lead to sudden, drastic, surprising and seemingly discontinuous change, change which can cause conventional forecasting methods, based on some form of linear extrapolation, to "go haywire". To give a physical analogy, let's look at gravitational motion in a vacuum. The same gravitational equations of motion, which cause planets, comets, and asteroids to move in a smooth and predictable way, can also cause asteroids to "tumble" in an erratic, chaotic and seemingly random way.

It's important to stress here that we use terms like "equations of motion" or "linear trend" simply as metaphors. We have no intention of reproducing a fallacy known as historicism (See H. Meyerhoff, 1959), the attempt to divine the underlying causes of history. Our aim here is not to divine the underlying causes of history, but simply to gain enough historical intuition; to enable us, not merely to extrapolate from current trends, but also, as much as possible, to "see around corners", and to predict "surprises" in a way which is useful.

Before finishing this chapter, we would like to deal with yet another potential objection to our approach, which is: Why can't one worry about the future without attempting to predict it? Why can't one simply strive to stay as flexible as possible and to be prepared for any contingency? To answer this objection, we will again quote from ourselves:

"Why not just forget about the long term future, say that it is unknowable, and make no assumptions whatsoever about it, simply stay flexible and 'be prepared for anything'? Indeed, that seems to be a recent approach to managing investments and business, make no assumptions about the future and be prepared for anything.

There are two fallacies with that point of view. First of all everyone, whether they know it or now, makes assumptions about the future. Everyone is born into a certain culture and has certain cultural predispositions which include strongly held beliefs about how the world should work; assumptions which in many cases operate on a subconscious level. So you can tell yourself a thousand times over that you are prepared for anything and that you are not going to be surprised by whatever happens, but the fact is that when the future unfolds you are still going to be surprised and disoriented because one or another of your unconscious assumptions has been challenged.

It is only by an analysis of the overall structure of human society on a global scale that one can free oneself from unconscious and inaccurate assumptions about the future. One of the reasons for the failure of the econometric forecasting models in recent years is that many of them were constructed with inaccurate basic assumptions, assumptions which arose from the cultural biases of the model builders.

But there is another thing wrong with the attitude that says, 'Forget about the long term. Let's just concentrate on the short term.' The long term and the short term are interlinked. Each of the economic and political crises of the last twenty years, the oil shocks, the inflation crises, the exchange rate crises, the protectionist crises, the Third World debt crisis, the Israeli invasion of Lebanon, the American budget and deficit crises, the Iranian upheaval, are intimately interlinked with the overall long term trends in the global political economy. Each of these local crises contains within it a great deal of information about the overall direction of the global political economy and conversely each of them is actually incomprehensible unless one analyzes and understands overall global political and economic trends.

Let's look at an analogy to explain this, Let's compare long term trends to the motion of tectonic plates in geology and short term crises and upheavals to the rumblings and earthquakes produced when the tectonic plates rub up against each other. Obviously, it's going to take a long time for California, say, to separate itself from the American mainland (and if human beings invent some way of controlling the motion of tectonic plates, then maybe it never will) but the process of its doing so is very likely to have very critical short term consequences at some point. The analysis of the long term trends whether or not these trends actually work themselves out in the future is critical to understanding the short term crises and upheavals. One has to know the long term in order to understand the short term." *Toward the 21th Century,* CFG, 1985

We conclude this chapter with an outline of the book. In chapters 2, 3, 4, and 5, we will analyze and predict overall socioeconomic and political global trends. In these chapters, we will not make any speculations about future technologies or about future global environmental changes. We will not speculate, for example, about the political and moral implications of transplanting a brain from one body to another, or about what will happen if all the world's land masses turn into deserts. When, and if, such things come to pass, so much else will have changed, that predictions made now would have little relevance. Instead, the methods of analysis we will use will be confined to history, geography, economics and political science. In chapters 6 and 7, we will discuss some widely (although not universally) accepted technological and environmental prognoses, and will analyze their potential impact on the general trends discussed in the earlier chapters.

Chapters 2 and 4 will deal with economics. Our goal will be to see what economics has to say about future patterns of global economic growth. Briefly, in the future, this growth is likely to come from two sources; new technologies and new markets. Therefore, in chapter 2, we will discuss economic theories of technological change, and, in chapter 4, we will discuss economic theories of those regions of the world that will likely constitute the "new markets"; namely the less developed countries and the Eastern bloc countries.

To be more precise, in chapter 2, we will discuss an area of economics known as the new growth theories. The new growth theories, developed in the 1980's, investigate the economics of knowledge, skills, ideas, information, technological advance. These theories were developed in response to the economic events of the last 20 years, and might not be familiar to the average reader of the business and financial press. They are also, controversial, highly technical and not that easy to describe in simple English. However, they are important because much of the economic growth in the recent past has come (and much of the economic growth in the future is likely to come) from the production and exchange of intangible factors such as knowlege, skills, technologies, ideas and information. As Peter Drucker, (1993) says;

"How knowledge behaves as an economic resource we do not fully understand. We have not had enough experience to formulate a theory and to test it. We can only say so far that we need such a theory. Such a theory alone can explain the present economy . . . So far there are no signs of an Adam Smith or David Ricardo of knowledge. But the first studies of the economic behavior of knowledge have begun to appear."

It is these first studies that we will be concerned with in chapter 2. These first studies are controversial, and there is an essential reason for this controversy. Namely, how is it possible to construct an purely economic theory of knowledge when knowledge depends as much on the laws of physics, chemistry, geology and biology as it does on the laws of economics? In other words, as J. Stiglitz (1990) says, "can one really explain by economic models, the discovery of the transistor, or the laser, or the host of other breakthroughs of the last century?" We will discuss this difficulty further in chapter 2. For the moment, let's leave it to one side, and assume, for example, that knowledge means knowledge based on physical science that is already known. It means incremental improvements, incremental innovations and incremental adjustments to a currently existing base of technology, rather than a radically new, currently inconceivable, technology that could hardly be predicted by an economic theory.

In describing the new growth theories, the *Economist* (1991) says "economists are developing plausible theories that give technical progess its due weight ". In fact, modern economic growth theories have always given technical progess its due weight. The problem is that economics prides itself on being the most scientific of the social sciences. It tries, to the greatest extent possible, to confine itself to the study of phenomena that are quantifiable and measurable, and to frame its conclusions in ways that are empirically testable. Economics usually treats intangible factors, such as technology, skills, ideas or knowledge in the same way as it would treat, for example, "culture" or "mass psychology"; i.e. as factors which obviously influence economic growth, but which are not themselves explainable by economic laws.

Clearly, however, when technology and knowledge have themselves become economic commodities, then economics has to accept them into its domain of study. In doing this, economics has two choices. It can either confine itself to purely qualitative descriptions (along the lines, say, of J. Schumpeter, 1934). Or it can try to develop mathematical, empirically testable, theories, as was done by the new growth theories in the 1980's.

The achievement of the new growth theories is not simply the realization that knowledge and technical progress are very important sources of economic growth. It is rather the attempt to quantify the importance of these sources and to explain their role by means of mathematical equations which are empirically testable.

Thus, it is very difficult to explain the nature or significance of modern economic growth theories without recourse to mathematics. This is why there are so few explanations of these theories in the business and financial press. In chapter 2 of this book, we provide a survey of these theories which is 98% English. Our survey can be followed by anyone who remembers their high school algebra or who has taken a quantitative business course in college. For those who have more mathematical background, (who have an MBA for example) we provide copious notes and references.

There are also many factors in economic development, (political, institutional, and social factors, etc.), which are impossible to quantify. No mathematical theory, however ingenious, can possibly capture them all.

In order to analyze these non-quantifiable factors, we will examine the the very, very long term historical development of global society. Why the very, very long term historical development? Because, in order to analyze the future, it is not enough simply to know the present or the immediate past. The evolution of world society depends on its entire past history. To paraphrase P. Anderson (1974), a society's past lies behind it, but, in many cases, a society's past also lies in front of it. Anybody who reads the newspapers knows how often the past, even the distant past, will reemerge to play an important role in the present. In other words, (to paraphrase E. L. Jones (1994)), we will need "a very long runway" for even our relatively short "flight into the future"

Our "runway" will start in the middle of the last millennium, when most of the societies that comprise the modern world were already in existence.

"In a primitive cross section, taken about the year 775, . . . the area of (Western Society) is almost restricted to what were then the dominions of Charlemagne together with the English 'successor states' of the Roman Empire in Britain. Outside these limits, almost all of the Iberian Peninsula belongs at this date to the domain of Muslim Arab Caliphate . . . Let us call. (Western society). Western Christendom; and, as soon as bring our mental image of it into focus by finding a name for it, the images of its counterparts in the contemporary world come into focus side by side with it, especially if we keep out attention fixed on the cultural plane. On this plane, we can distinguish, unmistakably, the presence in the world today of at least four other living societies . . .:

(i) an Orthodox Christian society in South-Eastern Europe and Russia;
(ii) an Islamic society with its focus in the arid zone which stretches diagonally across North Africa and the Middle East from the Atlantic to the outer face of the Great Wall of China;
(iii) a Hindu society in the tropical sub-continent of India;
(iv) a Far Eastern society in the sub-tropical and temperate regions between the arid zones and the Pacific . . . It is interesting to note that when we turn back to . . .

775AD, we find that the number and identity of the societies on the world map are nearly the same as at the present time. Substantially the world map of societies. has remained constant since the first emergence of . . . Western Society. In the struggle for existence, the West has driven its contemporaries to the wall and entangled them in the meshes of its economic and political ascendancy, but it has not yet disarmed them of their distinctive cultures." A. Toynbee, 1959.

The West, the Islamic world, and Byzantine civilization all developed out of the wreckage of the Roman empire. While it is probably stretching it a bit to say that contemporary Russia is a descendent of Byzantium, if we make that connection, we can then say that all the societies of the contemporary world, the developed societies of the West, the transforming societies of the East and the underdeveloped societies of the south, were, from a cultural point of view, already in existence, or emerging, as far back the 8th century AD. At that time, a sort of "critical mass" of knowledge and capabilities seems to have built up in world society, so that the succeeding 1000 year period was to see a series of rapid and explosive advances in different parts of the world successively, the last and most significant of which was the European industrial revolution.

In chapter 3, we will survey the history of the various regions of the world, and the history of their interactions, in order to project the basic, overall global trends that will constitute our "stable platform".

In chapter 5, we will describe, in detail, how, for the past 13 years, the day to day and month to month political and economic changes in this country, and around the world were, to a greater extent than you might have thought possible, and to a greater extent than any time previously, "generated" and "driven" by the overall, long term historical trends outlined in chapter 3. In chapter 6, we will extend this analysis to forecast the medium and long term future.

A word about references. As you will notice, this book is based on an enormous number of references. Each chapter, however, has several main references. These main references were chosen, not necessarily because we agree with their conclusions, but because the authors of these references have the courage (some would say chutzbah) to deal with the very broad topics that this book is concerned with, and because we believe that their expositions are very good. For chapter 1, the main reference was by historian Paul Kennedy. For chapter 2 the main references are by economists Kenneth Arrow, Robert Lucas, Paul Romer and Robert Solow. For chapter 3, the main references are by historians Samir Amin, Perry Anderson, economist P. T Bauer, and historians Marc Bloch, E. L. Jones and David Landes. For chapter 5, the main references are by Zbigniew Bzrezinksi, political scientist David Calleo, supply side economist Lawrence Lindsay and Paul Volcker.

Books about the long term future usually begin with a disclaimer, something along the lines of "this book is not about prophecy but about the changes that must be made if humankind is to confront the awesome challenges., . . . etc., etc."

For our part, however, we wish to state, by way of disclaimer, that prophecy is exactly what this book is about, in the sense that we are interested, not in advocacy, but in making predictions that are useful, non-obvious, and more right than wrong, most of the time.

HOW TO THINK ABOUT THE FUTURE

[1]At least it has often seemed strange to the pagan and secular western mind if not always to the Christian western mind.

Although obviously not to all.

The Abbassid Caliphate, the Song dynasty, Tokugawa Japan, and Western Europe.

Surely, (as much as science has progressed within the last century), there are many facts of nature which remain unknown. The so-called theories of everything are not really theories of all possible natural phenomena but theories of elementary particles, which are the fundamental building blocks of "everything".

Actually, *The Great Reckoning* is a very cogent analysis of the current economic climate. It has already made a great many very impressive economic and financial predictions, but it has done this primarily by historical comparisons of market behavior throughout the centuries and not by technology forecasting.

At the time of the signing of the Montreal CFC reduction treaty in 1987, it was projected there would be a global average ozone loss of around 2% by the middle of the 21th century. Later studies in the late 1980's revealed that an ozone loss greater than this had already occurred. See R. E. Benedick, 1991.

In fact, many technologies replace labor. Modern plumbing replaces water carriers. Computers replace figure clerks. If a technology is productive, and not environmentally destructive, then it can't do anything but make global development more likely, not less. There are plenty of uses for labor that is freed up by more productive technology. Of course, in many cases, technology can lead to social upheaval. The civil wars in Central America were intensified by landlessness caused by the mechanization of agriculture. On the other hand, history is full of violent agrarian conflict that had nothing to do with the mechanization of agriculture.

Unless, of course, the nanotechnology described by Rees-Mogg and Davies above becomes a reality. Then maybe all 10 billion of us can retire.

With or without biotechnology and robotics, there are many obstacles to development in the underdeveloped countries. We cannot assume, however, that the underdeveloped countries have to follow the same development path as the Asian "tigers", namely low wage manufactured exports to the markets of the developed countries, or that a large population makes development impossible in the absence of labor intensive agriculture. Such an assumption is a "reverse anachronism". A better way to state Kennedy's point would be to say, "an astonishingly large and increasing number of human beings are not needed or wanted to make the goods or to provide the services that the paying customers of the world can afford", which is simply another way of sayng that most of the world's people live in the underdeveloped parts of the world. As R. J. Barnet says, even if all production is automated, "there is a colossal amount of work waiting to be done by human beings". Global economic development would, in fact, constitute the doing of such work.

"'North/South issues' are issues relating to the relations between the developed and the underdeveloped areas of the world. The Iranian revolution and the oil price shocks of the 70's brought these issues into the awareness of the U.S. public but there was a tremendous disinclination to discuss these issues in a systematic way and they remained in the 'subconscious' of the American political climate in the early and mid-80's finding their way in a symbolic form into movies, fashion, cults, and religious and ethnic politics. One of the big reasons for Reagan's popularity is that he was seen as a 'Third World basher'." *Toward the 21th Century,* Cambridge Forecast Group, Tokyo, 1985.

This is a very common feature of nonlinear dynamical systems, namely a phenomenon of 'scaling' or 'self-similarity' in which the structure of the system as a whole is reflected in any of the details no matter how microscopic, and conversely, each of the details no matter how microscopic can be 'decoded' or 'transformed' into the structure as a whole. (D. Campbell, 1987).

Quote taken from S. Amin, 1990.

This "chaos theory of history" is overblown. For example, we ourselves predicted, in early 1990, that there would be an intense conflict between the US and Israel over settlements, a conflict which might end George Bush's Presidency, and that there might be a Persian Gulf crisis, possibly an upheaval in Iraq. However, we were as flabbergasted as anybody when Saddam Hussein invaded Kuwait. Obviously, the decisions of individual leaders are not totally predictable.

A "stochastic process" such as a nuclear holocaust could throw the entire system off course permanently, and a completely "deterministic" future deterioration in the global environment could completely determine all future human history (end it) and still be totally unanalyzable at the present juncdture with the current state of scientific knowledge.

Beyond this time span, the factors of human unpredictability, chance, technical change, (and possibly global environmental change) will inevitably come to the fore, and any attempt to analyze them from the present vantage point would simply be science fiction.

Of course, if some all-embracing, world shaking event occurs which originates from outside of human society, say some revolutionary new technical innovation based on some totally unexpected facts of nature, or some totally unanticipated global environmental disaster, or the arrival of visitors from another galaxy, or the collision of the earth with a large comet, etc; then historical analysis would be of little use. For example, the effect on Russian society of the Tunguska meteor, which slammed into Russia in 1908, had very little to do with the history of Russian society and everything to do with where the meteor landed (in an unpopulated area).

This is why we put the term "deterministic processes" in quotes.

To some extent, we agree with G. Vico's obervation (1725) that, "the world of civil society has certainly been made by men, and its principles are therefore to be found to be within the modifications of our own human mind. Whoever, reflects on this cannot but marvel that the philosophers should have bent all their energies to the study of the world of nature, which, since God made it, He alone knows; and that they should have neglected the study of the world of nations or civil world, which, since men made it, men could hope to know." Of course, Vico was totally wrong about the of ability of 18th century scientists to uncover the mysteries of nature. The mysteries of human historical evolution turned out to be far more complicated than the mysteries of nature. However, at this point in time, he is right in this limited sense: that if one is interested in prediction, an analysis of socioeconomic, political and historical trends is far more productive than speculating about future technological and environmental "discontinuities" (facts of nature) which, while not necessarily unknowable, are not yet known.

By mass psychology we mean "irrational mass psychology" and not "rational decision making under uncertainly", or the market fluctuations caused by everybody trying to second quess everybody else's decisions (so called "sunspot equilibria").

The extent to which these attempts have succeeded is still a matter of intense controversy. Most economists agree that they "ask the right questions"

Fortunately, many of the founders of modern growth theory are excellent writers, and parts of their work can be profitably read by anyone with a quantitative MBA.

S. P. Huntington (1993) maintains that many of the world's future conflicts will occur on the "fault lines" between the world various civilizations (what Toynbee called "societies"). Perhaps the Gulf war can be seen in this light. When the news of the Mongol invasion of the Middle East reached Western Europe in the 13th century, many Europeans thought that an army of Asian Christians led by King David had come to join the West in its conflict with the Muslims. The invasions of Baghdad by the Mongol leaders IlKhan in the 13th century and Timur at the beginning of the 15th century were particularly genocidal and destructive. Shortly after the beginning of the gulf war, President Bush received Mongolian President Punsalmaagiyn Ochirbat in the White House. President Ochirbat told Bush that the United States and Mongolia shared something. They had both made war on Baghdad. One can speculate that the the timing of this meeting, was a form of "civilizational" psychological warfare against Iraq. (*New York Times*, January 24, 1991).

The Frankish empire in western Europe devolved into European feudalism. The Japanese state created by the Taiko reforms of 646AD devolved into Japanese feudalism. Today's "Eastern Bloc" arose from a synthesis of Byzantine, Western European and nomadic steppe societies.

CHAPTER 2

ECONOMIC GROWTH AND HUMAN CAPITAL

Rosa Luxemburg was an early 20th century labor organizer who is best known today for her accurate prediction of just what a far reaching catastrophe World War I would turn out to be. Tugan Baranovsky was an obscure early 20th century economist who is best known today for being a partial inspiration behind the *Feldman-Mahalanobis model* of development planning for India in the early 50's.

The Polish economist Michal Kalecki—pronounced "Kaletski"—(1971) gives an analysis of an obscure economic debate between Rosa Luxemburg and Tugan Baranovsky called the *underconsumptionist debate*. We begin this chapter with an oversimplication of the Kalecki's analysis of this *underconsumptionist* debate.

This debate went as follows: As labor saving automation replaces labor, will not unemployment eventually become so acute and downward pressure on wages so intense that business activity will falter for lack of a market? No, according to Tugan Baranovsky. As long as businesses keep investing flat out, they will always constitute a market for each other's products until, ultimately, the economy consists of "machines producing machines for the sake of producing more machines" as in the science fiction movie "Terminator".

Quote taken from M. Kalecki 1971.

Not a desirable outcome perhaps, but a possible one. According to Rosa Luxemburg, however, Tugan Baranovsky's outcome was not possible. Eventually the "chain letter effect" of "investment for investment's sake" would be broken as some businesses slacked off in their investment and the whole process imploded.

Rosa Luxemburg, maintained that the only way for economic growth to continue was for more and more geographical areas, formerly outside the market economy, to be brought into it by Western colonization of non-Western countries For those who are interested, J. Robinson in the introduction to R. Luxemburg (1968) describes Luxemburg's growth model as follows:

"As soon as a primitive (pre-industrial) closed economy has been broken into, by force or guile, cheap mass-produced consumption goods displace the old hand production of the family or village communities, so thata market is provided for the ever increasing output from theindustries of the (consumer goods sector) in the old centresof capitalism, without the standard of living of the workers who consume these commodities being raised. The ever growing capacity of the export industries requires the products of the (capital goods) sector thus maintaining investment at home. At the same time, great new works such as railways are undertaken in the new territories." Though this pattern certainly represented the dreams of many Western businessmen ("If every Chinaman added an inch to his coattails, the mills of Lancashire could be kept running forever"), few economists would say that demand from the European colonies was an indispensible factor in early 20th century global economic growth.

This process would come to a halt when all countries were colonized or, more likely, when it precipitated a period of calamitous global upheavals, as the colonizers fought over colonies, and as the colonized rebelled. On this latter point, at least, Rosa Luxemburg was indeed right, although, today, her economic growth theory would be viewed as farfetched (as would Tugan Baranovsky's) and not an explanation for the catastrophes of the 20th century.

Economic growth theory has become far more sophisticated since Rosa Luxemburg's day. We bring up this archaic argument between Rosa Luxemburg and Tugan Baranovsky to illustrate the kinds questions we want to ask about future global economic growth.

Namely, where and how is it likely to occur? Will it involve the inclusion of more and more people into the world market economy? Perhaps the hundreds of millions of people in the former centralized economies?

Or the billions of people in the less developed economies? Or will it involve more and more growth in the already developed industrialized economies, and more and more stagnation in the rest of the world, leading to what Z. Brzezinski (1993) calls a global clash between "insatiable consumers and starving spectators"? Will it be blocked by environmental constraints or propelled forward by constantly evolving new technologies?

Here's a simple growth model. Businesses hire workers to produce economic output. Part of this output is consumed by the workforce and part is invested by businesses in order to create more economic capacity. This greater capacity is, in turn, used to hire more workers, which are used to produce an expanded amount of output, part of which is consumed by the expanded workforce and part of which is invested to create still more economic capacity to hire still more workers, and so on, the only limiting constraint being the size of the potential workforce.

Given the billions of people outside the industrial market economies, such a growth model would certainly seem to have a lot of potential. The Malthusians often look at the burgeoning populations of the underdeveloped world as an unmitigated disaster.

But to many investors, the enormous amount of talent, resourcefulness, ingenuity and drive for material betterment that must be present among so large a number of people, is often seen as an opportunity for unbounded economic expansion. The economist Milton Freedman (1992) has compared it to "the equivalent of a second industrial revolution". A good idea of how some investors look at this model of "economic growth through geographical expansion" is given by an interview between *Barron's* magazine and Barton Biggs, manager of Morgan Stanley Asset Management:

"Barton Biggs: The domestic demand in these (large Latin American) countries is so big, and they are not like the Asian Tigers—Singapore, Taiwan, Korea, etc.—who had to rely on export demand. I mean their domestic demand is big enough so that they can bootstrap themselves by that. They can't grow 8% or 10% a year, the way the Tigers did in their prime, but they can grow 5% or 6% a year . . .

Barron's: What we're asking is not so much whether latent demand exists as whether there realistically is any way of satisfying it? Barton Biggs: But you see, that's the magic—when you start opening these economies up to foreign capital and equity capital, that's the spark that gets them going, and you start creating virtuous circles. You get people to work, you pay them wages, so they can buy washing machines and all that stuff.

Barron's: Well, I think it's much more complex than you suggest.

Barton Biggs: "Gotta dream! Gotta dream!" *Barron's International Roundtable*, September 16, 1991.

In what way is it "much more complex" as *Barron's* suggests. As we shall see, the exact nature of these "complexities" embody some of the most important issues of present day history.

Here's another simple model of economic growth, this time with a fixed number of workers. Businesses produce economic output. Part of this output is consumed by the workforce and part is invested in industrial innovations which yield productivity improvements. Let's say (for the sake of argument) that these productivity improvements are labor enhancing rather than labor replacing so that nobody gets fired, and the workforce remains the same.

Part of the increased output goes into wage rises for the workforce (as opposed to hiring more workers) and part goes into investment in yet more industrial innovations which yield still more productivity improvements (which are labor enhancing as opposed to labor replacing). This is followed by more wages rises and more productivity improvements, and so on. This is growth with a fixed labor force and a constantly rising level of consumption per capita (a rising standard of living). This is the type of economic growth that the U.S. experienced from 1945-1973 and the alleged end of which was the main issue in the 1992 presidential elections. ("Will your children have a higher standard of living than you" and so on).

Can such a model of economic growth continue indefinitely? Can it continue indefinitely in the absence of revolutionary technical innovations (something along the lines of "cold fusion" say)?

This is another important question of present day history.

So the main question we address is this: will future economic growth consist of more and more economic activity in the same geographical areas, or will it consist of the spread of economic activity to more and more geographical areas?

Suppose that the whole world except for Massachusetts sunk into the ocean. Would Massachusetts be able to experience economic growth indefinitely? Suppose that the whole world except for the United States sunk into the ocean. Would the United States be able to experience economic growth indefinitely? Suppose that the whole world with the exception of the developed countries sunk into the ocean. Would the developed countries be able to experience economic growth indefinitely?

By indefinitely, we mean within a very long-term planning horizon.

Let us now briefly examine some of the old and new economic growth theories. First, we will describe the so called *Harrod-Domar* growth model which was developed in the late 40's. This model says, basically, that in order to achieve a desired increase in economic output, the economy needs a proportionate increase in the amount of capital stock, (so many railroads, so many roads, so many bridges, so many machine tools, etc. are needed in order to achieve a unit of output increase).

In other words, the ratio of incremental economic output to incremental increase in capital stock is fixed, the so called *incremental capital output ratio (ICOR)*.

Suppose, for example, that the incremental *capital-output ratio* for a particular economy is 2. Then, in order for the economy to increase its output by 1 unit, it needs to acquire 2 units of additional capital. Of course, once it has acquired 2 units of additional capital, it also needs to acquire additional workers to operate this capital (to drive the trucks, operate the machines, etc.) However, if it has acquired less than 2 units of additional capital, then, no matter how many additional workers it acquires, it's output will increase by less than 1 unit. This is because, in the Harrod-Domar model, labor can operate capital, but it cannot substitute for it. No amount of runners, for example, carrying packages, can substitute for even an infinitesimal proportion of the economy-wide stock of locomotives.

In other words, in the Harrod-Domar model, the economy needs capital and labor in fixed proportions. For this reason, it can be shown that, in the Harrod-Domar model, in order for an economy to achieve long term balanced growth, the capital stock has to grow at the same rate as the labor force, otherwise unemployment or shortages will result. Actually, the situation is even worse than this. In the Harrod-Domar model, the amount of economic output saved is assumed to be a fixed percentage of total output, the so called *savings rate*. Thus, in order for *balanced growth* to be achieved, the savings rate, the amount of output invested and the rate of population growth all have to be in balance, otherwise gluts, shortages, unemployment or labor scarcity will develop.

The Harrod-Domar economic is very much in the tradition of the Keynesian revolution with its concern for economic stability and unemployment and also for the rigid assumptions useful primarily for short-term economic analysis. The Harrod-Domar model neglected the effects of relative prices on factor proportions, such as capital and labor, implying that they were in fixed ratio. Thus, the Harrod-Domar model is generally thought to be more applicable to a developing country with a capital constraint on growth.

The World Bank uses a Harrod-Domar type model, a "two-gap model", called the "Revised Minimum Standard

Model (RMSM)" in its evaluations of LDC structural adjustment programs. The "Shimomura strategy" for doubling Japan's national income in the 60's was based on a Harrod-Domar growth model.

This strategy, devised by Dr. Osamu Shimomura, said that if firms invested flat out and consumers save the maximum amount that they could, then Japan's GNP would double in the 60's. The basis behind this reasoning was the low capital/output ratio made possible by investing in the latest, most productive technology. This enabled the instability inherent in the Harrod-Domar model to be circumvented. (See H. Takenaka, 1991).

Thus, the Harrod-Domar model suggests that balanced economic growth in the absence of central planning is a highly unlikely occurrence. This is clearly not an accurate description of reality, since there have been long periods in history when balanced economic growth has been propelled largely by private decentralized investment decisions.

"This sort of growth theory is essentially uninteresting because no economy could function if it did not contain definite stabilizing features that the permitted the system to absorb the shocks that it regularly receives froms outside. What we want to know is how much we can rely on these stabiliy properties and for that purpose we need more flexible growth models. This explains why recent developments in growth theory have gone far beyond Harrod's original formulations." M. Blaug (1962)

To address the flaw described above, the economist Robert Solow developed the so called *neo-classical* model of economic growth (R. Solow, 1956)

We concentrate on the neoclassical growth theory and its variants in this chapter, as opposed to the *structuralist* growth theories of N. Kaldor, N. Kalecki, L. Pasinetti, and J.Robinson, not because we wish to slight these other growth theories, but because we're not writing an encyclopedia, and the neoclassical growth theory is better known and has attracted a larger body of empirical research.

For those interested in other growth theories, see H. Wan, 1971.

According to the *neo-classical* model of economic growth, the assumptions of the Harrod-Domar model are highly unrealistic. In a modern economy, according to the *neo-classical* model, there are many different kinds of techniques, some more capital intensive, some less capital intensive, for performing the same economic functions. This means that capital and labor are partially substitutable, one for the other, and different combinations of capital and labor can yield the same amount of total economic output. It is this partial substitutability of capital and labor, one for the other, that ensures balanced long term economic growth. (As we shall see below.)

A simple formulation of neo-classical growth model can be stated as follows:

$$Y = F(K,L),$$

where Y is total economic output, L is total labor, K is the total capital stock, and where F is a *production function*. What is a *production function*? To explain this, (for those unfamiliar with functional notation) imagine that the entire economy consists of a single factory. The *production function*, F(K,L), of this factory, then, is a sort of schedule (or computer program), which, given inputs of labor (L) and capital (K), tells you how much output (Y) the factory can produce

Equivalently one can regard the economy as consisting of a large number, M, of identical firms each of which has theproduction function F(K/M,L/M). The total economy then has the production function MF(K/M,L/M) which, by constant returns to scale, is F(K,L).

For the purposes of this discussion, labor (L) is taken to be the number of people in the workforce. The measurement of total capital stock (K), on the other hand, is much more complex. There are many different kinds of capital stock (inventories, durable equipment of various kinds, structures, land and so on).

For purposes of simplification, capital stock (K), in the Solow growth model, is assumed to be a uniform homogeneous substance, which is measurable in some sort of unit, a "unit of capital".

Obviously that is a drastic oversimplification of a real economy. After all, "what does it mean to say that the capital stock was (say) twenty times larger in 1980 than 1880?

How many spinning jennies equal a personal computer?"

(B Bernanke, 1987).

In fact, the *aggregation* (lumping together) of all the different kinds of capital stock into a single homogenous substance was probably the most controversial aspect of the Solow growth model. It started a long theoretical debate, called the "battle of the Cambridge's", between the economists of Cambridge Massachusetts and the economists of Cambridge England. The details of this debate are far beyond the scope of this book.

Those interested in this arcane debate, see R. Solow, 1960.

For our purposes, we will simply accept the this simplification.

The *production function*, F(K,L) above, is assumed to exhibit *constant returns to scale*, by which we mean that, if both K and L are multiplied by a factor, then F(K,L) will be multiplied by the same factor. For example, doubling both K and L will double F(K,L), tripling both K and L with triple F(K,L), increasing both K and L by 5% will increase F(K,L) by 5%, and so on.

In other words, for any constant z, $F(zK, zL) = zF(K,L)$.

One of the consequences of constant returns to scale is that output per worker (Y/L) is solely a function of capital per worker (K/L). (For a proof of this, see the notes at the end of this chapter)

If $Y = F(K,L)$, where Y is economic output, K is the totalcapital stock, and L is the total labor force labor used, then dividing both sides of the above equation by L yields $Y/L = 1/L * F(K,L)$. Because $F(K,L)$ has constant returns to scale, $1/L * F(K,L) = F(K/L,1)$. Thus, $Y/L = F(K/L,1)$. Defining y as Y/L, k as K/L and $f(k)$ as $F(k,1)$, we have $y = f(k)$. In otherwords, output per capita is a function of capital stock percapita. If an increase in K and L were to cause a larger thanproportionate increase in economic output Y, the economy is said to have *increasing returns to scale* The standard Solow economic growth model postulates that increasing returns to scale are not an important factor in a large economy. New variants of the Solow growth model, the so called "new growth theories" study the role of increasing returns to scale on an economy-wide level.

If one makes the not unreasonable assumption that adding more and more capital to a single worker will cause output of this worker to increase very rapidly at first and then at a slower and slower rate as more and more capital is added (the *Inada conditions*)

For those familiar with elementary calculus, the Inada conditions can be stated as follows; (letting $k = K/L$, $y = Y/L$ and $f(k) = F(k,1)$), $df/dk > 0$, $d2f/dk2 < 0$ and df/dk increases without bound as k goes to 0.

For those familiar with elementary microeconomics, the Inada conditions state that themarginal product of capital is always positive, the marginalproduct of capital always diminishes as capital per capitaincrease, the marginal product of capital is infinite when there is no capital at all in the economy. In other words, adding on more and more capital to a single worker yields *diminishing returns.*

And, if one makes the additional three assumptions that the savings rate is constant over a long period of time, that all savings are invested, and that the work force is growing at a constant rate, then it is possible to show, using calculus, that economic growth will converge towards a *stable path*, where the capital per worker (K/L) is constant, and where output (Y), and capital stock (K), are all growing at the same rate as the labor force.

Although, it can take a fairly long time for an economy to converge to its "stable growth path." (K. Sato, 1966)

Let's explain (not prove) why this is so in English. At low levels of capital per worker, the gain in output from adding on additional capital is large (the *Inada conditions*); hence, at low levels of capital per worker, additional capital is being added to each worker, and the amount of capita per worker is increasing. At high levels of capital per worker, on the other hand, the gain in output from adding on additional capital is small. Thus, at high levels of capital per worker, it pays to simply let the workforce grow and not to add on capital, and the amount of capital per worker is decreasing. This provides a "thermostatic mechanism" which, in the "long run", causes the amount of capital per worker to even out at a constant level

A level which depends on the *savings rate*, the proportion of total economic output which is saved.

Suppose that, "in the long run", the rate of growth of the labor force is 5% per annum. Since, in the long run, the amount of capital per worker, is constant, the rate of growth of the capital stock is also 5% per annum. Because of *constant returns to scale*, the rate of growth of economic output is likewise 5% per annum.

This is a very incomplete, oversimplified explanation, nota proof. For those familiar with elementary calculus, let the proportion of output saved be designated by s. The amount invested in a unit of time is the rate of change of total capital stock per unit time, which is dK/dt. The amount saved is then sY.

Since what is saved is invested, dK/dt = sY. Defining, k, f, and y as above, setting the rate of growth ofthe workforce dL/dt to be a constant n, and differenting both sides of dK/dt = sY logarithmically, yields the equation dk/dt= sf(k)—nk. Let k* be the value for k* at which dk/dt = 0;i.e. sf(k*) = nk*. A simple version of the 'phase diagram' technique, shows when k is less than k*, dk/dt is positive (k is increasing), and when k is greater than k*, dk/dt is negative (is decreasing) and, therefore, k will converge to k*as time goes to infinity. k* is the capital per worker which the economy will converge to as it grows. It depends on the savings rate and the rate of growth of the workforce, n.

Output per capita (or standard of living) will also depend on the savings rate. However, the rate of growth of output isequal to the rate of growth of the workforce, and does not depend on the savings rate, a result which has seemed counterintuitive to many economists, and which is addressed inthe newer variants of the Solow model, the so called "new growth theories".

Thus, the Solow model removes the instability inherent in the Harrod-Domar model.

The Solow model also shows that, in the absence of technological change, the economic growth rate will be determined by the rate of growth in the labor force, a fact which would seem to make a stable population a potential impediment to growth

This is not strictly true of the model presented here, but is true in a more complex version of the Solow neoclassical growth model called the *optimizing version* which takes long term consumer demand into account. For another model (using different methods) of the drag that a finite population puts on economic growth, see P. Samuelson, 1988.

However, technological change does occur so that the same amounts of labor and capital yield more and more output as time goes on. In a simple version of the Solow model this fact is dealt with as follows:

$$Y = F(K, L, t),$$

where K is the capital stock, L is labor and t is time.

If the above equation is converted into rates, this is done by means of logarithmic differentiation.

It can be shown that the overall economic growth rate can be decomposed into the following three constituents:

- growth in the capital stock;
- growth in the labor force;
- another factor called *total factor productivity, tfp*.

Growth accounting studies have shown that economic growth in most of the developed countries has largely consisted of growth in *total factor productivity*.

"The developed economies are characterized by little growth in labor inputs (1.1%), moderate growth in capital stock (5.4%) and a relatively large contribution of tfp to economic growth (50%)."

From H. Chenery, 1986.

Tfp has been described as "technological change", "growth in productive skills", "human capital" and "everything we don't know about growth". Thus, essentially, in the Solow growth model, technological advance is considered to be something arising from "outside" the workings of the economy ("manna from heaven"), something determined, say, by the general state of scientific knowledge and which interacts with capital (K) and labor (L) to make them more productive. In his work on economic growth theory, Solow demonstrates that assuming a "constant rate of technological progress", economic growth will converge towards a rate which is the sum of the rate of growth in the labor force plus the "rate of technical progress".

More precisely, the technical progress has to be of the type known as "labor augmenting" i.e. where output, $Y = F(K, e^{bt}L)$, where t = time and b is a constant which is the "rate of technological change". In other words, the technicalprogress should be labor enhancing not labor replacing.

From the point of view of the present discussion, the important factor about the Solow neo-classical growth model is that it would seem to imply optimism about the growth prospects for the underdeveloped economies.

"It would seem to follow that all national economies with access to the same changing technology should have converging growth rates. There might be temporary or even prolonged differences in growth rates because countries that are still fairly close to their initial conditions having started with lower ratios of capital to labor than they will eventually achieve in the steady state, will be growing faster than countries that are further along in that process."

(R. Solow 1989)

"If a technology is 10 times more advanced in one country than another, there should be large returns to anyone who can cause the advanced technology to be used in the less advanced country. If technology has the kind of public good character attributed to it in the neoclassical world, it should not be hard to put it to use somewhere else in the world"

(P. Romer, 1991)

Indeed, the 50's and 60's were times of optimism about prospects for economic growth in the less developed areas of the world. In fact, the only obstacle to capitalist growth in the less developed world was seen to be the threat of Communist takeovers which American foreign policy in the Third World was largely dedicated to preventing.

However, in the 70's and 80's a series of economic upheavals and "growth failures" began to take place in large parts of the less developed world, (the Iranian upheaval, the oil shocks, the Latin debt crisis, the unraveling of the African economies), upheavals which also had profound repercussions on the economies of the developed world.

So that even as the economic, social, political and cultural linkages between the developed and the underdeveloped world continued to rapidly increase, doubts and confusion began to arise in the West about the prospects for economic growth in the latter.

In addition, in the late 80's, fears began to arise about environmental constraints to economic growth, (the thinning of the Ozone layer, the projected Greenhouse effect).

It was at this point that the so-called "new growth theories" began to emerge to replace the "neo-classical growth theory". Two of the main originators of these new growth theories were the economists Paul Romer and Robert Lucas.

From our point of view two of the most important features of these "new growth theories" are (1) attempts to construct plausible models of perpetual growth in the presence of "fixed factors" such as a fixed population base or a rigid environmental constraint, (2) attempts to model technological advance as a predictable function of economic activity rather than as "manna from heaven" which arrives from outside the economy and then interacts with it.

In our opinion, the motivations behind these "new growth theories" are: (1) a desire to find a model in which economic growth is free from the necessity of having to wait for the next big "breakthrough" in human scientific knowledge (i.e. superconductivity, nuclear fusion, artificial intelligence) and in which technical progress is controllable by economic agents, (2) a desire to find a model in which growth is not hampered by environmental constraints, and (3) a desire to find a model which explains the growing gap between the West and the underdeveloped world, and does so in a way that avoids the controversy and facile argumentation that always swirls around this topic.

"Economic growth being a summary measure of all of the activities of an entire society, necessarily depends, in some way, on everything that goes on in a society. Societies differ in many easily observed ways, and it is easy to identify various economic and cultural peculiarities and imagine that they are the keys to growth performance.

For this as Jacobs (1984) rightly observes, we do not need economic theory. 'Perceptive tourists will do as well'. The role of theory is not to catalog the obvious, but to help us sort out effects that are crucial quantitatively from those that can be set aside.", R. Lucas, 1988.

In order to do this, it is necessary to construct "a mechanical artificial world, populated by the interacting robots that economics typically studies, that is capable of exhibiting behavior the gross features of which resemble those of the actual world."

(R. Lucas, 1988).

In other words, the idea is to find the economic equivalent of "cosmological equations", equations which describe how the "economic cosmos" coalesces into "stars and galaxies" of development and vast empty voids of underdevelopment (empty, that is, of commercial prospects). This is accomplished by the addition of two new factors of production. *knowledge* and *human capital*.

What is *human capital*? To answer that questions, let's ask another one. In 1946, after a large part of its physical capital stock was destroyed, was Germany an underdeveloped country? The answer is obviously no. The wars which shattered Europe in the twentieth century did not render it underdeveloped. In other words, there must be some factor other than the size of the capital stock in a country which makes a country "developed".

It must be something to do with the people of the country, both individually and as a social aggregate.

This "something" is called *human capital*.

To take another example (in discussing the 19th century classical economist, John Stuart Mill) M. Blaug (1962) writes:

"Mill notes. that the average durability of capital goods is only about ten years. This accounts for the fact that countries recover so quickly after destructive wars; skills, technical knowledge and the more durable buildings ususally remain umipaired and make possible a rapid recovery. This obviously valid argument has never received the attention it deserves; it could be elaborated into a complete theory of the causes of economic growth."

Using *human capital* as a factor of production is an attempt to do that.

For those who are familiar with the so called *Cobb-Douglas* production function, and the concept of 'marginal product', R. Lucas (1990) is a simple, readable introduction to human capital calculations. We'll give a brief summary of this paper. Recall that in the neoclassical growth model above, because of contant returns to scale, economic output per worker is solely a function of capital stock per worker.

It is also a feature of this model that the smaller the amount of capital stock per worker the greater the gain in output from increasing the amount of capital stock per worker (the Inada conditions). In other words, capital investment should yield much greater returns in a capital poor country like India than a capital rich one like the United States.

So Lucas (1990) asks the question, "why doesn't capital flow from rich to poor countries?". Given India's large population and low average wage, the flow of capital from the United States to India, should be enormous, in fact all new investment capital should flow to the poorer countries. This is obviously not the case in fact. The reason why this is not the case in theory, is because there is another factor of production called *human capital*. A high level of human capital per worker makes physical capital more productive and a low level makes physical capital less productive. Poor countries have a low level of human capital, and this counteracts the low amount of capital per worker. Suppose that India has a human capital per worker of 1, and suppose that the United States has a human capital per worker of h, (which means that a worker in the U.S. would be, on the average, 'h' times more productive than a worker in India, even if India were to be given the same physical capital per worker endowment as the United States

Note that this refers to the average productivity of the population as a whole not whether an Indian fork lift operator, say, is more or less productive than an American forklift operator.

Lucas (1990) postulates a simple production function of the form:

$$Y = F(K,hL,h) = A K^b (hL)^{1-b} h^c,$$

which applies to production in both countries, where K = capital, h = human capital per worker

In the discussion of the Lucas article, "per worker" should actually read "per capita" because that is how the statistics were compiled. h = 1 in India, L = labor and A is independent of K, L and h. Those who are familiar with college level economics, will recognize the above equation, A Kb (hL)1-b, as an extension of the so-called *Cobb-Douglas function*, a production function often used in economic models because it is easy to work with. However, the exact form of this equation need not concern us here. For our purposes, there are two important things to stress. First of all, the term (hL) above implies that a worker in the U.S. would be, on the average, 'h' times more productive than a worker in India even if India were to be given the same physical capital per worker endowment as the United States. Secondly, the term 'hc' above is called an *external effect* and expresses the fact that workers in the U.S. are collectively more productive, more productive as a society, as well as being individually more productive. A migrant from India, whatever his or her skill level, can have his or her 'productiveness' multiplied by this *external effect* simply by *being* in the United States. Hence the incentive for migration from poor countries to rich.

Lucas (1990) uses the results of three economic surveys to calculate b, h, and c. A study by A. Krueger (1969) of labor efficiency in the U.S. and India allows h to be calculated as 5. On the average one American worker is the equivalent of 5 Indian workers, even if India were to be given the same amount of capital per worker as America. A study by E. Dennison (1962) of the sources of economic growth in the United States from 1909-1959 shows that output per worker has grown at a rate 1% faster than would be explained by growth in capital per worker. Attributing this difference to growth of "human capital" allows c to be calculated as .36. From other economic data b is estimated at .4.

A survey by R. Summers and A. Heston (1988) of real economic output and price levels in 130 countries is used (together with the above equation) to calculate the difference between gains from capital investment in India and gains from capital investment in the United States. This difference is shown to be approximately 4%. The proofs use elementary algebra, elementary microeconomics, and elementary calculus

For those who are familiar with college level calculusand college level economics, the "gain from capitalinvestment" is the *marginal product of capital* which, ofcourse, is the partial derivative of the production function with respect to K. Thus, the proofs of assertions above are partial differentiation and the chain rule.

Thus, human capital is the "missing ingredient" or, at least, a "missing ingredient" which shows why returns to capital invested are not an order of magnitude greater in capital-poor countries than capital-rich ones.

What then is human capital? It has been attributed to skills, training, experience, literacy, schooling etc. Denison (1962) attibutes unexplained growth in per capita output as due to schooling. Does this mean that, if every middle class person in India gets a Ph.D. in Hindi love poetry, Indian economic output will double? Obviously such a thesis would be preposterous.

Human capital must consist of more than schooling. It must consist of skills at economic, industrial, commercial, manufacturing and entrepreneurial activity, both on an individual basis and collectively as a society.

K. Arrow (1962) attributes it to experience gained by cumulative capital investment of a continually new and improved capital stock. Newer theories of human capital formation have stressed manufacturing, industrial and commercial skills acquired while going up against the world market.

Defining human capital as knowledge, the *Economist* survey of Asia, entitled *A Billion Consumers* (*Economist*, 10/20/93,page 9), denies that human capital is the source of total factor productivity, since the Soviet Union slid into economiccollapse despite an impressive accumulation of human capital.

One of the inspirations for the concept of human capital comes from the concept of *learning by doing*:

"The role of experience in increasing productivity has not gone unobserved though the relation has yet to be absorbed in the main corpus of economic theory. It was early observed by aeronautical engineers. that the number of labor hours expended in the production of an airframe. is a decreasing function of the total number of airframes of the same type produced . . . (another example) The Horndal iron works in Sweden had no new investment (and therfore presumably no significant change in methods of production) for a period of 15 years, yet productivity rose on the average close to 2% per annum . . . which can only be imputed to learning from experience."

K. Arrow (1962)

The term *human capital* is not used in K. Arrow's formulation. Instead, cumulative production of capital goods is used an an index of *experience* or *learning by doing*.

"Each new machine produced and put to use is capable of changing the environment in which production takes place. so that learning is taking place with continually new stimuli. This at least makes plausible the possibility of continued learning in the sense, here, of a steady rate of growth in productivity"

K. Arrow, (1962)

In Arrow's formulation, capital investment increases economic output directly, because it is a factor of production. It also increases economic output by generating *experience* and *learning by doing* which increase economic productivity.

In 1967, E. Sheshinski developed a simpler version of the Arrow model. In his formulation the economy consists of N identical firms and the production, function for each individual firm is written: y = F(k,(Nk)cw), where k is capital per firm, w is labor per firm and c is an exponent less than 1, and y is output per firm,

In the equation above, labor w is *augmented* or *scaled up* by the factor (Nk)c where (Nk) is the total economy-wide capital investment. The greater the total amount of capital investment, the more effective is labor. The process by which this happens is *learning by doing*.

As we mentioned above, in the recently developed new growth theories, human capital is a separate factor of production. Such growth theories have mathematical formulae which describe how economic activity generates human capital, i.e. *production functions* for human capital.

For example, in Lucas (1988), an invididual's human capital is simply his or her general skill level, so that a worker with human capital h is the productive equivalent of two workers with human capital h/2. The percentage growth of human capital per annum is proportional to the percentage of non-leisure time devoted to human capital accumulation (schooling, training, on-the-job learning, etc).

If all workers have human capital h and devote fraction u of their non-leisure time to productive work, and fraction 1-u of their non-leisure time to human capital accumulation then: percentage increase in h per annum = c(1-u) where c is a constant

The production function for the economy is similar to Lucas (1990) above. The mathematics in Lucas (1988) is well beyond the scope of this book, but the significant feature of the human capital equation above is that, since there are no diminishing returns to the production of human capital, human capital can act as an "engine of growth" in the presence of a fixed population. Thus, human capital allows long-term growth in the demographically stable developed countries, and explains the differences between the developed and underdeveloped countries.

R Lucas (1988) also postulates that 'external human capital' (hc above) could be an explanation for why economic development tends to cluster in certain geographical areas i.e. such as cities for example.

R. Barro once said, "I never knew what geographical region the Solow growth model was supposed to refer to.

A city? A state? A country? The world?"

"But we know from ordinary experience that there are group interactions that are central to individual productivity and that involve groups larger than the immediate family and smaller than the human race. Most of what we know we learn from other people."

This is an explanation for the economic role of cities.

"The theory of production contains nothing to hold a city together. A city is simply a collection of factors of production-capital, people and land. Why don't people and capital move outside, combining themselves with cheaper land and thereby increasing profits? . . . It seems to me that the 'force' we need to postulate to account for the central role of cities in economic life is of exactly the same character as 'external human capital' I have postulated to account for certain features of aggregative development. If so, then land rents should provide an indirect measure of this force . . . What can people be paying Manhattan or downtown Chicago rents for, if not for being near other people."

Another factor of production in the new growth theories is *knowledge*. *Knowledge* consists of ideas, designs, scientific theories, technology etc.

Unlike skills, knowledge is independent of the people possessing the knowledge. Sometimes it can take the form of private property through the use of patents or trade secrets, etc. Sometimes is is freely available to everyone. In the new growth theories, in contrast to the neoclassical growth theory, knowledge is generated by economic activity, for example, industrial research. The more resources directed to research, the more knowledge. Sometimes knowledge is regarded as a homogeneous mass (P. Romer 1986) like capital in the neon-classical model above. At other times, capital is regarded as a list of different types of capital equipment and "knowledge" is postulated to be the length of that list (P. Romer 1990) so that the economy grows by generating a greater and greater variety of products rather than more and more of a homogeneous mass.

These models often have a "production function" for the generation of knowledge such as "capital invested in research in, knowledge out" or "knowledge and human capital in, more knowledge out". A sample "production function" for knowledge might look like: "The amount of increase in knowledge per unit time is proportional to the currently existing stock of knowledge multiplied by the amount of human capital allocated to research."

(P. Romer 1990)

However, from our point of view, the most interesting thing about these growth models is what they have to say about the patterns of future global economic development. First of all, unlike technology in the Solow growth models, "human capital" is not freely transferable across national boundaries. Since human capital is a critical determinate of the growth rate, in many of these models, growth in the developed and undeveloped economies need never converge, and it is entirely possible for an economy to permanently experience a greater rate of growth the greater its level of development.

Furthermore, it can do this in the presence of a "fixed factor" such as a fixed population or an environmental constraint.

On the other hand, it will often benefit an underdeveloped country, even one with a large population, such as China or India to seek external trade with a developed one because "what is important for growth is integration not into an economy with a large number of people, but rather into one with a large amount of human capital" (R. Romer 1990).

How well have the new growth theories stood up to empirical tests? Obviously, the new growth theories have not had the same amount of time to attract empirical research as has the Solow growth model, which has inspired an enormous number of *growth accounting studies*. None the less, there have been an increasing number of empirical studies of the new growth theories.

In the October 1992 edition of the *Economic Review of the Federal Reserve Bank of Atlanta*, E. W. Tallman and P. Wang discuss the empirical evidence on the relationship between human capital, and economic growth. First of all, there is the question of how one goes about measuring human capital. This is done by means of *proxies* (substitutes). Some of these proxies are literacy rates and enrollment in primary and secondary schools.

Secondly, there is the question of the reliability and consistancy of the data from different countries. Thirdly, "human capital proxies are necessarily crude. For instance, although the literacy rate may be a fairly consistently measured variable, it may only tangentially measure the human capital concept of interest (that is, a measure of knowledge or achievement)." Thus, the empirical evidence regarding the controversial new growth theories is itself controversial.

Paul Romer (1990) investigates whether the 1960 literacy rate, affects the economic growth of a cross-section of countries in the subsequent 25 years. Romer finds that the initial level of human capital and the change in literacy has a significant effect on the rate of investment, and, thus, on economic output growth as a whole. Robert J. Barro (1991) studies the relationship, for many different countries, of the 1960 enrollment rates in primary and secondary schools (human capital) and the average economic output growth for the period 1960-1985. He finds that the 1960 human capital level, has, on average, a positive impact on subsequent economic growth. C Azariadis and A. Drazen (1990) find that possessing a literacy rate of 40% or greater has a positive effect on economic output growth for the sample of countries that they study. R. Levine and D. Renelt critize the above studies from a statistical point of view. See D. Renelt (1991) for a more detailed review of the empirical work on the new growth theories.

The new growth theories are a very rapidly expanding field. We have touched on only a very small fraction of the questions that are being currently investigated by these theories. There have been studies on growth and inflation (N. Roubini), growth and government macroeconomic policies (G. Saint-Paul), growth and international trade (E. Helpman, G. Grossman), growth and international capital flows (S. Rebelo), and growth and individual decision making under uncertainty (R. Lucas, N. Stokey, 1989).

One of the problems in writing about the new growth theories is that these theories make heavy use of advanced mathematical concepts, such as the "Kuhn-Tucker theorem" and "dynamic equilibrium theory". Some of their most interesting results, concern the extent to which individual, decentralized decisions lead to "optimal" or "suboptimal" outcomes.

Thus providing a theoretical justification of government intervention in the economic growth process through "industrial policies" or the promotion of education and research a la Clintonomics.

Results, or the extent to which government policy changes have permanent as opposed to one-shot economic effects, cannot even be adequately described in English. For those who are familiar with college level microeconomics, (and those who aren't can skip this paragraph) some other highly technical issues that the new growth theories are forced to deal with are the issues of "externalities", "non-convexities" and "economies of scale". Such concepts are difficult to model using the assumptions of "perfect competition" and "marginal cost pricing".

For example, perfectly plausible production functions using human capital and knowledge as factor inputs can be shown by elementary calculus to contradict the assumptions of "marginal cost pricing", something which would seem to render the generation of new technologies incomprehensible under a regime of perfect competition and profit maximization.

Let A be technological knowledge say in the form of industrial designs and let X be other inputs say raw materials. Then a plausible production function might have the form $F(A,X)$ where $F(A,QX) = Q. F(A,X)$. In other words, you only need the design once, but if you multiply the inputs X by a constant

Q then the output is also multiplied by Q. Assuming A is "productive", then increasing A should also increase output, so that $F(QA,QX) > F(A,QX) = Q. F(A,X)$.

Differentiating both sides of this inequality by Q, using thechain rule, and then setting Q equal to 1, one can show that producers with the above production function must always losemoney if they pay for their inputs at their "value marginalproducts". In this case, how can private, profit maximizingbehavior generate new technologies? See P. Romer, 1990 for details of this argument.

Some of the new growth theories address this dilemma by constructing mathematical models which use "Marshallian external increasing returns" to make human capital and technology compatible with perfect competition and "price taking" (P. Romer 1986). Others abandon perfect competition altogether and construct growth theories with "monopolistic competition" (P. Romer 1990). For those who are familiar with advanced college calculus, and who are willing to take a great deal on faith, P. Romer (1989) is a readable, heuristic overview of the new growth theories.

There are two widespread points of view concerning long term economic growth. The first point of view is that economic growth ultimately needs more and more participants in order to sustain itself, because, without them, it will end up producing only labor shortages or gluts. The second point of view is that economic growth does not need more and more participants in order to sustain itself

In fact, P. Romer (1987) implies that a large populationmay inhibit economic growth because an important part of

thegrowth process may be labor-saving technical innovations
induced by shortages of labor.

The populations of the already developed economies are
quite sufficient.

"The developed countries no longer need (the LDC's) as
they did during the nineteenth century. It may be hyperbole
to say, as Japan's leading management consultant Kenichi
Ohmae, has said that Japan, North America and Western
Europe can exist by themselves with out the two-thirds of
humanity who live in developing countries. But it is a fact
that during the last 40 years the countries of this so-called
triad have become essentially self-sufficient except for
petroleum. They produce more food than they can consume
in glaring contrast to the 19th century. They produce
something like three fourths of all the world's manufactured
goods and services. And they provide the markets for an
equal proportion." P. F. Drucker (1988)

To state Ohmae's point of view above in its most extreme
form, one could say that, even in a stable population, human
wants and desires are infinite, human inventiveness equally
infinite. Therefore, no matter how advanced technology
becomes, people will always be able to find ways to occupy
their time in the production of commercially viable goods
and services. In other words, technological advance will not
make people redundant, but will, on the contrary, make
them more and more able to interact commercially in a way
that magnifies their capabilities and satisfactions.

Before writing off such visions of perpetual economic
growth on a fixed population as "too good to be true", one

should note that there have been many such prognoses of limits to economic growth on a fixed population.

Some of the prognosticators have included Malthus, Ricardo, Marx, Luxemberg, and Schumpeter. During the depression of the 30's, there were predictions that growth in the West had reached a stage of "maturity", and that further economic growth would be confined to the European colonies.

All these predictions were invalidated by technological innovations that the prognosticators had no way of forecasting. Therefore, forecasters have become very leery about predicting that the West "needs" the Third World for future economic growth.

As R. Heilbroner (1990) puts it:

"Fears that capitalism will run out of things to doappear much less plausible than they did in the past. There's no doubt that important markets may become saturated . . . but the long term process of expansion hasbypassed saturation by discovering or creating new commodities, and that process does not suffer from the same fixed capacities for absorption that limit the demand for specific goods."

To be sure, this type of intensive economic growth might be possible only for the minority of the world's population in the already developed economies, but it is possible nonetheless. Indeed, it is the type of growth that has actually taken place in the West since 1945.

That is, since 1945, much of the economic growth in the West has not consisted of increases in the aggregate mass of capital stock (a la Tugan Baranovsky) nor of increases in the number of participants (a la Rosa Luxemburg), but rather in the increased ability of the same number of participants to generate more and more economic output, and to consume a greater and greater variety of goods and services. The standard Solow growth model has no economic explanation for the latter type of growth, and, indeed, maintains that no such economic explantion exists.

After all, "can one really explain by economic models, the discovery of the transistor, or the laser, or the host of other breakthroughs of the last century?" (J. Stiglitz, 1990). And yet, according to the new growth theories, technology, knowledge and skills are themselves economic commodities, which are "produced" by economic activity, and which should, therefore, obey economic laws.

The new growth theories investigate these economic laws. They do so in order to explain the phenomenon of long term growth on a stable population, and also to explain the widening gap between the developed and underdeveloped parts of the globe.

The new growth theories have generated an enormous amount of excitement both in the economics profession and, increasingly, in the business press as well. Part of this excitement is due to the fact that these theories have had to overcome formidable theoretical difficulties in order to model the economics of technology and human capital.

And part of this excitement is, let's face it, due to a desire on the part of people in the West to find a type of economic growth which is free from the problematical and potentially catastrophic condition of the four fifths of the human race not in West.

The new growth theories, (which project perpetual growth on a stable population), satisfy this desire, because, in these models, the participation of people outside the West, either as producers or consumers, is not needed to ensure economic growth in the West.

To sum up, the new growth theories purport to demonstrate the possibility of perpetual economic growth on a stable population. In addition, these growth theories, according to some economists, have been remarkably successful in explaining economic growth from 1945 to the present.

What about the future?

To address this question, let's examine some of the assumptions behind the new growth theories

Or rather the assumptions behind some of the new growth theories.

First, there is the assumption that the payoff to commercial and non-commercial research, in the form of growth-inducing technologies, will be the same or greater in the future than it was in the past.

"Assuming that the increasing returns arise because of increasing marginal productivity of knowledge accords with the plausible conjecture that, even with fixed population and fixed physical capital, knowledge will never reach a level where its marginal product is so low that it is no longer worth the trouble it takes to do research.

If the marginal product of knowledge were truly diminishing, this would imply that Newton and Darwin and their contemporaries mined the richest veins of ideas and that scientists must sift through its tailings and extract ideas from low grade ore."

P. Romer, 1986

This point of view certainly coincides with the commonly held belief that "the future = now + new technology"

Certainly, the history of the past 200 years has been that of a constant stream of new technologies, steam engines, railroads, autos, electronics, petrochemicals, etc. each of which has "changed everything" and powerfully stimulated economic growth. It would not seem unreasonable to expect this to continue in the future. Indeed, when the claims of "cold fusion" were advanced in 1989, on the flimsiest of scientific evidence, they were accepted by a large number of people on the belief no doubt that the world was "due" for just such a technological fix for its economic and environmental problems.

However, there is a sense in which the technologies that are now being investigated, (high temperature superconductivity, fusion, artificial intelligence, climatic and global environmental modeling, genetic engineering, etc.) are fundamentally different from the technologies which propelled global economic growth up until now.

The latter technologies were "reductivist technologies" which employed isolated chemical, electro-magnetic, physical and quantum reactions which were controlled by "clockwork mechanisms", such as gears, levers, pipes, circuits, hydraulics, etc. The new technologies being looked at now are far more complex, involving intricate "non-linear" systems, plasma control, complex molecular systems, "holistic" pattern recognition, etc.

Is it really so obvious when these technologies will yield commercial applications whose growth inducing effects are so powerful as to constitute a "technological fix" for the current global economic crisis? Will it be months, years, decades, centuries? Will an ad hoc "production function" for technological development really predict this? In other words, isn't it true that revolutionary new technologies are, to some extent, "manna from heaven" and outside the realm of purely economic analysis?

"There is something not quite right with the idea that an increasing allocation of labor-time (or just output) to research activity can buy increases in the rate of growth of knowledge. If anything like that were true, then R&D outlays equal to 2% of the GNP would be unaccountably small. The numbers get much larger when the activity in question is understood to include all education and training. It still seems to me to play fast and loose with the rates of growth. . . . Fundamental technological change probably is more nearly exogenous. Anyone who has ever done research knows that. Given a functioning research activity, a lot depends on chance and erratic insight."

R. Solow, 1990

Of course, this doesn't mean that perpetual economic growth on a stable population is impossible. It only means that such growth cannot be predicted using economic arguments alone. Will such economic growth in fact occur?

Our own opinion is that, barring some completely revolutionary technological development such as, for example, "cold fusion", it's hard to imagine perpetual economic growth in the West that does not also involve the participation of large numbers of people outside the West.

In other words, to paraphrase Paul Romer, a great deal of future economic growth will, inevitably, consist of "causing advanced technologies to be used in the less advanced countries" whether this be easy or hard.

Everyone agrees that the new growth theories provide valuable insights into the economic growth process. However, they remain controversial. They have been criticized for being too ambitious, for attempting to explain too much by means of mathematical formulae.

J. Stiglitz (1990), for example, describes them as being characterized by "a certain amount of *chutzpah* combined with a high level of technical ingenuity". In the same way that the new growth theories attempt to model the generation of new technologies some of which will inevitably involve "facts of nature" which are not as yet known and could be quite surprising when they are discovered, so to do these new growth theories propose to explain institutional, historical, social, cultural and political change as well:

"Changes in institutions can solve the problem of explaining the time trend in growth rates but they do so by exchanging exogenous technological change for exogenous institutional change. Making institutional change exogenous allows economists to conduct a provisional analysis that focuses on issues that they understand relatively well and sets aside ones that they do not. But ultimately, one would like to be able to explain the evolution of institutions as well. It seems quite plausible that increasing rates of return and increasing opportunities for private investment caused the evolution of institutions that supported these activities." (P. Romer, 1991)

Many historians think the important chain of historical causality went in the reverse direction:

"In Europe, . . . the private trade sector had evolved from the wreckage of central authority during the Dark Ages. The small scale of early government attached itself to trade—for the sake of the revenues that sector could quickly provide. In China and Asia generally the private sector emerged only after government on sufferance. No independent laws arose to shield it. Contractual legalism never replaced statist morality. The Chinese (in particular) showed signs of development nevertheless but was turned aside by the dead-end opportunity of internal colonization." E.L. Jones (1981)

During the early feudal ages in Europe. a pattern of development began in which technology (the water mill

(Roman), the heavy plough (Slavic), the three field system, the horseshoe (Celtic), and a new method of harnessing draught animals (China)) began to be assimilated and applied to agricultural production at a very rapid rate promoting a growth in output which, over the long term, exceeded demographic growth, something not true in the classical civilizations. Furthermore, the institutions to block these activities had not had time to arise (the Carolingian empire fell apart, the Mongol invasion of the 13th century stopped short of Western Europe, etc.)

In other words, the division of human society into a developed West, a centralized East and an underdeveloped South began a thousand years ago.

It was at this time, in Western Europe, that a new type of society emerged in which productive growth in advance of population growth emerged as a "social organizing principle" involving the formation of decentralized stocks of capital and decentralized political power centers. It involved the growth of feudal society, the growth of contractual relations, the dependence of the monarchs on the merchant classes in the towns, the rapid expansion of trade and ultimately the "scientific" and "industrial" revolutions.

Why, after so many thousands of years of agricultural civilization, such an unprecented and unique form of social and historical evolution should have occured in the small Western promontory of Eurasia is ultimately a mystery.

It had something to do with Christianity, something to do with the prior Celtic and Germano-Roman cultures, something to do with the nature of decaying Western

Roman society, something to do with the geographic, climatic, environmental and epidemiological nature of Europe. Its eastward spread was hampered by the nomadic invasions of the 13th century, which, in turn, determined the centralized shape of the Russian political economy.

The "South" was formed by 500 years of colonization, by the West, of what is now the "underdeveloped world"(South America, Africa, the Ottoman Empire, Mughal India, Safavid Persia, the Ching Dynasty and East Asia).

All of this greatly influenced the differing amounts of "human capital" in different sectors of the world. It's no accident, for example, that Japan, the only non-Western country to fully join the developed world, was spared both the Mongol invasion and European colonization, and had a feudal social structure closer to that of pre-industrial Europe than to the centralized political structure of the "classical civilizations" of antiquity.

Can the results of such long term historical evolution really be described by means of mathematical equations? If not, it certainly won't be for lack of trying. Some new growth theorists are attempting to do just that (M. Kremer, 1992, A, Ades and T Verdier, 1993).

However, for the purposes of this book, we will stick to purely qualitative exposition when we discuss very long term economic development in the next chapter.

ECONOMIC GROWTH AND HUMAN CAPITAL

CHAPTER 3

A DIGRESSION ON DEVELOPMENT ECONOMICS

What does economic theory have to say about the growth prospects of the underdeveloped world? We start with this region first, not because we are examining the world's regions in order of demographic size, but because, there is, at this point, a greater body of theoretical and empirical research about Third World development.

To begin with, some brief comments on the various branches of economic theory. The first is classical economics. The major classical economists were Adam Smith (1723-1790), David Ricardo (1772-1823) and Karl Marx (1818-1883).

One of the problems addressed by classical economics was the question of what caused a commodity to be valuable (i.e. to command a high price). It couldn't simply be how useful the commodity is. After all, water is very useful, but has a very low price, whereas diamonds are far less useful, but have a very high price. This was the famous "diamond-water paradox" of Adam Smith. The answer given by classical economists was that the value,(cost price. essential price, or price of production) of a produced good or commodity must,in some sense, be a numerical measure of the amount of effort involved in obtaining or producing the good.

The classical economists assumed that each commodity must have a natural or essential price, which was determined by the ease or difficulty of producing it, and around which the market price would fluctuate as, supply and demand conditions changed. For example, in a hypothetical primitive economy, in which everybody obtained or produced their own goods, the value of a good should be the number of hours required to obtain or produce it. If it took one hour to hunt a deer and two hours to hunt a bear, than one bear should be worth twice as much as one deer, and two dears should exchange for one bear in the market. If the exchange, were less than that, then people who wanted bears, would find that it took less effort to hunt deer, and exchange them for bears, than to hunt bears. The supply of deer would increase and the supply of bear would drop until the two-for-one deer for bear exchange rate obtained.

Of course, the classical economists were aware that, in a more advanced economy, where the production of goods required intermediate products, hired labor, tools and instruments of production, which themselves had to be produced, different amounts of time to completion, etc., goods would not, in general, exchange with each other according to the amount of labor time embedded in each.

None the less, the classical economists felt that the essential value, if not price, of a good should, in some sense, be its labor-time equivalent. Smith maintained that the value of a good should be the number of hours somebody would be willing to work to obtain the good, (the amount of labor time commanded by the good.) Ricardo sought to measure the labor-time equivalent of a particular good by determining how much of a good, that required only labor to produce, the good in question would exchange for. Marx specified the labor time embodied in a particular good as the amount of labor required to produce that good, including the amount of labor required to produce all intermediate inputs to that good, together with the amount of labor required to produce all the inputs to the inputs, and so on, ad infinitum.

The classical economists sought to determine the laws by which the total amount of values produced per year, (the total economic output), was distributed among the three main social classes of the time, (land owners, laborers and capital-owners). They also sought to determine the laws by which the values of goods were transformed into prices of production. Marx claimed to have found a solution to these two problems, but his solutions were shown to be mathematically flawed by the Austrian economist Eugene Von Boehm-Bawerk. In short, the classical economists never really succeeded in adequately defining their concepts of value and natural price.

More recently, a group of economists known as neo-Ricardians (Piero Sraffa, Ian Steedman, Michio Morishima), using a branch of mathematics known as matrix algebra, have again returned to the problem of calculating prices of production independent of market prices and monetary measures. Also, there have been attempts to develop an energy theory of value in order to calculate, independently of the future energy prices,the rate of return on investments in alternative energy sources.(M. Slesser (1989), and N. Georgescu-Roegen (1972)).

To summarize, the classical economists, investigated the concept of natural price, divided consumers into social classes, (land-owners, capital-owners and laborers), and divided industries into branches,(i.e. agriculture and manufacturing, or capital goods and consumer goods). Natural prices were calculated by assuming that the rate of return to capital invested was equalized among the various branches of industry.

The neoclassical economists (Leon Walras (1834-1910), Stanley Jevons (1835-1882), Vilfredo Pareto (1848-1923)) took an entirely different approach to economic research. They maintained that rapid technological change made the concept of natural price or value meaningless. They also maintained that society was changing too rapidly to be divided into social classes. The method used by the neo-classical economists was to examine an economy at its maximum level of detail (maximum disaggregation). That is, they tended to view an economy as consisting of an enormous number of individual commodities, individual consumers and individual producers (firms). This is called an atomistic way of looking at an economy. The feeling was that economics can only deal scientifically with individual agents, whether consumers or producers, that it was very difficult to speak scientifically about economic aggregates.

On the face of it, it would seem that this approach converts a difficult problem into an impossible one. After all, how, can one analyze the behavior of millions of individual consumers, workers and producers? Only, it turns out, by making a number of drastic simplifying assumptions about such behavior. The most important of these assumptions, is the assumption that this behavior is describable mathematically.

To explain this, let's examine the most important doctrine of neoclassical economics, the so-called theory of general multimarket equilibrium. This theory, due to Leon Walras, was essentially an approach to determining relative prices. It maintained that if some "all knowing being" possessed enough knowledge about:

- all the types of commodities used for consumption or production (including land and labor);
- the preferences, material desires and material assets of each of the consumers;
- the methods and technologies of production of each of the producers (firms), this knowledge would suffice to determine the relative prices of each of the commodities, assuming (among other things) that the economy was in a state of perfect competition. The relative prices so determined would be such that the market for every commodity "cleared". What do we mean by "perfect competition"? We mean that no one individual consumer or producer is large enough to have more than a vanishingly small effect on market prices. What do we mean when we say "the market for every commodity clears"? We mean that there is a set of relative prices such that:

- every consumer or producer who wants and is able to afford to buy a good can find a seller of that good;
- every consumer or producer who wants to and, has, or is able to make a particular good to sell can find a buyer for that good.

Furthermore, the theory of general equilibrium, maintains that perfect competition will bring about exactly the set of relative prices that would be calculated above by the "all knowing being". In other words, perfect competition is an "all-knowing being" who is able to perfectly allocate goods among individuals with no shortages or wastage.

To most of the economists of the time, to prove such an assertion seemed like an insanely ambitious task. Yet Leon Walras gave very convincing arguments that it could be done. A. Wald (1936) and K. Arrow and G. Debreu (1954) gave rigorous mathematical proofs of much of Walras's general equilibrium theory. Walras suggested that equilibrium prices are reached by a process known as tatonnement or "groping", suggested by his observations of the Paris stock exchange. In the process of tatonnement, there is a sort of "market machine" which coordinates all production and exchange. This "market machine" operates as follows: It begins by posting a list of prices for each commodity. It then asks each producer how much of each commodity the producer would be willing to produce at those prices, and how much of each commodity (including labor) the producer would need in order to carry out the production. It then asks each consumer how much of each commodity (including labor) the consumer would want to purchase (or sell) at those prices. If there is a shortage of any commodity, the "market machine" raises the price. If there is a surplus of any commodity, the "market machine" lowers the price. After this is done, all the producers and consumers are polled again. This process is continued until a list of prices is found, such that (1) all commodities produced at those prices will find a buyer, and (2) every consumer's and every producer's buying plans at those prices are realizable. In other words, all the bargaining takes place before any physical production or exchange takes place. While this might be a realistic description of an auction, say, it is obviously not a realistic description of most actual markets. The actual process by which "equilibrium prices" are reached in actual markets is extremely difficult to analyze mathematically, and is an object of continuing research (and acrimonious controversy). (See F. M. Fisher, 1989.)

Leaving such difficulties to one side, let's give a little more detail about Walras' general equilibrium theory as described above. How does one go about measuring a particular consumer's "preferences"? Sometimes this is done by means of a utility function which gives a numerical measure of the amount of "satisfaction" a consumer would derive from the consumption of any particular combination of commodities. Sometimes by a concept known as ranked preferences which ranks the various commodities in the order in which they are preferred, and sometimes by a more involved concept known as revealed preferences. How does one go about describing the "technologies of production" of a particular producer? This can be done by a mathematical concept known as a production function or by a mathematical concept known as a production possibility set. How does one describe the various assets owned by a particular consumer before the trading and producing takes place?

This is done by describing the amount of each commodity initially possessed by the consumer, including his or her ability to provide labor services, and his or her ownership shares in each of the producers (firms). Having done this, how does one predict the behavior of each of the consumers and each of the producers? How is one able to tell what kinds of exchanges and what kinds of production will take place? This is done by assuming that each consumer will strive to maximize his or her utility and that each producer will strive to maximize its profit. The actual mathematics of Walras's general equilibrium theory is far beyond the scope of this book. It involves the solution of a very, very large number of "simultaneous equations" A description of the proof requiring college calculus can be found in Henderson and Quandt (1986) and a detailed proof can be found in Arrow and Debreu (1954).

With Keynesian economics, (John Maynard Keynes, 1883-1946) the emphasis shifts back to the study of large economic aggregates (total economic output, total consumption, etc.) Such a study was not an issue in neoclassical economics, where it was simply assumed that competitive pressures would force the economy to make the most efficient use of the resources and techniques available to it. If there was unemployment, for example, wages would drop until all labor was employed. Simultaneously, output would rise as the additional labor was put to use. The additional output, for its part, would be consumed by the larger work force, and what was not consumed would be invested.

However, in the 1930's, many of the world's economies were clearly operating below capacity amid widespread unemployment. Thus, Keynes was confronted with the problem of explaining an economic decline occurring amid gluts rather than shortages. Furthermore, the economic failure was "system-wide" rather than confined to any particular sector. Therefore, Keynes needed to study the behavior of large, economy-wide aggregates. But how are such aggregates to be measured? In classical economics, the answer was (deceptively) simple. The value of any good, or any agglomeration of goods, no matter how large, was simply the number of labor hours needed to produce it. In modern macroeconomics, however, the measurement of economic aggregates is an extremely complicated issue. In general, economic aggregates have two measures, a nominal measure (the total monetary value) and a real measure (which is actually less "real" than the monetary measure, consisting of the monetary value "adjusted for changes in the general price level"). Hence, it can be immediately seen that modern macroeconomics has a lot of complexities which weren't present in classical or neoclassical economics. In fact, modern macroeconomics is an enormous field. It addresses such areas as the collection, evaluation and aggregation of economic data (national accounts), the modeling of the economy, economic forecasting, policy advice to governments, the formulation of economic theories to explain changes in the economy, and the formulation of statistical methods to test the conclusions of these theories.

There are very few people who don't have some idea of "what Keynes said". In fact, there such a large number of popular books on this topic, that there is no need for us to dwell on it here. The question we address here is: "what theoretical techniques did Keynes use, and in what way did these theoretical techniques differ from the techniques of neoclassical economics?". For those who have a background in college calculus, A. Stevenson et. al. (1988:1-56) gives a very clear summary of this topic. The version of Keynesian theory it presents is known as the Hicks-Hansen IS-LM model. The IS-LM model is a simple general equilibrium model which is similar in, some ways, to the general equilibrium models of neoclassical economics. However, unlike neoclassical equilibrium models, it does not rely exclusively on consumer preferences and production technologies. It consists of a small group of simple equations which express the interrelationships between the following variables (known as macroeconomic variables); the money supply (M), the general price level (P), the wage rate (W), total employment (N), the real interest rate (r) and real economic output (y). For example, one such equation would be:

$$y = e(y,r);$$

where e(y,r) is real expenditure (demand) as a function of y and r.

Another equation would be:

$$M/P = l(y,r);$$

where M/P is the supply of "real purchasing power" (real balances) and l(y,r) is the demand for it.

In some cases, it can be shown that the function l(y.r) can have a shape which makes it impossible for markets to clear. In other cases, the function e(y,r) can have a shape which likewise make it impossible for markets to clear. Thus, one can use the IS-LM model to construct plausible systems of economic equations which have no realistic market clearing solutions. This gives one the "theoretical permission", as it were, to drop the assumption of market clearing for the labor market, assume unemployment, and vary the parameters e, M and P in order to observe the effect of these variations on employment (N) and real output (y). Out of this kind of analysis comes the "Keynesian multiplier", "the liquidity trap", "the Keynes effect", etc., and all of the other Keynesian terminology which you may or may not be familiar with. A more detailed explanation of the IS-LM model is given in the notes.

One of the purposes of modern Keynesian macroeconomics is to study statistical and historical economic data to search for economic structure. Economic structure consists of mathematical relationships between economic aggregates which persist over a long period of time.

An econometric forecasting model consists of a great many equations expressing structural relationships between economic aggregates. These equations are derived by means of statistical analysis of historical economic data, as well as by economic theory. Econometric models are used to predict future economic activity. They are also used to analyze and forecast the future ffects of proposed changes in government economic policies; i.e. to push economic reasoning "beyond historical experiences". (L. R. Klein and R. M. Young 1980:9) It was Professor Lawrence Klein who pioneered the construction and application of large-scale econometric forecasting models.

In the early 1970's, the economist Robert Lucas developed a very significant critique of Keynesian econometrics. This critique was called the Lucas critique.

Briefly stated, the Lucas critique maintained that there were severe limitations on the use of structural relationships between macroeconomic aggregates, either in economic policy making or economic forecasting. This is because a change in government economic policy would be observed by consumers and producers who would adjust their economic behavior in response, and structural relationships which held prior to the policy change, would no longer hold after it.

The Lucas critique means that economic theory must take into account the way in which consumers, workers and producers change their economic behavior in response to changes in government economic policies. It is now necessary to describe how consumers and producers develop forecasts of future economic conditions in response to changes in government economic policies. This study is known as the theory of rational expectations or the new classical economics. In this branch of economics, prices are not just a means of allocating resources. They are also a source of economic information about the current and future state of the economy as a whole. Consumers and producers, when confronted with a price change, face a problem of "signal extraction"; they have to decide how much of this price rise is due to inflation and how much to a change in the demand or supply of the product they are making (buying). Consumers and producers make "random errors" when doing this (according to rational expectations theory) but not systematic errors, because systematic errors would eventually be noticed and compensated for.

Rational expectations economics is a sort of "souped up" version of neoclassical general equilibrium theory. It assumes that (1) markets clear very, very rapidly at all times, (2) consumers and producers maximize their expected economic benefit, and (3) consumers and producers make decisions based on forecasts which have random errors but no systematic biases. Cycles in real wages, employment levels and real business activity are explained by means of forecast errors ("signal extraction problems"), changes in consumer preferences and changes in production technologies. Unlike Keynesian economics, rational expectations economics is pessimistic about the ability of government to manipulate the economy in a beneficial way.

In recent years, an enormous amount of empirical research has been devoted to testing the predictions of rational expectations economics. There have also been extensive searches for testable predictions of rational expectations which differ from the predictions of alternative theories. Elaborate statistical studies have been made to determine when, and to what extent, the Lucas critique of Keynesian econonometric models applies in practise.

The above summary is by no means a complete survey of the various brands of economics. Nor is the chapter to come a complete survey of development economics (which is why it's entitled "a digression on" rather than "a survey of"). For a layman's survey of the various branches of economics, we recommend Economic Theory in Retrospect by Mark Blaug (1978).

Now we are ready to address the following question: "What do the various branches of economics have to say about the prospects for Third World development?

In fact, the answer to that question is not at all obvious, since none of these branches of economics was actually formulated with Third World development in mind. Classical economics was formulated to explain the development of the first "underdeveloped" country to develop, namely England. It wasn't designed to describe development in a world market dominated by already developed countries. Keynesian economics was designed to explain the development of a mid-20th century developed country whose economic output was constrained a lack of demand, rather than by lack of supply. It wasn't designed to describe a Third World economy suffering from supply and capital shortages.

When it comes to describing Third World development, neoclassical economics certainly has the advantage. This is because the "laws" of neoclassical economics, like the laws of physics, are presumed to be the same in one area of the world as in another, and should, therefore, be able to explain economic behavior in one area of the world as well (or as badly) as in another. After all, (according to neoclassical economics) what's so special about a developing country? Isn't every country "a developing country"? Isn't every country undergoing rapid structural transformation?

And the answer, of course, is "yes, rapid structural change has been pervasive in the world economy in recent years". Indeed, this is one of the reasons why neoclassical methods have come into vogue, since the 70's, both in the developed and developing worlds. (See R. Takachi, 1993) In times of rapid and pervasive structural change, the tendency (for better or worse) is to "go back to the fundamentals", back to the "equations of motion" of individual "economic agents", where firms maximize profit and consumer maximize "utility".

As for the other branches of economics, their perspective is that a country is "developing" until it "develops", after which it is "developed". Once it "develops" then it can be described by "economics". But, until it develops (if ever), then it must be described by "development economics". "Development economics" is economics "customized", in various ways for the particular problems faced by a "developing country".

So, rather than concentrating on branches of economic theory, let's concentrate on what D. Hunt (1989) calls paradigms of Third World development. Some of these paradigms, such as structuralism and dependency theory, are rather pessimistic about the prospects for Third World development. Others, such as the neo-Marxian paradigm, are very pessimistic about the prospects for Third World development. Still others, such as the neoclassical paradigm, are optimistic. The neo-Marxian paradigm depends on the labor theory of value ala classical economics. Structuralism and dependency theory are Keynesian in orientation, and the neoclassical paradigm is obviously neoclassical in orientation.

Let's start with the most pessimistic paradigm first. We do this by using an example incorporating the labor theory of value. Now the great majority of modern day economists regard the labor theory of value as an anachronism.

Expressed in its mathematically correct version, the labor theory of value is a labyrinthine tangle of matrix algebra and, in its classical form, it is mathematically incorrect! However, in its classical form, the labor theory of value does have the advantage that it yields simple examples that can be presented using arithmetic only.

To examine such an example, suppose that there is a completely self-sufficient (closed) economy that has, over its history, accumulated 140 labor units of capital stock, (where each labor unit is a very large number of labor hours). Suppose that the useful life of this capital stock is seven years. Using straight line depreciation, all firms in the economy, put together, incur a capital depreciation cost of 20 labor units yearly. Suppose, furthermore, that, in addition to the 20 labor units of capital used up annually in production, 40 units of labor must be applied to produce the economy's annual product. The total 'value' of the economy's annual output is then 40 + 20 which is 60 labor units. Suppose that total wages paid to all the laborers is the equivalent of 12 labor units of goods. Thus, the total wage cost incurred annually by all firms in the economy is 12 labor units, Hence, the total "cost of production", in labor units, is depreciation cost plus labor cost, or 20 + 12, which is 32 labor units. Since the total value of annual output is 60 labor units, the 'profit' expressed in labor units is the total value produced less the total cost of production, which is 60 less 32 which is 28 labor units.

What is the average "profit rate" of this economy expressed in labor units? It is equal to "total profits divided by total capital stock" which is 28/140 which is 20%.

Of course, in actuality, the profit rate expressed in labor unit terms is not equal to the actual profit rate, which is, of course, the profit rate in monetary terms. It is not even a close approximation. However, for the sake of argument, let's assume that the profit rate in labor unit terms is a very, very rough first approximation of the actual profit rate, and thus for the remainder of this example, we'll continue to use it as the real profit rate.

Now, let's continue with the example. What is one of the major differences between Third World countries and developed countries? Certainly, one of the major differences is that Third World countries, with very few exceptions, have a much lower standard of living and a much lower wage rate than developed countries. So let's divide our economy above into two sectors, a rich sector and a poor sector. Assume that the rich sector has accumulated 70 labor units of capital stock and that the poor sector has likewise accumulated 70 labor units of capital stock. Assume that labor in the poor sector has the same productivity as labor in the rich sector. Assume, furthermore that:

- the capital stock in both sectors has a seven year useful life;
- in each sector 20 labor units must be applied to the capital stock to produce the total annual output;
- capital and goods are completely mobile between sectors but labor is completely immobile between sectors;
- the "wage cost" in labor units is 10 for the rich sector but only 2 for the poor sector even though equal amounts of labor are performed in each sector.

Thus, each sector produces 30 labor units of output which includes, in each case, 10 units of capital stock used up in production, and 20 units of applied labor. Thus, the total value produced by both sectors taken together is again 60 labor units. The total cost of production of both sectors taken together is again 20 labor units depreciation cost plus 12 units labor cost or 32 labor units. Total profits for both sectors is again 28 labor units. In other words, the "average rate of profit" for both sectors taken together is "total profits / total capital stock" which is 28 / 140 which is again 20%."

Since capital is completely mobile between sectors the profit rate in each sector taken individually should identical and be equal to the average rate of profit for both sectors taken together! Thus, the profit rate in each sector is 20%. Since each sector has 70 units of capital stock, the total profit in each sector is 20% times 70 units which is 14 labor units.

. This allows us to calculate the total price of produced goods in each sector individually. (Each in the table below is assumed to be in labor units).

Sector Depreciation Labor Cost Profit Price of Production

rich 10 + 10 + 14 = 34
poor 10 + 2 + 14 = 26

To conclude the example, the total value of goods produced in the rich sector is 30 labor units, but its total price is 34 labor units. The rich sector has gained 4 labor units of value. Conversely, the total value of goods produced in the poor sector is 30 labor units but the total price is only 26 units. The poor sector has lost 4 units of value. Because the poor sector has a lower standard of living, capital mobility and trade have worked to its disadvantage. Wealth in the form of "value" has drained out of the poor sector and into the rich sector.

And, indeed, over the past several decades, a great many poor countries, (including very poor countries such as Haiti) have been the recipients of an enormous amount of "industrial redeployment" from the rich countries without becoming wealthier and, in many cases, becoming poorer. According to the above argument, this is because capital infusions have "sucked wealth" out of those countries, rather than put wealth into them.

To take an example, S. Amin (1976) estimates the amount of "value" transferred from the undeveloped world to the developed world in 1966. He proceeds as follows. Total exports of the underdeveloped world to the developed world, in 1966, were on the order of $35 billion. Of this, the "ultra modern sector" (oil, mining, modern plantations, primary processing) contributed approximately 75% or $25 billion worth of exports. Amin calculates the total cost of these same products, if produced in the developed world, as $34 billion. He makes the following assumptions in this calculation. He assumes that, since the sectors in question are "ultramodern", the same techniques would be used in the developed world as in the developing world. He also assumes that, given the same techniques, the productivity of the workers in the developing world would be the same as that of the workers in the developed world. (Compare with R. Lucas, 1988). He assumes, furthermore, that the average rate of profit on total capital stock is 15%, and that the average useful life of ths capital is 7 years. He assumes that the average rate of surplus value (total production in labor units from which is subtracted depreciation in labor units and labor cost in labor units) is 100% Under those assumptions, Amin calculates that, in 1966, $8 billion of value was transferred from the developing world to the developed world by means of trade in the "ultramodern sector" alone.

Why are wages lower in the poor countries? Because of the growth of population and the lack of high productivity industries to employ this expanding population. This drives down wages.

In other words, underdevelopment leads to low wages, which (according to the above example) leads to economic losses through trade, which, in turn, perpetuates underdevelopment, which, in turn, leads to low wages, and so on. This, phenomenon is known as the theory of unequal exchange

Before we continue, it must be pointed out that there are a great many flaws with the above examples. First, of all, studies have shown that labor in poor countries is generally not as productive as labor in rich countries. Furthermore, the example, presented above, fails to explain why capital doesn't simply keep flowing from the rich sector to the poor sector, until wages rates equalize in both sectors. For a much more complete exposition of the theory of unequal exchange see A. Emmanuel (1972). For a critique of logical inconsistencies of this theory see P.A. Samuelson (1976).

Later on in this chapter, we will discuss several examples, neo-classical, new classical and neo-Keynesian which present "unequal exchange" in a logically and mathematically consistent form, (without recourse to "labor values").

Before doing that, however, we will discuss a more mainstream economic theory which also analyzes the obstacles to Third World development. This theory is known as the ECLA school of development economics or Latin American structuralism. This theory was developed by the Argentinean economist Raul Prebisch (1901-1986) in 1949 and is also known as the Prebisch-Singer hypothesis.

Here is a brief description of the Prebisch-Singer hypothesis. The vast majority of Third World countries began their integration into the global market economy via the export of raw materials and agricultural products, (i.e. sugar, coffee, tea, nitrates, raw silk, rubber, copper, tin, cotton, etc.) to the developed economies. In return, they imported manufactured goods from the developed economies. In some cases, these Third World export industries were developed directly by European colonizers (an example being the Dutch industrial plantations in Indonesia.) In other cases, they were the result of political and economic deals between the European colonizers and local elites such as the Zamindars in India or the Islamic Cofraternities in Nigeria. In the case of Eqypt, several thousand highly placed Egyptian government bureaucrats were converted into landowners to produce cotton for export to Britain. In the case of Latin America, the rural oligarchy, which had gained control after the liberation of Latin America from Spain, and which had acquired ownership of the bulk of the land, set up export industries to the industrial countries, primarily Britain and America.

To summarize, the underdeveloped countries exported raw material and agricultural products to the developed countries and the developed countries exported manufactured goods to the underdeveloped countries.

The economic demand for a particular commodity depends on many factors. Two of the most important factors are the price of the commodity and the income of the consumers of the commodity. The lower the price of a commodity the greater should be the economic demand for it. The higher the income of the consumers of a commodity, the greater should be the economic demand for it. As economic development takes place, the income of the consumers in the developed countries rises, and the income of the elites in the underdeveloped countries rises. Consequently, the economic demand, both for the manufactured goods of the developed countries and the raw materials of the underdeveloped countries, rises. But, according to the Prebisch-Singer hypothesis, the demand for manufactured goods rises to a much greater extent than does the demand for raw materials and agricultural goods. After all, if a consumer's income doubles that doesn't mean he or she will consume twice as much coffee or twice as much sugar. The extra income will be rather more likely to increase the person's demand for manufactured goods. Similarly, if the output of manufactured goods increases, This doesn't mean that the demand for raw material inputs to the manufactured goods will increase by the same percentage. Developed countries are always developing ways to conserve on raw material use and are always developing substitutes for raw materials (i.e.

such as the substitution of fiber optics for copper cable). Thus, the price of the underdeveloped countries' exports tend to decline in relation to the prices of their imports from the developed countries; i.e. the terms of trade move against the underdeveloped countries.

Can the underdeveloped countries compensate for this disadvantage, by increasing the productivity of their raw material and agricultural export production, thereby lowering the price of and increasing the demand for their exports? No, according to the Presbisch-Singer hypothesis. If the price of coffee or sugar is halved, this doesn't mean consumption in the developed countries, will double. There is a limit to how much agricultural produce consumers, in the developed countries, will consume, no matter how low its price goes. Similarly, if the price of a raw material input to a manufactured good drops, this will generally not cause the price of the manufactured good to drop by much. The price of a raw material input is generally a very small percentage of the price of a manufactured good. Thus, the strategy of dropping the price of raw materials in order to stimulate demand for manufactured goods which use these raw materials as input is not likely to succeed. (The reader should have, by now, noticed two important exceptions to this discussion, namely oil and cocaine, but more of this later.

Actually, the Prebisch-Singer hypothesis involves more than just the type of commodity produced. It also involves the type of country which produces it (developed or underdeveloped). First of all, according to the Prebisch-Singer hypothesis, the developed countries maintain a permanent technological superiority over the developing countries; a fact which gives them a sort of "technological monopoly".

This tends to put upward pressure on the prices of their exports. In addition, wage rates in the developed world tend to rise as productivity rises (a fact which is due partially to unionization and partially to custom). Therefore, technical progress and increased productivity in the developed world tends to result in higher factor incomes (higher wages for workers and higher profits for owners) rather than lower prices for consumers. In contrast, the results of increased productivity in the developing world tend to show up as lower export prices, rather than higher factor incomes. Industries in the developing world do not generally enjoy a "technological monopoly" and, secondly, wage rates in the developing world are held down by chronic labor surpluses caused by rural-urban migration. Thus, there is a "tendency for productivity improvements (to benefit) consumers in industrial countries but not in. developing countries" and this "clearly (will) affect terms of trade and international income distribution." (H. W. Singer, 1989)

The Prebisch-Singer hypothesis was based on empirical studies by Singer of Britain's terms of trade between 1873 and 1938. The specific prediction of the Prebisch-Singer hypothesis is that the terms of trade of the underdeveloped countries with the developed countries show a long term tendency to decline. Has this, in fact, been the case? The empirical evidence is mixed. It depends on exactly how "terms of trade" are defined and on what the base year of the study is.

Both the Unequal Exchange argument of Emmanuel and the Prebisch-Singer declining terms of trade hypothesis can be presented as simple, highly aggregated, general equilibrium models called North-South models. For those who have had a course in intermediate microeconomics we recommend the formulation in E. I. Bacha 1978.

More recently, in the late 60's and early 70's, the Prebisch-Singer hypothesis has been extended to an even more pessimistic analysis of the losses to trade of the developing countries. This analysis is known as Dependency Theory. Some Dependency Theorists are Celso Furtado, Fernando Cardoso, and Theotonio Dos Santos. For a readable description of *Dependency Theory* (no graphs, formulas, or Greek letters) see R. A. Packenham, 1992.

Let's continue with the structuralist analysis of the barriers to Third World economic growth. Many Third World countries tried to solve their trade problems by adopting a policy of import substitution and the promotion of manufactured export goods. Import substitution is the substitution of domestically produced manufactured goods for imported manufactured goods. It usually took place behind tariff barriers, was based on the use of imported capital goods and technology, and involved the production of light manufactured goods such as textiles, certain types of machinery, leather goods, construction materials, and so on. Industrial import substitution took place in many of the large Third World countries during the breakdown of global trade during the depression and the World War II when manufactured inports became unafforable or unavailable. In fact, during the 1930's when the United States was plunged in depression, the large Latin American countries underwent an industrial expansion! At the end of World War II, Argentina was considered to be on the verge of becoming a developed country. A. Fishlow (1989) gives a readable discussion of Latin American economic performance during the 1930's and it's contrast to the Latin American debt crisis of the 1980's.

The problem with import substitution as a solution to the trade problems of Third World countries is that, ultimately, it requires the importation of more and more capital goods, technology and intermediate goods from the developed countries. Eventually, (during the late 40's and early 50') Third World countries began to experience the same trade problems with the import of capital goods and industrial technology as they had experienced with the import of light manufactures. They were then confronted with the task of developing a domestic capital goods industry. But this involves enormous economies of scale, and very large and costly initial investments. Thus, a very large market was needed over which to amortize startup costs. The export market was not an option because it would require being internationally competitive at the outset, an impossible task.

"(In Argentina in the 50's), although substantial early success was achieved in import substitution—in terms of growth and diversification of output—the promotion of industry fell short of providing incentives to increase productivity and product specialization that would have made possible the achievment of sufficient scale of production and economies of scale. The shelter of protection prevented industry from achieving lower costs, and the high costs deterred from further expansion of production. The lag of investments in energy and transport—basic imputs to all sectors of industry—also had very adverse repercussions on the industrial cost structure. The initial phases of IS in in Argentina were also characterized by insufficient backward linkages with supply sources at the primary and intermediate input levels at a time when imports were discouraged by high tariffs—Argentina's industry was thus caught in a vicious circle, with the inefficiency in production preventing entry into international markets and the lack of competitive pressure from domestic and export markets to improve quality and lower costs contibuting to not attaining economies of scale and efficiency" (S. Teitel, F. E. Thomas, 1986).

A potential solution to this dilemma is to possess a suffiently large internal market. But very few Third World countries possessed such a market. In fact, none of them did. This is because the internal market of even populous Third World countries, such as Brazil and India, was limited by widespread inequality in wealth and land distribution, widespread poverty and landlessness, and the unproductive nature of much of the agricultural sector.

The strategy tried by many Third World countries to get around this dilemma was the institution of land reform programs. A land reform program is the redistribution of landed property titles by the government in order to make land distribution more equal.

There are several goals behind land reform programs. One is to enlarge the internal market by restributing wealth (which in many Third World countries is largely in the form of land). Another is to increase productivity and efficiency in the agricultural sector by making it less monopolistic and more competitive (See T. W. Schultz, 1964). This allows the agricultural sector to act both as a market for and a source of food for industrial expansion. It is no accident (according to structuralism) that the East Asian developing countries which have more successful economies than other underdeveloped regions, also have a more equitable distribution of land! South Korea and Taiwan had notably successful land and rural credit reform programs imposed by Japanese and then American military occupation. Other countries in East Asia, such as Malaysia and Indonesia, have created greater equality in land distribution by crop extensification, and the resettlement of landless laborers to unused land (albeit at an environmental cost),

To understand the reasoning behind land reform, imagine a situation in America in which the Confederacy had won the civil war and, with the help of a foreign power, had occupied the agriculural land of the West and Mid-West and converted it into slave plantations producing cotton and other cash crops for export to Europe. Industry in the United States would have been deprived both of its domestic market of agricultural freeholders and of a significant source of food for its laborers. The region which is now the United States might have looked very much like a Latin American country today.

Fortunately, the United States won the civil war, but, unfortunately, successful land reforms in the Third World are very much the exception rather than the rule! The obstacles to land reform in Third World countries are very formidable.

First, there is the question of "fair compensation" to the large landowners. Since, land represents much of the wealth in underdeveloped countries, very few countries can afford to pay for widespread land redistribution. In other words, without the economic growth that land reform is supposed to generate, its implementation cannot be afforded, an obvious vicious circle. (Japan financed its post-war land reform by inflation.) In many cases, large landowners can easily evade land reform legislation, especially since most of the peasants seeking to defend their claims were illiterate. In many cases, large landowners were an important part of the government that was developing and executing land reform programs. Large land owners have preferential access to subsidized irrigation, fertilizers, and mechanization programs, and often control the seed farms necessary for HYV (High Yielding Variety) crops. Even in cases where land reforms were widespread and drastic, as were the land reforms under Lazaro Cardenas in Mexico in the 1930's, they were ultimately reversed:

" . . . The land reforms effected by Mexican President) Cardenas were reversed because. while large land ownerers were expropriated without any compensation . . . a very powerful sector dominated by large farmers survived, and this sector was allowed to aggrandize itself in later years. The political conditions for systenance of land reforms were, of course, upset as soon as Cardenas (left) . . ." (A. K. Bagchi, 1982)

A detailed examination of almost any land reform program will reveal the many obstacles to its implementation. To take one example, R. Carpano, 1990, gives an account of the difficulties and failures encountered by Comprehensive Agrarian Reform Program (CARP) in the Philippines under Aquino. It's no accident that some of the most successful land reform programs, (Japan, South Korea, China and Taiwan) were simply imposed by military occupation or revolution.

To summarize, land distribution in most of the underdeveloped world remains very unequal. A good, short, statistical survey of land distribution in the different regions of the Third World can be found in N. Quan and A. Y. C. Koo, 1985.

Some of the results of the new growth theories (see chapter 2) could be regarded as "pessimistic" for Third World development. However, we put the word "pessimistic", here, in quotes, because the new growth theories are, after all, "new", and many of their results have to be regarded as provisional. They are not meant to be hard and fast causal explanations of development and underdevelopment, but are meant rather to be mathematical models "consistent" with the actual patterns of development and underdevelopment. Keeping this in mind, recall, that, in many of the new growth theories (as in reality) economic development tends to distribute itself unevenly across the surface of global society. Areas with a greater accumulation of human capital tend to have more opportunities for profitable investment and, thus, tend to undergo still further development. Areas of low human capital endowment on the other hand, tend to have fewer opportunities for profitable investment, and, thus, tend to remain underdeveloped, even as they continue to undergo demographic, social and economic change (The so called "development of underdevelopment"). This can be seen intuitively by examining one of the postulated mechanisms of human capital accumulation. Successful, rapidly growing, Third World countries, such as the "Asian Tigers", have tended to follow the strategy of introducing a wider and wider variety of "higher and higher quality" industrial exports. This is known as "moving up the quality ladder". (See Grossman and Helpman, 1991). In fact, the very process of continuously learning-by-doing a greater and greater variety of more and more sophisticated industrial skills itself constitutes human capital formation.

The definition of a "high quality" industrial export is technical, but, in many of the formulations of human capital growth, it is defined in relation to the tastes and preferences of consumers globally. Since the global consumer market is dominated by consumers in rich countries and by the rich and middle classs elites in Third World countries, the successful Third World countries have achieved their success by acquiring a greater and greater skill at catering to the tastes and preferences of the world's rich minority, rather than the desperate needs of the world's poor majority. As A. Mackillop (1988) puts it, "illiterate people, who desperately need basic agricultural and industrial development, are not going to generate rapidly a market for yuppie goodies."

Thus, we can see that, almost by definition, development (human capital formation) is biased against the Third World. N. Stokey (1991) incorporates these ideas in a North-South equilibirium model to show that free trade between the North and South has a retardant effect on development (human capital formation) the South. The details of her paper are way beyond the scope of this book. In her formulation, "North" means "relatively well endowed with human capital". She obtains "a unique world equilibrium" where the "north" produces "high quality goods" and the "south" produces "low quality goods". She then concludes that "with free trade . . . human capital formation. is depressed in the poor country, which now imports high-quality goods from the rich country rather than attempting to produce them at home."

Lucas (1992) also points out that any North-South equilibrium model should also encompass an explanation of the "Asian miracles", the notable economic success of the East Asian economies.

"The main engine of growth is the accumulation of human capital—of knowledge— . . . Learning on the job seems to be by far the most (important way of doing this) . . . For such learning to occur on a sustained basis, it is necessary that (the workforce continuously takes on) . . . tasks that are new to (it), . . ."

This kind of "learning experience" can take place only if the country is a large scale exporter to markets that can afford "high quality products" (products whose manufacture provides the requisite learning stimuli). This, according to Lucas, is the way that the East Asian "tigers" accomplished their "economic miracle". However, it is not an approach that could be followed by the Third World as a whole, because "there is a zero-sum aspect, with inevitable mercantilist overtones, to productivity growth fueled by learning-by-doing."

The italicized sentence above means that the entire Third World is not going to grow at East Asian rates simply by exporting to the rich countries.

Some countries have tried to get around the above dilemmas by a "brute force" approach, i.e. by having the central government take over the construction of a capital goods industry "whole cloth". An example of this strategy is the Indian heavy industry strategy developed by Mahalanobis at the Statistical Institute in Calcutta. Under this strategy, the state planned, financed and built the capital goods industry and a large part of the intermediate goods industry. The import of technological knowledge and managerial know-how was permitted only until the knowledge was absorbed by domestic industry. Import licenses and production licenses were granted on a highly selective basis, by the central government, to ensure profitability of the new industries. This strategy led to a rapidly growing and integrated industrial sector. It also led to inefficiency, bureaucratization, corruption (the "License-Raj" system), enormous import costs, foreign exchange crises, and agricultural stagnation, which, in turn, (along with droughts) led to widespread famine in the mid-60's. For a critique of the strategy of government planned and controlled development see P. T Bauer (1972).

To sum up, there are many barriers to successful Third World development. These barriers include the lack of an entrepreneurial class, the enormous inequality in land and wealth distribution, the lack of free competitive markets in land, labor and goods, the feudal, oligarchic and bureaucratic restrictions on economic development, the hypertrophy of the service sector, the leakage of investment capital into speculation, the maldistribution of population and backwardness of agriculture (particularly in Africa), the unrepresentative nature of the political processes (particularly in the Middle East), the existence of overpopulation and excessive pressure on the carrying capacity of the land (particularly in parts of Asia), old diseases such as river blindness and cholera, and new diseases such as AIDS and drug resistant Malaria. In addition, as the global economy becomes more integrated, many of the blockages to development so long characteristic of the underdeveloped countries are beginning to manifest themselves in the developed countries as well.

Indeed, current economic debate in the United States centers on precisely such factors as increasing wealth inequality, the "hollowing" of the industrial sector, the growth of the speculative service sector (what the Japanese call the "bubble sector") of the economy and so on. Emil Luttwak describes these phenomena as "The Third Worldization of America" (See E. Luttwak, 1993). As De Long (1988) states ". . . the ability to assimilate industrial technology appears to be surprisingly hard to acquire, and it may be distressingly easy to lose." In other words, the blockages to Third World development have now become the blockages to global development as a whole.

Not an optimistic assessment to be sure, but there is also a brighter side to the picture. First of all, not withstanding the many North-South models which give pessimistic prognoses, the fact remains that, in certain regions, certain sectors, in certain time periods, and among certain groups, extremely rapid economic growth in the Third World has, in fact, taken place.

"(Most of the developing world) . . . is envisaged as . . . wretchedly poor, separated from the rich countries by a widening gap in income, . . . In fact, this picture bears no resemblence to reality. It does not do justice to. the rapid growth of many formerly poor countries and the prosperity of large groups there" P. T. Bauer (1991)

"We often fail to appreciate just how spectacular the rate of accumulation has been in the Third World compared to past historical standards. It took America more than six decades to do what the Third World has done in two or three." J. Williamson (1988)

Jeffrey Williamson believes that there is a lot more dynamism in Third World societies than most people recognize. In many Third World countries agrarian reform programs have been successful up to a point. In India, for example, in the 70's large landed estates were successfully redistributed to about 10% of the rural popoulation, and agricultural productivity was dramatically increased in several of the Indian provinces including Punjab, Haryana and Andhra Pradesh using irrigation and HYV technology. In Kerala a very equitable land redistribution was carried out but without a consequent increase in industrial growth.

Secondly, mainstream free market economics is inherently optimistic that private ownership, free, competitive markets and free trade will promote economic development. It happened in the developed free market economies. Why would it not eventually happen elsewhere? Much of mainstream economic theory stresses gains through economic integration between nations and betwqeen the developed and underdeveled economies. These gains include Ricardo's well known theory of comparative advantage, the realization of economies of scale through trade (emphasized by Adam Smith) and the benefits of technology transfer through foreign investment from North to South. Much of the advice given to developing countries by the IMF and the World Bank is to follow policies that encourage integration into the world market by reversing the governmental policies that were instituted during the import substitution phases of industrialzation. Such procedures are called structural adjustments. These include currency reform such as devaluations to promote exports, monetary reforms such as the elimination of monetary creation as a form of government financing, financial reform such as interest rate deregulation, tax reform such as replacing trade taxes with consumption taxes, regulatory reform such as easing of industrial licensing, trade reform such as ending or easing import quotas, privatization of government assets to encourage capital inflow, etc. Trade agreements such as the Uruguay Round of GATT (General Agreement on Trade and Tariffs) and NAFTA (the North American Free Trade Agreement) are designed to promote Third World development through North-South trade and capital and technology transfer. In fact, during the Reagan and Bush administrations, the West's main approach to North-South economic issues has been the use and proposed use of North-South trade to promote Third World development. (See R. Reagan 1985).

Another reason for optimism about the growth prospects of the underdeveloped countries is the so-called Gerschenkron thesis updated to include the experience of the East Asian countries, The Gerschenkron thesis maintains that there are "advantages to backwardness", especially in the ability to utilize the latest developments in technology to "leapfrog" the development paths taken by the developed countries. For example, the use of cellular telephones and satellite communications can allow telephone systems to be installed in the underdeveloped countries without the enormous infrastructural and labor costs associated with the development of telephone systems in the advanced countries. Containerization and robotization allow many types of industrial plants to be built in underdeveloped countries with less need for industrial insfrastructure and industrial skill pools. Electronic communication reduces the need for literacy in skill transfer, and can potentially allow activity in any part of the world to be coordinated and managed in any other part of the world. Electronic communication can reduce the need for the "geographical clustering" that R. Lucas (1988) talks about. In fact, the economist, W. Rostow (ever the perennial optimist) projects that the above technologies (". . . the fourth great technological revolution of past two centuries") will enable most of the developing world to develop rapidly.

"Despite current vissitudes, India, . . . China . . . and (most of) . . . Latin America . . . are likely to absorb the new technologies and move rapidly forward over the next several generations". W. Rostow, 1991.

The "advantages to backwardness" become particularly strong if an environmental constraint to global growth materializes (such as the projected greenhouse effect). It is precisely the underdeveloped nature of the LDC's that could give them the potential to develop in a way that circumvents environmental constraints. In other words, the underdeveloped regions of the world, precisely because they are underdeveloped, have the potential to be more flexible in their development. It is potentially easier for them to develop along a different path, since their physical and social structures are not locked into a preexisting path. For example, compare the rapid success of the Soviet Union's free market reforms in the early 20's, when it was relatively underdeveloped, to the extreme difficulties that the present day C.I.S. is having with its privatization and marketization plans. Compare, also, China's success with free market reforms to the current difficulties of the C.I.S.

For the sake of argument, let's suppose that scientific evidence clearly shows at some point that carbon emissions into the atmoshpere have to be severely curtailed. The developed economies are now "locked into" into various physical, infrastructural and economic patterns, which are "CO_2 emission intensive", centralized power grids, automobile-ization, chemical and energy intensive agriculture, fossil fuel generation of electricity. For example, the gains in CO_2 emission reduction that could be realized from the use of biofuels is limited by the fact that the production of the crops to be used for biomass energy is itself energy intensive and thus creates greenhouse gas emissions. In the underdeveloped countries, on the other hand, there are large sectors of agriculture, both subsistence and commercial, which have not, as yet, modernized. The use of crops from such sectors affords a much greater reduction of greenhouse gas emissions. For example, according to the center for energy and environmental studies at Princeton University, the percentage of total electricity generated by utility companies that could have been produced from sugar cane alone using advance gas turbines is 14.9% in Asia, 19.2% in Africa, 45.1% in Latin America and 200% in Oceania. To take another example, the lack of centralized power grids in many areas of the Third World has the potential of rendering profitable many forms of energy that would not be as profitable in a developed economy, photo-voltaics, wind, geothermal and others. According to J. C. Hourcade (1981), in many parts of the developing world, the new forms of renewable energy, specifically biogas, photovoltaics, solar, ponds, and geothermy, would already be competitive, for such uses as:

- cooking, especially in rural areas;
- agricultural irrigation;
- hot water heating in temperate and cold regions;
- pumping water;
- agricultural machinery and commerical vehicles.

He maintains that, "on the whole modern sources of renewable energy have a market potential covering 40% of final demand" and, therefore, "new renewable energy energies no longer appear as the energy of the distant future, but as the more appropriate to solve the present crisis in rural areas."

A DIGRESSION ON
DEVELOPMENT ECONOMICS

This theory had been called "the Magna Carta of modern economics".

The origin of this description of tatonnement is obscure. It did not originate with Walras.

This kind of study is known as macroeconomics.

This example assumes for simplicity that only labor and goods produced by labor are used in production.

In fact, for those who have a background in college calculus, Keynes's original classic The General Theory of

Employment, Interest and Money is quite readable, with the proviso that Keynesian economics is continuously being revised, amended and reinterpreted. The controversies about "what Keynes really said" are completed outside the scope of this book.

It has been maintained that the IS-LM model doesn't really describe Keynes's economic insights. For example, Keynes put great stress on expectations in analyzing economic activity, yet had no mathematical theory of expectations. Thus the IS-LM model gives a far too static view of Keynesian theory. However, since the IS-lM model is the way Keynesian theory is usually presented, we describe it here.

More precisely, in the IS-LM model, the "demand side" (in its original form) is based on "rules of thumb" rather than on reasoning about the "utility functions" of consumers and investors. expenditure is usually divided into investment, i(y,r), and consumption, c(y,r).

For example, e can be increased by postulating an increase in government expenditure.

Later on, the IS-LM model was augmented by the inclusion of real wealth (w) as a variable in the equations. It was shown that, in this expanded model, given flexible prices, markets would clear even in the "limiting cases" discussed by Keynes. (D. Patinkin 1965). In addition, Keynes' decision to drop the assumptions of general equilibrium (such as market clearing) has remained controversial to this day, because if these assumptions are dropped then it's not clear how prices are supposed to be determined? For a survey of the economics of "sticky prices" and "disequilibrium" see D. Romer et. al (1991).

The definition of economic structure is actually more restrictive than this. See notes at the end of the chapter.

Following L. R. Klein (1980:2) we can say that the IS-LM model described above is the "mother" of Keynesian econometric models, which can be described as "extensions of the IS-LM relationship". For a (mostly) English description of a Keynesian econometric model see L. R. Klein (1980:11-45).

Economic theory, after having gone from the study of economic and social aggregates (classical economics), to the study of individual economics behavior (neoclassical economics), and from there back once again to the study of economics aggregates (Keynesian macroeconomics), has to go yet again to the study of individual economic behavior.

In many current econometric models such as, for example, the IMF/MULTIMOD model, it is assumed that the participants in the economy actually use the model itself to make their forecasts. (See S. Hall, et. al, 1994) subject to the economic information available to them.

Rational expectations economics is sometimes called "new classical economics" (not to be confused with economic theories which still use the classical labor theory of value such as neo-Ricardian or neo-Marxist economics). "New classical economics" also includes the new growth theories.

These changes are assumed to be random and are called "demand shocks" and "technology shocks".

This is because government macroeconomic policy can often increase the problems of "signal extraction" and thus worsen business cycles rather than ameliorate them.

J. G. Williamson (1983) maintains that England's development is not a bad model for the development of contemporary developing countries, that a great many of the "pathologies" (such as income inequality and "overurbanization") attributed to LDC development were also true of England in the early 19th century.

In all societies, (See Chapter 3) there is often a tendency to "go back to the fundamentals" in order to find answers in the face of a confusing crisis. During the chaotic "middle periods" at the beginning of this millenium, Islamic civilization went back to "Sunni orthodoxy". During the 19th century, Chinese officials tried to "go back to Confucian fundamentals" in order to find some way of absorbing Western technology without convulsing the society.

There are actually many reasons why the neoclassical paradigm has come into vogue in the 80's and early 90's. Not least of them is the explosive advance in transportation, communication and information technology in recent years, an advance which has shaped world economic activity in ways which make it more describable by neoclassical methods. (The "transaction costs" of economic activity have been lowered. More and more economic activity is able to pass through "auction-like" markets. The globalization of production weakens the market power of monopolies and labor unions. Contracts are replaced or supplemented by spot and futures markets.) In addition, there are political reasons for the success of the neoclassical paradigm; for one thing, it's a good way of avoiding debates about global and national economic inequities. But more of this in the next chapter.

This corresponds to a capital-output ratio of 3.5.

The theory of unequal exchange is a revision of Ricardo's theory of comparative advantages to show that it doesn't hold in the LDC's.

"The market for industrial goods, apart from textiles, hardly exceeds 50 to 60 million people, or hardly 10% of the population" P.T. Patai Indian Minister of Industries, 1975

See R. Lucas, 1992.
See Chapter 2 of this book.

Notice the similarity of this assumption to the assumption of Western Christian and Islamic medieval cosmology that the motion of heavenly bodies is perfectly describable by means of mathematics. It was this assumption that ultimately gave rise to the Galilean union of mechanics, physics and astronomy. (See Chapter 3 of this book.) Neoclassical economics tries to replicate this breakthrough by assuming that the behavior of individual economic agents is describable mathematically. It's no accident that many of the neoclassical economists started out as physicists. Thus, (see Chapter 3) modern mathematical economics can be viewed as a modern variant of neoplatonism (along with popular astrology and "near death experiences").

Other requirements for the existence of an "equilibrium" are: (1) returns to scale are constant or diminishing; (2) there are no joint products or "external effects" either in production or consumption (an example of the latter is, for example, pollution, or economy-wide economies of scale); and (3) all goods are "gross substitutes" for eachother, in the sense that a rise in the price of one good will always produce positive excess demand for at least one other.

For example, suppose the three commodities are coal, wheat and coal. An iron manufacturer might say: "At those prices, I would be willing to produce 5 units of iron. I would need to purchase 3 units to grain to feed the miners (or equivalently I would need to pay the miners enough to purchase 3 units of grain), and I would need to purchase 2 units of coal to run the equipment."

Most of the proofs of the so-called "stability" of general equilibrium usually assume that the price of a commodity somehow rises in response to "excess demand" and falls in response to "excess supply" (or negative "excess demand") without specifying how this actually happens in a real market. For those who know intermediate calculus, if p – $(p1(t), \ldots, pn(t))$ is the vector of prices as a function of time t, then $dpi(t)/dt = Hi(Zi(p(t)))$, where $Zi(p)$ is the "excess demand" for the ith commodity and $Hi(.)$ is a sign-preserving continuous function.

The extent to which the assumptions of "general equilibrium" (such as market clearing) are valid is central to many of the doctrinal disputes of economics. Supporters of general equilibrium maintain that one has to be very cautious about dropping its assumptions, since the mathematics of economics becomes onerously difficult without them. Opponents of general equilibrium counter that many aspects of economic reality such as unemployment and business cycles violate these assumptions. Supporters of general equilibrium (such as the "rational expectations" economists) counter that general equilibrium can be combined with probability theory to explain these phenomena (R. E. Lucas and T. J. Sargent 1978:49-72). Critics of general equilibrium counter, in turn, that "rational expectations" mathematics is hairy enough, that the mathematics needed to test its conclusions hairier still, and that there is no escaping the need for adhoc judgements when constructing economic models. (L. Taylor 1983:1-11)

To oversimplify enormously, the proof of Walras' equilibirum theory goes as follows. The "all knowing being" writes down a list of prices for each commodity. Using the producers' "production functions" and assuming that each producer would produce an amount of each commodity which would maximize its total profit, the "all knowing being" calculates, for each producer, how much of each commodity the producer would want to produce at those prices and how much of each commodity (including labor) the producer would need in order to carry out the production. Using the consumers' "utility functions" and assuming that each consumer "maximizes his or her utility", the "all knowing being" calculates, for each consumer, how much of each commodity (including labor) the consumer would want to purchase (or sell) at those prices. If there is a shortage of any commodity, the "auctioneer" raises the price. If there is a surplus of any commodity, the "auctioneer" lowers the price. After this is done, this process is continued until a list of prices is found, such that (1) all commodities produced at those prices will find a buyer, and (2) every consumer's buying plans at those prices are realizable. The proof that such a list of prices would, in fact, be found, depends on a mathematical result, which is way beyond the scope of this book, and which is known as a topological fixed point theorem. For the present purposes, we wish to make only one observation about the description of general multimarket equilibrium given in this chapter. The use of a mathematical equation such as a "utility function" to describe the behavior of an individual consumer often seems very strange to an economic novice (much stranger, say, than the use of a "production function" to describe the behavior of an individual firm). And yet, (to paraphrase the famous British neoclassical economist Francis Edgeworth), short of keeping tabs on each of the hundreds of millions of individual consumers in an economy, and short of trying to second quess the behavior of each of them, how else would one model the behavior of an economy consisting of hundreds of millions of individual agents. For a discussion of the behavioral assumptions behind "utitily maximization" see D.C. North (1990:3-26.)

For those who have a background in intermediate college calculus, here is a brief (oversimplified) summary of some of the mathematical aspects of the IS-LM model. Capital letters will represent nominal quantities and lower case letters will represent real quantities. We will assume that the labor supply (N) and the money supply (M) are fixed. We will also assume that labor is the only factor of production in the period under discussion (although investment for the next period will be included in the analysis). Furthermore, we will suppose that the economy produces only one commodity which is both an investment good and a consumption good.

Designate the general price level by P, the wage by W, the real interest rate by r and real output by y. In addition, let q(N) be the economic output as a function of N, where dq/DN >0, and d2q/D2N < 0. Let e(y,r) be total expenditure as a function of y and r. Let c(y,r) be consumption as a function of y and r. Let i(y,r) be total investment as a function or y and r. let l(y.r) be the "demand for real balances" as a function of y and r.

The equations of the IS-LM model can now be written as follows:

$$y = q(N) \text{ (the production function for the economy)};$$
$$y = e(y,r) = c(y,r) + i(y,r) \text{ (total output = total expenditure}$$
$$= \text{consumption + investment)}$$
$$M/P = l(y,r) \text{ (the demand for "real balances" = the supply)}$$

The second equation above is called the IS curve and the third equation above is called the LM curve. Now, Let y lie along the horizontal axis and r lie along the vertical axis.

Expenditure, e(y,r), will obviously increase as total output (y) increases. It will also increase as the real interest rate (r) decreases, because the lower interest cost will make more investments profitable. Thus, the IS curve is downward sloping.

Because markets clear, the economy will produce at a level (y) that uses all of the available labor (N). The real wage rate (W/P) will adjust to ensure such an outcome. What will this real wage rate be? Well, in addition to clearing the labor market, firms in the economy will also produce at a level that will maximize their profits, i.e. will maximize $Pq(N)$—WN. Thus, the derivative of $Pq(N)$—N must be zero, or, in other words, $W/P = q'(N)$. Since we know N, this gives us the real wage rate (W/P). How does one determine the real interest rate r? One equates the demand for economic output (which is equal to $e(y,r)$) to the supply of economic output y and solves for r.

Now that we know y and r, we can determine $l(y,r)$ (the demand for "real balances"). Since this demand must be equal to the supply of real balances (M/P), we can solve for P and hence for W.

This essentially is the neoclassical view of things. Once the labor supply is determined, everything else follows.

Now, let's throw more and more labor on the market, so that N keeps increasing. This means that $q(N)$ (or y) keeps increasing (since $q' > 0$). Because the IS curve is downward sloping, r will decrease. Therefore, as we keep throwing more and more labor on the market, y will keep increasing, and r will keep decreasing.

Thus, in the above system of equations, a rise in the labor supply leads to a drop in the real interest rate. Is this a realistic description of the economy?

In some circumstances, according to Keynes, yes it is. As more labor is thrown on the market, wages drop. This leads to a general price drop, which, in turn, leads to an increase in the supply of real balances (M/P). This in turn, lowers the real interest rate (r). This chain of causality is known as the "Keynes effect". So far, so good.

Suppose, however, that there is a lower bound below which the real interest rate cannot fall. Then the ability of the economy to absorb labor has to stall at a certain point.

Can such a lower bound exist. In some circumstances (according to Keynes) the answer is again yes. To show this, Keynes divides the demand for real balances (l(y,r)), into two parts: (1) a demand for transaction balances, and (2) a demand for "speculative balances". The first demand is a demand for the real balances needed to facilitate economic transactions. It will increase as y increases, and as r decreases. However, the second demand, the demand for "speculative balances" is a demand for money to be kept in reserve just in case the real interest rate has hit bottom. Investors don't want to be locked into an investment with a low rate of return, when interest rates rise, and, therefore, they will want to hold a certain amount of precautionary balances. Below a certain point, a drop in the real interest rate will increase the demand for precautionary balances. In fact, this demand for precautionary balances "may tend to increase almost without limit in response to a reduction of r below a certain figure" (J. M. Keynes 1953:203). In other words, as r approachs its minimum value from above, the function l(y,r) will "blow up". This unfortunate state of affairs is known as "the liquidity trap".

Suppose that we respond to the "liquidity trap" by simply making y large enough to clear the labor market, solving the IS curve for r, plugging r into the LM curve, and solving for P. If we do this, we end up with an absurd situation in which everybody is working for nothing and everything is free; "from each according to his abilities, to each according to his needs"; exactly the kind of situation Keynes was trying to avoid.

Fortunately (as pointed out by A.C. Pigou in 1941), long before we reach this alarming situation, the real value of the already accumulated wealth will be so large that enough of it will be spent to clear the labor market. If prices and wages have fallen so low that a single dime will suffice to employ everybody at a living wage, then obviously the labor market will clear. However, this could take a very long time to happen.

A complete explanation of "economic structure" and "the Lucaas critique" depends on some rather arcane technical statistical concepts. For those who have some background in statistical regression analysis, structural equations are those which allow analysis of the effect of policy changes. The parameters of structural equations should be invariant to the policy changes. However, in many cases, the structural equations are not regression equations. In order to make them into regression equations, they have to be transformed into reduced form equations, which are regression equations. However, in many cases, it is impossible to go from the estimates of the parameters of the reduced form equations back to estimates of the parameters of the structural equations (a difficulty known as the identification problem). In order to do this, it is necessary, in many cases, to put simplifying restrictions on the structural equations. Lucas challenged the way in which these restrictions were introduced. Particularly suspect, according to Lucas, was the way in which expectations of future economic variables were handled. They were treated as functions of past observed values. In other words, people were assumed not to take policy changes into account in forming their expectations. But if the structural equations forecast the effect of policy changes, then why don't the people whose behavior the equations were describing also forecast the effects of policy changes? Were they stupider than the equations themselves?

Improvements in computers in recent years have had an enormous influence on economic modeling. For example, it might seem that Walras' theory of general equilibrium, while of theoretical interest, would not be of much practical use in devising models of a real economy. After all, even a small national economy consists of an enormous number of goods, consumers, and firms. And the number of equations needed to solve the general equilibrium system of such an economy would be astronomical, far beyond the power of any computer to solve. None the less, over the past 20 years, as the power of computers has grown, computer programs have been written which mimic Walras' "all knowing being". Such programs are called, Computable General Equilibrium Models, or CGE's. These CGE's obviously do not account for each individual good, consumer and firm in an economy. Instead, goods, consumers, and firms are grouped into aggregates or sectors. For example, producers might be grouped into forestry, fishing, mining, construction, export agriculture, etc. Consumers might be grouped into rural workers, landlords, capitalists, skilled urban workers, unskilled urban workers, etc.

CGE's are often used to evaluate economic policy changes by national governments, (such as, for example, a devaluation, or a tariff change). In evaluating an economic policy change, it not enough to ask whether the national economy was "better off" after the change. An economy might be impacted by an external factor, that has nothing to do with the policy change, (such as a rise in global interest rates). The relevant question is whether the economy was better off with the policy change than it would have been without it. The analysis of such a question is called a counterfactual analysis. CGE's can often be useful in performing such a counterfactual analysis.

CGEs can be very complex. For example, A. Kelly and J. Williamson (1983) used complex CGEs to investigate the reasons for Third World city growth. Their study examined several possible reasons for rural-urban migration in Third World countries, a demographic reason (population growth) and an economic reason (greater productivity growth in urban industry than in rural agriculture). In other words is rural-urban migration "driven" by "demographic push" or "economic pull"? Both factors occurred simultaneously in many Third World countries. Thus, a counterfactual or what if analysis was necessary to assess the importance of each factor individually. The construction of CGEs made such an analysis possible.

To take another example, W. J. McKibbin and P. J. Wilcoxen (1992) developed a multi-sector computable general equilibrium model of the global economy to quantify the costs of curbing CO_2 emissions.

At the other end of the scale, economic models have been developed which are purely empirical and embody as few economic theories or assumptions as possible. These models "let the data speak for itself". They are known as Vector Autoregression (VAR) models, and are based on older method of economic forecasting known as time series analysis.

Times series analysis is basically a method of mathematically "filtering" past economic data in order to "extrapolate" future values. It cannot be used to do "policy analysis" or to answer "what if" questions. Since the Lucas critique, however, and since the failures of economic forecasting models in the 1970's, time series analysis has made a comeback. It is now used extensively in economic modeling and in economic research (See P. Kennedy 1993:249).

A time series is essentially a series of observations over time, whether on a daily, monthly, quarterly or yearly basis. Examples of times series are daily stock prices, quarterly economic growth numbers, or annual GNP figures. One of the earliest ways of analyzing a time series was to assume that it consisted of a superposition of cycles of various types, a form of analysis known as harmonic analysis. Harmonic analysis is still used extensively in economic research. For example, C. W. J. Granger (1969:424-438) used it to devise a statistically testable definition of "economic causality".

During the 1920's, the Russian economist Eugen Slutsky and the British economist G. U. Yule showed that weighted sums of "random shocks" exhibit cyclical behavior that look very much economic time series. This led to the technique of analyzing times series by treating them as weighted sums of random shocks (Autoregressive, Moving Averages).

A time series can exhibit a trend, a cyclical pattern (such a seasonal fluctuation), or a unit root (a random error which can propagate itself in an additive fashion to produce misleading trend-like behavior). Various techniques are available to remove trends, cycles and unit roots, The resulting time series can then be extrapolated mathematically into the future.

For those who've had some encounter with time series, here's a question about times series which might seem too silly to ask, or it might not. The question is: how can one analyze a time series without going back in time? Suppose, for example, that we are looking at, say, money supply figures and unemployment figures from 1970-1990. If we could keep "resetting" the economy back to 1970, and then letting it run forward to 1990, then we could say, "Yes, I see! In 95% of the run-throughs, if the money supply does such and such, then unemployment goes up!". Obviously, we can't do this. The economy is an experiment which happens only once, and in only in one direction. An economic time series, therefore, is a sample of one from a single experiment. If this is the case, then why does a time series have any significance at all?

If you've never been troubled by this kind of question about times series, then forget it.

But if you have, then the answer is as follows: A time series is an instance of a statistical phenomenon known as a dynamic random process. If a dynamic random process is sufficiently "well behaved", then one "realization" of it can tell us a great deal about its structure. This fact, which can be proved mathematically, is known as the statistical erodic theorem. Thus, we don't need a time machine to analyze a time series (according to the statistical ergodic theorem).

In most countries, the ratio of farmers to available land is much smaller than in the United States or Europe. Farms of less than a hectare characterize China, Bangladesh, and Java. In India the average farm size is approximately 1 to 2 hectares, and in Latin America farms of less than 10 to 20 hectares are the rule. In contrast, average farm size in the U.S. is well over 100 hectares and over 50 hectares in Britain. In most countries, the available farm land is not distributed equally among all potential farmers. See P. Timmer, 1988.

"A major problem (in industrialization) has been the lack of markets . . . The successful experience of three East Asian countries (Japan, the Republic of Korea and China) could, however, provide useful examples in this respect. The first major source of demand in these cases was a distribution of assets through land reform and a subsequent high and sustained growth of both agriculture and industry." *The Impact of Development Strategies on the Rural Poor*, FAO Publications, 1988.

Japan imposed land reform on its Asian colonies because it needed to increase food production for its industrial revolution. America imposed land reform in Asian countries after World War II because of fear of communism. The crucial difference between Asia and Latin America was that America occupied the Asian countries where it imposed land reform, but was dependent in Latin America on the rural oligarchies (who opposed land reform) to counter the leftists. America, not directly occupying most of Latin America, could not realize its ideal goals of a right wing land reform, and, therefore, after an abortive attempt under the Alliance for Progress in the early 60's to encourage land reform, ultimately opposed it as too destabilizing. Following Latin American structuralism, we can imagine that if Britain had fallen in World War II and if the US had decided to fight on, then the US might very well have been forced to occupy large parts of Latin America, impose land reform, encourage industrialization, and we would now be regarding Latin America as the world's "economic powerhouse" rather than East Asia. Incidently, the problems encountered by land reform efforts are nothing new. Both the Byzantine, Ottoman and Chinese empires tried unsuccessfully to prevent concentration of land holdings. Of course, the ancient, pre-capitalist "world empires" were infinitely weaker and more sluggish than a modern nation state. Even so land reform is a very difficult task at all times and in all contexts. The classic article on land reform was written in 1970 by Jacques Conchol, director of agrarian reform in Chile under Eduardo Frei. According to Conchol, a successful land reform must have the following characteristics. "(1) Agrarian reform must be a massive, rapid, and drastic process of redistribution of land and water rights. Agrarian reform and colonization must not be confused because the latter implies no change in the power structure. (2) Political forces and the entire community must be actively mobilized, so that the reform is carried out within an institutional framework and creates an awareness among the masses and political groups of . . . need for substantial changes in the power structure. (3) Indemnification payments for land must be minimized since the market value of agricultural lands is often determined by the possibilities of gaining speculative rents rahter than by true productivity . . . (4) Agrarian reform must be part of a broad development plan for the entire agricultural sector (J. Conchol, 1970:158-172)" (Quote taken from M. Edelmen, 1993:86).

Land reforms also have risks. Both the Iranian revolution and the Afghan civil war were, in part, the precipitated by flawed land reforms. In Peru, the rural power vacuum created by the land reform aided the rise of the Shining Path querrillas.

What do economic historians have to say about the prospects for Third World development? The doyen of gloomy pessimism, in this regard, is the economic historian David. S. Landes. (See D. S. Landes, 1992:99) In a recent article, he sums up the prospects for the Third World as a whole. Many countries in the Third World, he says, "do well in some regions and languish elsewhere", a pattern that Landes calls "mottled development". Although some analysts express optimism about the recent economic performance of the Third World, Landes maintains that "we are witnessing a selection process . . . a window of access", in which only some of the Third World countries "will be able to develop their own capacity for innovation and thereby" and avoid the calamities of underdevelopment. Landes's rhetoric evokes images of leper colonies ("mottled development") and concentration camps ("selection process"). He concludes by saying, "If a society cannot export merchandise, it can and will export people, or, in extreme cases, get them to sell their body parts. This too is not a basis for sustainable growth." (Good God!) In contrast, other economic historians, such as Walt Rostow, are as optimistic as Landes is pessimistic. For example, W. Rostow (1991:424), projects that ". . . the fourth great technological revolution of the past two centuries" will enable most of the developing world to develop rapidly, since most of the Third World is "likely to absorb the new technologies and move rapidly forward over the next several generations". In fact, the entire field of development economics tends to suffer from a sort of "bipolar disorder", in which prognoses tend to range from euphoric fantasies of billions and billions of middle class customers, on the one hand, to "Bladerunner"-like images of morbid despair (ala Landes) on the other.

Obviously such an approach would seem to leave the Third World economies very vulnerable to the failure of trade negotiations and protectionist pressure in the West. (Later on, we will see that the media manipulation and public mood manipulation practised by the Reagan administration and the secrecy of the Bush administration were, in many cases, attempts to distract the American electorate from protectionist sentiment). If such protectionist policies in the West should materialize, could the South expand its trade through South-South trade aggreements? C. Van Beers and H. Linnemann (1991) argue that the potential for South-South trade in manufactures is limited. This is because there is not that much complementarity betqeen the export sectors of the various Third World economies. This would seem to imply that the potential for Third World industrialization via South-South trade is limited. `. Van Beers and H. Linnemann's paper is summarized as follows:

"Using two different measures, the degree of correspondence between a country's export vector of manufacturers and a trade partner's import vector is determined. These export-import similarity measures are shown to contibute to an explanation of bilateral trade potential in manufacturers for 34 developing countries, and an index showing the potential to replace LDC imports presently originating from developed countries. Given the existing LDC commodity composition, the possibility of subsituting imports of DC manufactures by LDC supplies is found to be limited only", C. Van Beers and H. Linnemann, 1991

Thus, not only are the industrial sectors of most Third World countries "hollow", but the industrial sector of the Third World as a whole is "hollow". And this situation is difficult even for a South-South trading bloc to ameliorate by import substitution. Nonetheless, the free market reforms in the former Soviet Union could offer some promising opportunities for East-South trade in the event of a protectionist upsurge in the West. According to Boris Yeltsin's advisor Sergei Stankevich.

"A rapid move (by Russia) into the markets and full-fledged integration into the system of economic relations of such states as the United States, Japan and the economically developed states of Europe are highly problematical. . . . At the same time, on the other hand, are far broader and qualitatively better opportunities connected with other states, . . . which are at a historical fronter similar to ours— . . . These are the countries lying to the south of our traditional partners: in Latin America, Mexico Brazil, and Argentina, in Africa . . . Turkey, Asia, India, China and the Southeast Asian countries. . . . Interaction with them, use of the potential available to both parties, movement into their markets, and the use of the potential of our market-these are opportunities which must not be overlooked" S. Stankevich (1992)

CHAPTER 4

THE WORLD ECONOMY FROM CHARLEMAGNE TO THE PRESENT

From 1000AD-1700AD, while Europe was making the transition from feudalism to early capitalism, the rest of the civilized world on the Eurasian continent[1] was being periodically battered by Mongol, Turkic and Tungusic nomadic invasions. These invasions half depopulated Russia, decimated China, and practically annihilated Persia and large parts of the Middle East. They ultimately led to the pre-colonial governments of much of what is now known as the "Third World" (the Ottoman Empire, Mughal India, and Manchu China). They also strongly influenced Russia's political and social evolution, (Ivan the Great was a tax collector for the Mongol empire) and, in fact, the development of the entire "Eastern bloc".

The western tip of the Eurasian continent (Western Europe) and the island of Japan, to its east, were spared the nomadic invasions. If you take these two regions and throw in the United States (a European implant) you have the geographical area now known as the "developed world". [i]

We wish to address the following questions: Why, when the rest of the world was being "driven from pillar to post", first by the nomadic invasions and then by European expansion, did the small continent of Europe develop a scientific and industrial revolution and a form of society that "changed man's way of life more than anything since the discovery of fire." (D. Landes 1969)? If an industrial revolution had not taken place in Europe, would it have taken place elsewhere? Was the industrial revolution a "natural" occurrence, something that would have inevitably taken place somewhere sooner or later, had it not occurred in Europe? Or was it a "fluke", the result of an unlikely conjuncture of circumstances, that could very well never have happened at all had it not occurred in Europe?

Before addressing these questions, however, we will touch on another, far more fundamental, question, which is: Why do we care why the industrial revolution occurred in Europe and not elsewhere, or whether it would have occurred elsewhere had it not occurred in Europe? What practical use does the answer to that question have today, 200 years later? In other words, why does history matter, and does history matter? Does it matter, for example, that Russia started out as Scandinavian colony? Does such an origin for Russia have any implication at all, say, for present day Swedish investment in Russia? To take another example, did the fact that the words "pound" and "lira" originate as names of coins minted by Charlemagne have any bearing at all on the recent European monetary crisis?

144

In his book "The Historian's Craft", the French historian Marc Bloch discusses these kinds of questions. The book, written during the second world war, attempts to defend the study of history against the charge of total irrelevance. Marc Bloch admits that he, like most historians, has an "obsession with origins", a desire to claim that everything in the past is terribly significant for the present. He also maintains that such an obssession is not as crazy as it seems, that, in the past, it was even widely shared by most educated people.

"Must we believe that because the past does not entirely account for the present, that it is utterly useless for its interpretation? The curious thing is that we should be able to ask the question today. Not so very long ago, the answer was almost unanimously predetermined. 'He who would confine his thought to the present time will not understand present reality.' So Michelet expressed it at the beginning of his Peuple-a fine book but infected with the fever of the age in which it was written. And Leibnitz before him ranked among those benefits which attend the study of history 'the origin of things present which are to be found in things past; for a reality is never better understood than through its causes.' But since Leibnitz and since Michelet, great changes has taken place. Successive technological revolutions have immeasurably widened the psychological gap between generations. With some reason perhaps the man of the age of electricity and of the airplane feels himself far removed from his ancestors."

With each new invention of the industrial revolution, the railroad, the steam engine, the telegraph, electricity, the study of the past began to seem less and less relevant. In the 19th century, for example, Marc Bloch's high school teacher could say, "Since 1830 there has been no more history." And, finally, in the early 20th century, Henry Ford could say, "History is bunk.". Marc Bloch, on the other hand, defends Leibnitz's statement about history:

"A society that could be completely molded by its immediately preceding period would have to be a structure so malleable as to be virtually invertebrate. It would have to be a society in which communication between generations was conducted so to speak in 'Indian file'—the children having contact with their ancestors only through the mediation of their parents".

In other words, the historical evolution of a society is not a "Markov process", where the future state depends only on the immediate past. The future evolution of a society depends on its entire past history.[ii] To give a simple physical analogy, let's look at the physics of snowflake formation. The exact shape of a snowflake depends on the air pressure at every point of its entire previous trajectory; i.e. depends on its entire history, not just on its immediately preceding state.

Let's assume, for the moment, that the above analogy is accurate. Surely (to play the devil's advocate), the study of past history is not always useful. For example, once the snowflake melts (or is squashed), then its present shape does not depend on its entire past history. In other words, if some sufficiently momentous event (such as the collision of the earth with a large comet, or the invention of a new source of cheap, limitless, nonpolluting power) takes place, then, for many purposes, its impact on human society overwhelms the effect of past history. When Henry Ford, for example, (who conceptualized and implemented a totally new technique of manufacturing) said "history is bunk", wasn't he right? Wasn't the study of past production techniques as misleading as it was useful for his purposes?

So in answering the question, "Does history matter?", we first have to answer four other questions, "Whose history?", "Matter to whom?", "Matter in what way?" and "When?". To the vast majority of people in 19th century Europe, a knowledge of Japanese history had no practical use whatever. Yet, to the Japanese reformers of the Meiji period, a knowledge of Western history proved to be very useful indeed. The Spanish Conquistadors had little use for the intricacies of pre-1942 South American history. Yet, for North American investors, a knowledge of pre-1992 South American history might be useful.

So to answer the second question above, "Matter to whom?", we say "Matter to corporate planners". Does history matter to corporate planners? Well, obviously, an accurate prognosis of future conditions matters to corporate planners. But when, and under what circumstances, does a study of past history matter to corporate planners? For example, suppose that some revolutionary new technology (i.e. "cold fusion") materializes, whose commercial repercussions are immediately apparent and enormous. In such a case, wouldn't time be better spent in analyzing these commercial repercussions, and not in worrying about past history? Conversely, in a period of benign and stable economic expansion (such as occurred, for example, in the postwar period prior to the 70's), purely mechanical techniques of forecasting give reasonably useful results. Under such circumstances, to study, say, the history of the various regions of the world, and the history of the interactions between these regions, and to try to anticipate how these historical tendencies will work themselves out in the future, would be, to put it mildly, "overkill".

However, if it turns out to be the case, that the primary engine of world economic growth in the future is the spread of capitalist economic development from the areas of the world where it exists (the G7 countries) to the areas of the world where it does not (the Eastern bloc and the underdeveloped world) then precisely such a study is what is needed. Furthermore, many of the egregiously wrong, "out of the ballpark", predictions that have been made in the last 20 years result precisely from the failure to do such an analysis! This is because, with the globalization of the world's economies, many of the current economic and political events are "driven" by the complex interactions between the various regions of the world!

Before turning to our question about the industrial revolution, we would like to touch on yet another question. Is historical causality knowable? Does our question about the industrial revolution have an answer?. After all, human historical evolution is very complicated, far more complicated, say, than the evolution of the physical cosmos, or biological evolution. Human history is something which happens once and in one direction. It can't be "rewound" and "restarted" with "different parameters" in order to make a "scientific observation". Nor can it be separated into its "constituent parts", its "DNA" or "elementary particles". In fact, it's not at all obvious what its "constituent parts" would be. Technologies? Beliefs? Customs? Geography? Climate? Access to draught animals? Soil fertility? Diseases?

Crops? Natural disasters? Chance? The effect of very influential individuals such as Jesus, St. Paul, Muhammad, or Alexander the Great?[iii] Innate human biological tendencies? Of course, it's easy enough to pick out this or that feature of a society such as caste, primogeniture, bulk trade, irrigation or flood control, Confucian values, landed property, or whatever, and attribute to it some other feature, such as "cyclical dynastic change in Asia vice unidirectional historical change in Europe", etc., but very hard to come to conclusions that could be called "scientific". It's hard to imagine how even 100,000 statisticians with 100,000 time machines could come to scientific conclusions about historical causality.

"There are reasons why the search for statistical uniformities is of little use for the explanation and prediction of the general course of history. It is generally difficult or even impossible to specify the class or category of events from which examples should be selected, . . . And if certain statistical uniformities have been selected between clearly defined phenomena, we often cannot tell whether these uniformities reflect functional relationships between the variables examined. Nor is it possible to predict with confidence whether the uniformities or relationships will persist . . . There are many valid generalizations that can be made about the . . . conditions of humankind throughout the ages. But these generalizations are not about variables that predictably affect the course of history." P. T. Bauer, 1991

P. T. Bauer (1991) also makes the point that strongly held beliefs in "underlying laws of history", especially when applied to political advocacy or political movements, have led to the authoritarian tendencies that so plagued the 20th century.

"Many of those who have claimed to have discerned the laws of history have simultaneously claimed it as their mission to bring about and hasten an outcome that was in any case inevitable. And in pursuit of this march the proponents of these ambitious claims have been ready to tolerate or to perpetrate large-scale and lasting brutality."

Also, the search for broad patterns of historical development (patterns which can never be known in any objective sense) can divert scholarly attention and effort from more modest, but much more rewarding intellectual endeavors. Thus, we agree with P. T. Bauer that, if the goal is to (1) find some basis for a political doctrine, or (2) to find a fool-proof development strategy, or (3) to expand the sum total of objective human knowledge, then the questions we posed at the beginning of this chapter simply have no answer.[iv] However, if the goal is to find information which, although subjective, incomplete and provisional, is, nonetheless, extremely useful for long term business planning and decision making, then, as we shall see, these questions do indeed have an answer!

Thus, we ask again "Why did the industrial revolution occur in Europe and would it have occurred elsewhere had it not occurred in Europe?". Many historians have proposed theories to answer these questions. While these theories can, in no way, be called scientific, there's certainly "something to them", and we believe they can be extremely useful in thinking about present-day and future global trends. In this chapter, we will present a brief history of them.

The West and the Rest

P. Anderson (1974) (462-549) gives a succinct history of the
of attitude of post-renaissance Europeans to non-European
societies. After the renaissance, European philosophers
and travelers such as Machiavelli, Bernier, Adam Smith,
Montesquiue, and Hegel began to speculate about the nature
of non-European Society. Their speculations were primarily
based on observations of the Ottoman and Mughal and
Safavid Empires. Francois Bernier was a French physician
(and a perceptive tourist) who travelled widely through
the Ottoman, Mughal and Persian empires. For a period
of time he was the personal physician of the last Mughal
Emperor Aurangzeb. He wrote down his observations in his
book "Voyages" published in Amsterdam in 1710:

"How insignificant is the wealth of Turkey in comparison
with its natural advantages! Let us only suppose that
country as populous and cultivated as it would become if
the right of private property were acknowledged, and we
cannot doubt that it could retain armies as prodigious as
formerly. I have traveled through every part of the empire
and witnessed it is ruined and depopulated . . . Take away
the right of private property in land, and you introduce,
as an infallible consequence, tyranny, slavery, injustice,
beggary and barbarism, the ground will cease to be
cultivated and become a wilderness, the road will be opened
to the destruction of nations, the ruin of kings and states.
It is the hope by which a man is animated that he shall
retain the fruits of his industry, and transmit them to his
descendants, the forms the main foundation of everything
excellent and beneficial in this world; and if we take a
review of the different kingdoms of the globe, we shall find

that they prosper or decline according as it is acknowledged or condemned"[2]

Bernier also attributed Indian agricultural backwardness to restrictions placed on landed property. He put the following much quoted (and perhaps exaggerated remark) into the mouth of an Indian official with whom he was familiar:

"Why should the neglected state of this land create uneasiness in our minds. And why should be spend our money and time to render it fruitful? We may be deprived of it in a single moment (by the Mughal administration) and our exertions would benefit neither ourselves nor our children. Let us draw from the soil all the money we can, though the peasant should starve or abscond (flee to an area outside Mughal rule), and we should leave it when commanded to quit, a dreary wilderness." [3]

The early 18th century French political analyst, Montesquieu, was very influenced by Bernier's observations. In *De l'Esprit des Lois*, Montesquieu used Bernier's account to warn about the dangers of an overly powerful French monarchy.

"The Grand Seignior (European word for Turkish Osmanli Sultan) grants most of the land to his soldiers and disposes of it at his whim; he can seize the entire inheritance of the officers of his empire; when a subject dies without male descent, his daughters are left with mere usufruct of his goods, for the Turkish ruler acquires the ownership of them; the result is that the possession of most assets in society is precarious. There is no despotism so injurious as that whose prince himself proprietor of all landed estates and heir of all subjects; the consequence is always the abandonment of cultivation, and if the ruler interferes in trade, the ruin of every industry".[4]

The point made by Bernier and Montesquieu was that, in India and Turkey, the existence of an "all powerful" sovereign who owned all the land, and could interfere in commerce at will, blocked agricultural and commercial progress. As European colonial expansion and exploration led to more and more knowledge of Manchu China, Montesquieu's and Bernier's generalizations were applied to China as well. This led to the general European theory of Asiatic despotism which was believed to apply to non-European societies generally. The theory of Asiatic despotism is known as a Eurocentric theory because it lumps (the very different) Mughal, Ottoman, Safavid and Manchu societies into the general category of "not Europe". An Asiatic Despotism, according to European social philosophers, consisted, at its base, of a large mass of peasant villages, indifferent to dynastic changes above them, and engaged in a primitive and unchanging form of agriculture. Above these peasants, were a class of people who "ate food but didn't grow food", officials, warriors, priests, scholars, clerks, artisans, domestic retainers, tax collectors, and, where taxes were paid in cash rather than in produce, rural money lenders. At the top was an all powerful sovereign, an emperor or sultan, who owned all the land, controlled everyone below him and could interfere in commerce and trade at will. An Asiatic Despotism was devoid of legal codes, religion (Hinduism and caste, Islam, Confucianism) or the emperor's whim acting as a substitute. Property in land and the free flow of commerce were not protected by a legal system. The emperor and the "non-producing classes" formed a tiny fraction of the population which consisted mostly of peasants. Asiatic societies were believed to be decrepid, stagnant and unchanging:

"China and Indian remain stationary and perpetuate a natural vegetative existence even to the present time" G. W. Hegel

Adam Smith emphasized the centralized nature of the capital stock in Asia; capital investment consisted primarily of large public works, particularly hydraulic works for irrigation, transport and flood control. This led to the centralization of political control. An all powerful sovereign and a strong, centralized bureaucracy is necessary to construct and maintain an extensive system of hydraulic works. It was this centralization of political power and capital stock that made non-European political structures brittle and fragile, vulnerable to periodic disintegration into civil chaos through maladministration, factional fighting, natural disasters, peasant uprisings or nomadic invasions.

In fact, the non-European societies that Europe was observing were already beginning to come under economic and military pressure from Europe. The Ottoman empire had lost its monopoly of the East-West trade routes, its finances had been depleted by the European "price revolution", and its territorial expansion (a large source of revenues) had been stymied by European military power. The Europeans monopolized India's foreign trade. In addition, the Qing dynasty in China was beginning to encounter severe internal crises, as evidenced by the peasant uprisings of the 18th century, the precursors to the massive Taiping rebellion of the mid-19th century. However, historically, as Anderson (1974) points out, these non-European societies were anything but stagnant. On the contrary, during many periods in history, these societies were extremely dynamic. During the Song dynasty (960-1279), the Chinese invented water driven machinery for pumping and milling, water-powered spinning machines for hemp, piston bellows for iron manufacture, fire arms, compasses, movable type, paddle wheels for shipping, and pound-locks for canals. Prior to that, the Chinese had invented the seismograph, iron chain suspension bridges, porcelain, paper and steel. In addition, there was considerable progress in mathematics, astronomy and medicine. In the 13th century, the Mongol invasions led to the Yuan dynasty whose policies promoted advances in mercantile enterprise, commerce, international shipping and the introduction of a national non-convertible paper currency. In 1368, a massive peasant uprising led to the replacement of the Yuan dynasty by the Ming dynasty. The Ming dynasty (1368-1644), oversaw an "agrarian revolution" based on drought resistant rice, alternating crops, and the use of aquaculture to control malaria. There were also significant advances in naval exploration. Chinese ships of a size and seaworthiness exceeding anything in Europe, or anywhere else, ranged from the Philippines to Africa. During that period, the Chinese possessed the technology and resources to explore and colonize North America. However, this naval progress was accompanied by a certain amount of technological retrogression in other areas. In addition, the Ming government, for reasons that are obscure, eventually called a halt to sea trade and naval exploration.

The Manchu conquest of China in the 17th century led to the Qing dynasty. During the Qing dynasty, there was a tremendous expansion of commerce and manufacturing, a gradual assimilation of outside technology, large increases in agricultural extension and productivity, improvements in the techniques of civil administration, and an enormous demographic increase culminating in a population of over 400 million by 1850. By the early 19th century, however, the Qing dynasty was already running into a severe crisis of soil erosion, declining land/man ratios and peasant unrest, when it began to be buffeted by European penetration starting with the Opium Wars.

The British chemist Joseph Needham compiled an extensive survey of technology and science in China. All the "constituent parts" for an industrial and scientific revolution seemed to have been present at one time or another in China, but they never quite came together in the right way.

"It is truly striking to see how earth-shaking were the effects of Chinese innovations upon the social systems of Europe when once they found there way there, yet they left Chinese society relatively unmoved" J. Needham 1981

In China, a new invention would be registered, perhaps a temple built to commemorate the inventor, and, in some cases, that would be the end of it. In other cases, the inventions would be gradually absorbed into Chinese society and put to use, but without generating the kind of economic and conceptual upheavals that occurred in the West. At the level of the craft guilds, manufacturing innovations often became family secrets and never diffused into the society as a whole. At the level of the "macro-economy", gains in agricultural output and extension were matched and then exceeded by a demographic increase which ultimately strained the carrying capacity of the land and the administrative capacity of the Qing government, resulting in famine, flooding, soil erosion and political upheavals.

If Chinese civilization was the world's most advanced civilization at the beginning of the current millennium, then Islamic civilization was the world's most advanced civilization at the end of the previous millennium. The Islamic world, the Byzantine empire and European civilization were all offshoots of the Hellenistic world, formed by the conquests of Alexander the Great of Macedonia. At the end of the previous millennium, European civilization consisted of Barbarian Kings, landed magnates and Christian clergy who were trying to patch together a society which was collapsing around them. (As we shall see later, a combination of political disintegration and technological dynamism was a critical feature of early feudal European society). In contrast, Islamic civilization was built by a coalition of urban merchants and nomadic fighters who took control of entrenched, pre-existing societies in the Hellenistic world and beyond. At first, these nomadic fighters were Arab caravaneers from the deserts. Later on, they were Turkic/Mongol invaders (or conscripts) from the steppes. The Arab/Isamic world was ". . . stamped by its merchant character, with Egypt the only peasant exception." (S. Amin, 1976). Its ruling class, the "cement" which held the Arab/Islamic world together, was urban and highly mobile. It spoke a common language and eventually came to adopt the same orthodox Sunni Islamic culture.

"Its prosperity was linked to that of long distance trade. The latter was the basis for this class's alliance with the nomad tribes (its caravaneers) and for the isolation of the agricultural areas, which retained a distinct personality." S. Amin, 1978.

Islamic civilization quickly brought a vast portion of the civilized world, extending from China to Spain, into a single culture and a single language. In this way, it was able to pool technology, ideas and knowledge from many regions of the world into a single body of work which included Euclidean geometry, Arabic numerals (actually from India), deductive logic and Hellenistic metaphysical and philosophical speculation. Arab and Islamic scholars made progress in astronomy, medicine, optics, chemistry and mathematics including the invention of algebra, trigonometry, and logarithms. The Islamic world bestrode the major East-West trade routes and unleashed a pre-modern global "commercial revolution" by its means of its political unification of the Roman and Persian domains, and its linking of the Mediterranean and the Indian ocean into a single maritime trading system. (See J. L. Abu-Lughod, 1989).

Contrary to the theories of "Asiatic despotism", Islamic and Asian societies were both very dynamic. They both experienced periods of advance in areas such as commerce, technology, theoretical and empirical knowledge. These periods of advance were both rapid and explosive.

However, the "equations of motion" of Chinese, Islamic and European societies were all very different. From 400AD to the present. European civilization experienced, what seems in retrospect, to be a sort of unidirectional, progressive, dialectical change, change that could be characterized by the word "development". It consisted of crisis, conflict, advance, crisis, conflict advance, etc. eventually culminating in an industrial and scientific revolution. In contrast, Chinese history consisted of cyclical, dynastic change; periods of economic and population growth culminating in social and political collapse, civil chaos, population loss, and then reconstitution of a new dynasty along the same centralized lines. In Islamic civilization, there was a bewildering succession of dynastic changes (Muhammad left no male heirs and no successor scheme), along with a continuing cultural, linguistic and commercial unity. To some extent, Islamic civilization can be regarded as the "solution" to the problem of linking together so many disparate societies for so long a period of time. (However, once this linkage was achieved, Arab-Islamic intellectual advance slowed down considerably.) To oversimplify enormously, Islamic history can be divided into three periods; the Caliphate period, the Middle Period and the period of the Gunpowder Empires. The Caliphate period, in the second half of the last millenium, was the period of the Arab conquests. The Caliphates based their legitimacy on claims of being political successors (Caliphs) to Muhammad. The Ummayad Caliphate founded in 661AD in Damascus was based on Arab tribesmen. It was overthrown in 750AD by the Abbasid caliphate, based on Persian administrators and structured along the lines of Sassanid Persia. The Abbasid Caliphate quickly evolved into the most advanced civilization of its time. Towards the end of the 10th century, along with the shift of the east-west trade routes due to the rise of commerce in western Europe, the center of the Islamic world shifted to the Fatimid caliphate based in the newly build city of Cairo (Al-Qahira), Egypt. The Middle Period, during the first half of this millenium, was a period of political fragmentation, internecine conflict, enormously destructive nomadic invasions, and the development of an international, cosmopolitican Islamic society which transcended the rapidly shifting political boundaries. Notable dynasties of this period include the dynasty of the Seljuq Turks, Saladin's dynasty, the Mamluk dynasty in Eqypt, (based on former Turkic and Circassion military slaves), and a succession of Mongol dynasties in Persia. An important feature of this period was the spread of the Muslim religion, in all directions, to all parts of the civilized world, a spread which continues to this day. The middle of this millennium saw the rise of the gunpowder empires, the Ottoman, Mughal and Safavid empires. Firearms rendered these empires more stable and protected them from further nomadic invasions from the steppes. However, there was a certain loss of commercial vitality due to the loss of the East-West trade routes to European navigation. The final declines of the Ottoman and Mughal empires unleashed a sort of "protoindustrialization" in both cases. (See R. Mukherjee, 1974 and S. D. Petmezas, 1990). There were upsurges in commerce and manufacturing, including a putting out system in India in the 18th century, and an abortive attempt at industrialization along English lines in Eqypt in the early 19th century. (All this was quickly overwhelmed by European economic expansion however.)

In the 14th century, the Arab historian, Ibn-Khaldun, worked out a theory of cyclical dynastic change in the Islamic world, a theory which involved a sort of cyclical interaction between urban societies and pastoral, nomadic societies. More recently, some historians have actually claimed that world history as a whole, can be divided into cyclical, "dynastic" cycles; cycles which consist of alternate periods of global expansion and contraction. According to these historians, the long term historical development of the world's various societies has always been synchronized via trade, conquest, technological diffusion, cultural influence, diplomacy, etc. For example, according to this perspective, the period from 100BC to 200AD was an expansionary phase in all of the societies along the entire "silk route"; in Rome, in Persia, in Central Asia and in China. The period from 200AD to 500AD was a period of disintegration in all of these societies. The period from 500 to 800AD was an expansionary period in many parts of the world (but not western Europe). During this period, Byzantium and Sassanid Persia expanded, collided, and then lost out to the rapidly expanding Islamic Empire. This period saw the rise and fall of the Chinese Tang dynasty and its collision with the Islamic world at the battle of Talas. The Abbasid empire was probably the world's "superpower" during this period. The period from 750/800AD to 1000/1050AD was a period of crisis which saw the fragmentation of the Carolingian empire into European feudalism, the breakup of the Abbasid caliphate, a Byzantine military revival, and the disintegration of the Tang dynasty into warlordism. The period from 1000/1050 to 1250/1300 was a period of widespread economic growth in the many parts of the world. Western Europe experienced an "agricultural and technological revolution", invaded the Islamic world in the crusades, enormously expanded both its internal and external trade, and acquired Hellenistic science, mathematics and culture via the Islamic world and Byzantium. The most spectacular economic, commercial, technological and demographic advance was in the Song dynasty in China which was the world's most advanced society of that time and came very close to having an "industrial revolution" 800 years before the West. North Africa, Eqypt and the Middle East experienced strong economic and commercial growth.

Byzantium, on the other hand, lost economic and military power to landed magnates, lost its eastern Provinces to an irruption of Seljuq Turks, became an arena for commercial competition between Venice and Genoa, and was finally conquered, and dismembered by a Venetian crusade. The period from 1250/1300 to 1450 was a period of severe crisis, a crisis of hemispheric proportions. This period saw the Mongol conquest of Russia, China and the Middle East, the hundred years war in Europe, the spread of the Black Death from its origins in the rodent populations of Mongol Central Asia outward to the Islamic world, to Europe and to China and elsewhere, resulting in a collapse of the Mongol empire and a massive global depopulation. Byzantium threw off the Latin occupiers, but remained an Italian economic colony, and went into a long decline. The period from 1450 to 1600 was another period of expansion, a period which saw the rise of the Ming dynasty in China, the rise of the Mughal empire in India and the Ottoman empire in Anatolia and the Middle East. It also saw the beginning of Europe's 500 hundred year long rise to dominance over the world.

The Advantages of Backwardness

So, to return to our original question, why did an industrial revolution take place in Europe and not elsewhere? In "The European Miracle" 1981, the noted historian E. L. Jones (1981) discusses this question. He maintains that the industrial revolution was by no means a sure thing, even in Europe.

"Europe's very long term development appears miraculous. Comparable development (elsewhere) would have been supermiraculous."

E. L. Jones (1981) presents an exhaustive discussion of reasons why "early Europe was different". Such reasons include a cultural propensity to restrain population; a cultural propensity to use non-human energy; the existence of extensive rivers and coastlines for bulk transport; a more benign epidemiology; a location which allowed it to be influenced by, or "educated by" other societies, without at the same time being overwhelmed (or overrun) by them; a more geophysically and climatically stable environment; the discovery and colonization of the new world; and so on. A discussion of "European exceptionalism" can also be found in J. Baechler et al (1988), P. Crone (1989) and in the introduction to D. S. Landes (1969).

For the purposes of this chapter, we present a more "universalist" and "globalist" theory due to S. Amin (1980,1989). S. Amin's theory is a "super super generalization" in the sense that it involves all periods of historical time and all types of societies. In fact, S. Amin's theory is the epitomy of everything that P. T. Bauer warns against in historical theorizing. As Amin himself puts it:

"Social reality considered in its totality, has three dimensions: economic,political and cultural. The economy probably constitutes the best-known dimension of social reality . . . Economics has forged instruments for its analysis and, with a greater or lesser degree of success, for (its management). The domain of power and the political is considerably less well known, and the eclecticism of the various theories that have been proposed reflects (society's) feeble mastery of this area of reality . . . As for the cultural dimension, it remains mysterious and unknown; empirical observation of cultural phenomena (religion, for example) has not produced, up until now, anything more than some intuitive essays." S. Amin (1989)

However, the very breadth and scope of S. Amin's theory makes it useful for the purpose of this chapter (which, after all, is "historical intuition" and not absolute scientific truth).

S. Amin's theory divides all societies into three types or modes. They are;

- a tribal, communal,kinship mode;
- a tributary mode;
- an industrial, capitalist mode.

Each mode has a socio-economic aspect (physical production and the social relations attendent to it), a political aspect (power and control relations), and a metaphysical, religious and spiritual aspect, (the realm of ideas, knowledge and beliefs). A tribal, communal, kinship society engages in hunting and gathering and/or agriculture. It possesses a certain amount of empirical knowledge in many areas such as navigation, astronomy, textiles, pottery, animal husbandry, etc. It possesses a local mythology which seeks to explain the origin and characteristics of the world in which the "tribe" finds itself; the physical universe, people, and the social order of the "tribe". This particular mode of social organization, as defined by Amin, can apply to societies at many different levels of development, from primitive tribes

to fairly advanced agricultural civilizations. An example of
a communal, tribal, kinship society would the Barbarian
peoples that invaded the Western Roman empire at the
beginning of the last millennium. In fact the English name
for the head of each group of barbarian people was king,
which is derived from the word cyning ("man of the kin").

Amin defines a tributary formation as an advanced
pre-capitalist civilization. Examples of the latter would
be the Hellenistic world (the Ptolomaic, Macedonian
and Seleucid Empires), the Islamic world, Byzantium
and China. To some extent, the European theory of
"Asiatic despotism" can be regarded as a over simplified,
one-dimensional description of a tributary formation.
To explain briefly, a tributary formation is still primarily
agricultural, but its political and social structure is much
more elaborate and its base of theoretical and empirical
knowledge is at a much higher level. There is a clear class
division of society into a mass of peasant producers at the
bottom and a group above them of "people who eat food,
but don't grow food". This class division is maintained by
an elaborate "political superstructure", usually a centralized,
"top-down" governmental structure, which can take a wide
variety of forms depending on the specific tributary form in
question. There is a considerable amount of manufacture,
but the primary mode of production is still agriculture,
There is a considerable amount of commerce and trade,
but the primary mode of distribution is "tribute"; a direct
commandeering of output or labor from the agricultural
producers (peasants, serfs, slaves or rural laborers). Some
of the forms that this "tribute" can take are taxes in kind,
taxes in money, crop sharing, corvee' labor, slave labor and
bonded labor. Tributary formations were more complex

and dynamic than would be implied by the theory of "Asiatic despotism". Contrary to this theory, there was land ownership in pre-capitalist China for example, and not all investment was centralized. For example, many of the investments in hydraulic works, marsh draining and land reclamation were undertaken by local officials.

A tributary formation also has a metaphysical, religious and "ideational" aspect. Centralized political control over a large area cannot be maintained by force alone. There has to be some accepted system of belief that "legitimates" central rule. In a tributary society, this role is played by religion. (Although there is nothing uniquely "Asian" about this. In Europe, for example, Charlemagne's rule was bolstered by the support of the Papacy.) A tributary formation is a centralized empire over a large geographical area, which contains many local cultures and religious beliefs. This leads to "conceptual crises" (how can all these beliefs be true), crises which are resolved, in many areas of the world, by the spread of belief systems with a claim to completeness and universality. Examples, of the latter would be Hellenistic thought, Islam, Confucianism, Hinduism, Byzantine (Eastern) Christianity and later European (Western) Christianity.

"The syncretisms of the Hellenistic period thus prepare the ground for Christianity and Islam, the bearers and sowers of a new universalist message. The social crisis which so frequently is used to describe the end of the Roman empire, . . . was above all a product of this general and complex questioning. The medieval construct unfolds in three time periods; a first Hellenistic period (approximately three centuries B.C.), a second Christian period, first appearing in the East (from the first until the 7th century

of the Christian era) and then, much later, in the West
(starting from the 12th century), and finally, a third Islamic
period (from the 7th until the 12th century). The core
of this construct . . . goes back to the Hellenistic period.
Neoplatonism serves as the base for the constitution of
the first Christian scholasticism (in the East), an Islamic
scholasticism and finally the second Christian scholasticism
(in the West), this last form being greatly imbued with
Islamic thought. Undoubtedly each of these periods has its
own specific traits and its particular interpretations; but,
in my opinion, the common characteristics far outweigh
the differences . . . The fundamental characteristic of
medieval thought is the triumph of metaphysics, henceforth
considered synonymous with philosophy (or wisdom). This
trait is to be found in Hellenism, as well as in subsequent
Islamic and Christian scholasticism. Metaphysics proposes
to discover the ultimate principle governing the universe in
its totality; namely, 'absolute truth'. It is not interested in
'partial truths' established by means of particular sciences;
or, more precisely, it is only interested in them to the extent
that these partial truths can contribute to the discovery of
the final principles governing the universe . . . The entire
enterprise of Islamic and Christian metaphysics will consist
in seeking to establish that there is no conflict between the
use of deductive reason and the content of the revealed
texts . . . What the new metaphysics—which will crystallize
into scholasticism—calls human reason is, in fact, exclusively
deductive reason . . . Medieval scholasticism . . . remains
superbly ignorant of scientific induction, although by force of
circumstances certain scientific practises, notably medicine,
always employed inductive reasoning", S. Amin 1989.

This "Medieval construct" contains deductive logic, pre-calculus mathematics, a large body of empirical scientific knowledge in astronomy, chemistry, medicine, geography, and a large body of technology in civil engineering, navigation, agriculture, and military combat. It contains a belief that everything which should be known can be known by deductive reasoning, historical revelation (i.e. the Quran, the Gospels), and/or direct personal perception of "divine reality" under religious guidance and instruction (i.e. Sufism).

The third type of society is the industrial, capitalist mode This is the type of society which we live in today and which embraces the vast majority of the human race. In the place of metaphysics and religion there is the "scientific method". The "scientific method" consists of controlled experimentation and the linking of mathematization to empirical observation. The goal of the scientific method is not the search for "absolute truth", but rather the search for a larger and larger body of "partial truths", (and the application of the latter to industrial innovation for profit). Unlike the former tributory formations, the "political economy" of capitalism is truly global in scope. Although billions of people on the globe have not, as yet, benefitted from it, all are affected by it. It has brought about an enormous increase in the gobal population, most of it occuring since 1950. It is causing unpredictable changes in the Earth's atmosphere and bio-physical environment, changes of a magnitude unprecedented in geologic time. It operates in a global economy of enormous wealth for a minority of the world's population and desperate poverty for the majority.

At the end of the last millenium, an "outside observer", looking at societies such as Byzantium, the Islamic world, China and the Frankish empire in Europe, would certainly have characterized Europe as "backward". And yet it was Europe which experienced the industrial and scientific revolutions and which went on to dominate the world. Why? According to Amin, it was precisely the fact that Europe was backward that allowed it to circumvent the barriers to further development characteristic of the tributory societies.

"The Roman empire might have evolved and developed into a complete tributary form. It fell before doing so. Three entities grew up on the ruins of Rome, the Christian West, the Byzantium and the Arab-Islamic world. The latter groups probably went further than Rome in developing the tributary mode . . . On the other hand, the West remained marked by the primitive societies of barbarian Europe. This is precisely the reason why feudal Western Christianity offered the most favorable conditions for transcendence of the tributary mode (and the rise of industry)." S. Amin 1980.

In other words, it was the fact that European feudalism was a backward, "underdeveloped" version of the tributary mode, that allowed Europe to transcend the tributary mode. E. L. Jones has described Europe as a "a mutant civilization in its uninterrupted amassing of knowledge about technology". In Amin's formulation, one could describe early Europe as a "hybrid" civilization. It was a mixture of Barbarian and Roman elements coalescing in a context of rapid technological and agricultural change.

According to most historians, the "genetic mutation" which produced European society took place some time between the sack of Rome by Alaric in 410 and the European crusades of the 11th century. In this period of time Europe was culturally and commercially "delinked" and then "relinked" with the outside world. In period of "isolation", it developed the characteristics of nascent "Western civilization". According to the famous Belgian historian Henri Pirenne, it was the Arab conquest of the southern Mediterranean that "delinked" Europe from the outside world and caused it to evolve in a different direction. This is the so-called Pirenne thesis. According to the Pirenne thesis, the wreckage of the western Roman empire could have reconstituted itself into a full fledged "tributory formation", either under the influence of one of the Romanized Frankish kings or under the influence of Byzantium. However, the Arab conquests of the 7th century cut off Europe's export trade and deprived the Frankish kings of the "hard currency" needed to finance their administrations. At this point, land became the sole source of wealth. The landed aristocracy translated this economic wealth into political and military power by the use of feudal institutions, such as land grants to warriors in exchange for pledges of military service, creating land tenureships known as fiefs or feudums. The first man to do this was Charles Martel.

"After (the battle of) Poitiers, Charles Martel decided to create a cavalry—following the example of the Arabs—which could rapidly confront the enemy and replace the advantage of numbers by that of mobility. . . . It was out of the question to expect freemen to maintain a war horse and acquire the costly equipment of the horse-soldier, or to undergo the long and difficult apprenticeship that would qualify them to fight on horseback. To attain his object, Martel had to create a class of warriers with resources to correspond with the part they had to play. A generous distribution of land made to the stongest vassals (bonded servants) . . . Each man at arms thus provided with a tenure—or to employ the technical term, a benefice—was required to rear a war horse and to do military service whenever required. An oath of fidelity confirmed his obligations . . . This institution (feudalism) was soon introduced throughout the kingdom. The immense (landed) domains of the aristocracy (landed magnates) enabled each of its members to form a troop of horse, which they did not fail to do." H. Pirenne, 1939.

The Feudal institutions, thus created, led to a geographical and social decentralization of political power. Pirenne (1939) gives a vivid picture of this process in his description of the coronation of Charlemagne:

"The kings no longer had any finances . . . The Merovingian king bought or paid men with gold; the Carolingian king had to give them fragments of his domain. This was a serious cause of weakness which was offset by booty as long as the country was at war under Charlemagne, but soon after his reign the consequences made themselves felt. And, here let it be repeated, there was a definite break with the financial tradition of the Romans. To this first essential difference between the Merovingian and Carolingian empire another must be added. The new king, as we have seen, was king by grace of God. The rite of consecration . . . made him in some sort a sacerdotal personage. The Carolingian was crowned only by the intervention of the Church, and the king, by virtue of his consecration, entered into the Church.

He now had a religious ideal, and there were limits to his power-the limits imposed by Christian morality."

A complex network of competing, yet interdependent political power centers developed in feudal Europe; the kings, the landed/warrior nobility, and the church. When Europe was commercially and culturally "relinked" with the outside world through the crusades, commerce, manufacturing and technical innovation could flourish with an unprecedented degree of freedom from outside authority.

"The genesis of urban commodity production is not to be located within feudalism as such: it of course predates it. But the feudal mode. was the first to permit it autonomous development within a natural-agrarian economy. The fact that the largest medieval towns never rivaled the scale of either antiquity or Asian empires has often obscured the truth that their function within the (feudal) social formation was a much more advanced one. In the Roman empire, with its highly sophisticated urban civilization, the towns were subordinated to the rule of noble landowners who lived in them but not from them; in China, vast provincial agglomerations were controlled by mandarin bureaucrats resident in a special district segregated from all commercial activity. By contrast, the paradigmatic medieval towns of Europe which practised trade and manufacture were self-governing communes enjoying corporate and military autonomy from the nobility and the church." P. Anderson (1974)

To summarize, the Pirenne thesis postulates a sharp transition between post-Roman Europe and medieval Europe. This transition occurred when the Arab invasions cut off Europe's export trade and precipitated a "financial crisis" in the Merovingian empire. The Carolingian empire responded to this crisis by founding its power on the land, moving its economic and political center to the north, and forming an alliance with the Papacy. This was the transition from antiquity to feudalism. according to the Pirenne thesis. More recent research has tended to cast doubt on the Pirenne thesis, particularly on the effect of Mediterrannean trade on the evolution of early Europe, and the effect of Arab conquests on this trade. Feudal social relations and feudal land tenure relations were very complex, and the origins of these institutions were equally complex. There was a gradual fusion of German and Roman societies. Both of these societies had institutions similar to vasalage and the benefice (a precursor to the fief). The Roman slave economy, under the impact of dynastic collapse and barbarian invasion, underwent a social and technological transformation to become the far more advanced European feudal economy. The importance of this transformation to Europe's long term development vastly exceeds the amount of source material available about it.

For those who are interested, there are hundreds of explanations for the failure of western Rome to reconstitute itself after the barbarian invasions. Perry Anderson (1974), for example, highlights the unsustainability of the western Roman slave economy, once the limits of territorial expansion and enslavement had been reached. According to this explanation, the fall of the western Roman empire was no mere dynastic collapse. It was the collapse of an entire socioeconomic "system of production". Therefore, when western Roman society collapsed, it left no "template" upon which a new dynasty could reconstitute itself. This, in turn, left the field open for a new and radically different type of society to evolve on the wreckage.

The important point to make is that feudal European society, whatever its exact origins, was decentralized. without, at the same time, being completely anarchic. It consisted of a complex and interlocking pattern of local governances; duchies, counties, royal domains, urban communes, ecclessiastical holdings, free towns, etc., loosely linked together by the church, the German emperors and the monarchs at the apexes of complex feudal hierarchies. This led to a pattern of constant feuding, urban factional fighting and endemic warfare. But it also gave European society a great degree of flexibility and openness to innovation. Viewed as a system, and in comparison with the tributory societies, European society was far more flexible, "fault tolerant", and had far more "degrees of freedom". Although European society was politically decentralized, "cultural connections and the competitive nature of the states encouraged continual borrowing" which facilitated the spread of technological and commercial advances. (E. I. Jones, 1981).

In Europe, as in other societies, powerful tendencies towards centralization arose. At a certain point, the process of feudal fragmentation came to a halt, and a complex and uneven pattern of centralization began, a pattern which was, for a long time, concentrated in areas outside Italy and Germany, and which was intensified by the prolonged European crisis of the 14th century. However this process of centralization was itself, shaped and molded by the existence of already entrenched and autonomous commercial, artisanal and scholastic sectors in the towns, so that what emerged was not a centralized "tributory formation", as in the pre-capitalist world, but rather a "states system" of competitive "city states" and then "nation-states". The competition between these states was mediated not only through conquest, and absorption, but also through commerce, innovation, exploration, and the competitive colonization of the non-European world. Thus, the last 500 years have seen, not the political, centralization of Europe, but its military, political, economic, demographic and cultural expansion into the rest of the world, creating what we have today, the world's first truly global society, linked together, not by a single political structure, but by a world market. (And Europe continues to have a surprisingly hard time creating a centralized political structure.)

In the realm of ideas, the European "world view" in feudal times was an incomplete version of the "tributory world view" (the "Medieval construct"). We will the discuss the way in which this fact contributed to the European scientific revolution. One of the important components of the "medieval construct" was Hellenistic thought, particularly Aristotelian thought. Ibn-Rushd (Averroes) was one of the scholars who introduced Aristotelian thought into the Islamic world. Saint Thomas Aquinas was one of the European scholars who "Christianized" Aristotle. S. Amin (1989) contrasts European Medieval thought with Islamic Medieval thought:

"Western medieval scholasticism takes shape beginning in the twelfth century, not by chance in regions in contact with the Islamic world; Arab Andalusia and the Sicily of Frederick II. It shares certain characteristics with its Islamic source of inspiration: an unlimited reliance on syllogism and formal logic, an appreciable indifference to facts and science in general, and an appeal to reason to confirm conclusions fixed in advance by revelation (principally the existence of God). But whereas the perfected metaphysics of the Islamic avant-garde purifies these conclusions of their textual dross, retaining only the abstract principle of immortality of the soul . . . Western scholasticism remains at at inferior level. Even St Thomas Aquinas, the most advanced mind of his age, does not go so far in his Summa contra gentiles as ibn-Rushd (Averroes), whose conclusions he rejects as too daring and potentially threatening for the faith. But this poverty of Western scholasticism is precisely what gave Europe it advantage. Necessarily leaving a greater sense of dissatisfaction that Islam's refined version, Western scholasticism could offer only slight resistance to the assaults of empiricism, in which Roger Bacon, restoring importance of experience over the dialectics of scholastic syllogism, initiates a process of development independent of metaphysical discourse. Historians of the Crusades know how much the Arabs were scandalized by Frankish practises. Their 'justice' founded in superstition (trial by ordeal) could not withstand comparison with subtleties of the Sharia. This is often forgotten today, when the Sharia is characterized as Medieval: It was easier to get rid of a body of 'law' as primitive as the Frankish one than it was to go beyond the erudite causistry of Moslem law."

Ironically, it was the primitive Frankish idea of "trial by ordeal" which was eventually to become one of the inspirations for the concept of a "controlled experiment" ("The secrets of nature, betray themselves more readily when tormented by art (outside manipulation) then when left to their own course". Francis Bacon, New Organum,

1620). The concepts of empirical observation and deductive logic were well known to Eastern Christian and Islamic scholarship, but the concept of a controlled experiment was a distinctive European advance and an essential feature of the European "scientific revolution". Another essential feature of the scientific revolution was the Galilean-Newtonian union of mechanics, astronomy and mathematics. In the 16th and early 17th centuries, after the Renaissance, European Christian cosmology was in a state of profound crisis. At first, this crisis was marked by an outburst of unbridled and heretical, non-rational metaphysical speculation, much of it derived from a collection of mystical Neo-Platonist texts known as the Hermetica. In 1543, Copernicus (who was influenced by the Hermetic belief in the divinity of the sun) published his work De Revolutionibus Orbium. In it, he suggested that the earth and planets revolve around the sun and that the earth rotates on its axis every 24 hours. By making these assumptions he drastically simplified the mathematics of medieval astronomy. The total number of circular motions needed to explain planetary motion was reduced from 80 to 34. However, his approach aroused widespread skepticism. If the earth was rotating rather than the heavens, then why didn't the earth fly apart? Why wasn't there a perpetual wind from east to west? How could an enormously heavy body such as the earth revolve around a supposedly weightless body such as the sun (which had to be weightless so as not to fall down to the earth). If the earth was revolving around the sun, then why didn't the stars appear to shift position or change brightness during the course of the year? In order for the stars to appear the same all year round, while the earth moved over enormous distances, they would have to be of a size, brightness and distance from the earth which was absurd. too large to be plausible. In 1572, a new star appeared in the heavens which was brighter than anything in the sky except for the sun, the moon and venus. It shone throughout 1573, contradicting the belief that the creation of the heavens had been completed on the 7th day, since something new had seemingly been created. In 1577, a new comet appeared. Measurements by the Danish astonomer Tycho Brahe, placed showed that this comet was at a greater distance from the earth than the moon, (previously comets were thought to be atmospheric phenomena), and that it was passing through space that was supposed to be occupied by the crystalline spheres that were supposed to be holding the planets in place.

To get an idea of the magnitude of ensuing conceptual crisis, imagine the impact on present day society of the discovery, say, of Bronze Age artifacts on Mars. Both lay scholars and the church were alarmed at the disorder into which the outside universe had seemingly fallen. ("'Tis all in pieces, all coherence gone", J Donne, 1611) The 17th century saw a flurry of attempts by many researchers to set things to right. These attempts included the gathering of more astronomical data, the use of new mathematical techniques (conic sections) to fit this data into mathematical patterns, experiments with weights and pendulums (under the assumption that the physics of terrestrial objects was similar to the physics of planetary motion), and advances in mathematics (analytic geometry and calculus). All this activity culminated in the late 17th century with Newton's synthesis of mechanics, mathematics, and astronomy. As Bacon predicted, the search for final truths and ultimate causes was left to religion and future scientific efforts were directed to discovery of a larger and larger body of partial truths by means of the scientific method.

The "tributory world view", by its very completeness and claim to universality, tended to inhibit such conceptual advances. Hellenistic thought, in particular, because it was such an impressive, all encompassing intellectual construct, especially when combined with a "universal" religion, tended to have an intimidating effect on researchers. The 9th century Arab scientist Al-Kindi was cautious in his approach to Hellenistic thought.

"It would have been impossible for us, despite all our zeal, during the whole of our lifetime, to assemble these principles of truth which form the basis of the final inferences of our research. The assembling of all these elements has been effected century by century, in past ages down to our own time . . . It is fitting then (for us) to remain faithful to the principles that we have followed in all our works, which is first to record in complete quotations all that the Ancients have said on the subject, secondly to complete what the Ancients have not fully expressed, and this according to the usage of our Arabic language, the customs of our age and our own ability"

Like the European world view, the Islamic "tributory" world view also went into a conceptual crisis, but one with a different outcome. "The discovery of the limits of the power of reason could have led to a questioning of metaphysics and its doomed project for arriving at absolute knowledge, but this did not happen. Renewed questioning of rational metaphysics (led to) . . . the affirmation of non-rational metaphysics" (S. Amin, 1989).

However, the European world-view, despite its post-Renaissance flirtation with non-rational metaphysics, (and partially because it was an "underdeveloped" version of the Islamic world view) was more able to advance to the "scientific revolution", when it encountered the limits of rational metaphysics.

In other words, it's wrong to think of religious or cultural belief systems as demiurges of scientific progress or stagnation. "It is better to think to think of (them) . . . as filters through which actions had to pass, to be slowed down, or (speeded up) . . . according to the occasions" (E. I. Jones, 1988,). The feudal Western "world view" was simply a "weaker filter" than the medieval Islamic world view. It was "weaker" in the sense that it offered less resistance to "the assaults of empiricism".

How did the medieval Western world view compare with the medieval Chinese world view? One important difference between the two was the very strong Western notion (derived from Aristotelian physics and Neo-Platonism) that the motion of heavenly bodies should be perfectly describable mathematically with no deviations. It was this notion that made anomalies in astronomical observations so threatening to Western cosmology. It was this notion, therefore, which led to the successful effort to resolve these anomalies by means of the "scientific revolution". Prior to that revolution, however, there was no a priori reason, other than faith, to believe that the motion of heavenly bodies should always be "perfect". The Chinese, for example, tolerated anomalies in astronomical observations ("Even the heavens occasionally go astray"). Thus, it is interesting to speculate how Chinese astronomy might have evolved had the European scientific revolution not occurred. E. L. Jones (1988) speculates that, in China, a continued progress in technology might have eventually led to a "scientific revolution" based on empirical observation, and from there to an independent discovery of Western mathematics and deductive logic.

In China, as in the Islamic world, the use of "cultural values" to explain progress (or the lack of it) has to be viewed with skepticism. For example, Weber used "Confucian values" to explain China's failure to industrialize, and later analysts have used the same "Confucian values" to explain the ability of the "Pacific rim" to industrialize. In fact, the real significance of "Confucian values", for our purposes, lies not in the differences between China and Europe at all, but in the differences between China and Japan. It was because the Japanese world view was an "incomplete", not yet fully developed, variant of the Chinese Confucian world view that it was more easily transcended by Japan's successful assimilation of the modern western world view.

This (according to Amin's thesis) was an important reason why Japan, as opposed to China, escaped the destructive effects of European colonialism, and went on to develop a successful capitalist economy. One of the important factors behind this outcome was the Japanese feudal system. Following Amin (1989), we can describe the Japanese feudal system as an "underdeveloped" version of the Chinese tributory system. Under the Taika reform of 646AD and the Taiho codes of 702AD, Japan instituted a country-wide administrative system modeled after the Tang dynasty in China. By the middle of this millennium, this system (which included an imperial dynasty and an official religion based on Buddhism and Shinto) had evolved into a feudal system with striking parallels to feudal Europe. The emperor had evolved into a sort of religious figure (analogous to the Papacy) but the real power was vested in a military structure known as the Bakufu (military regime), headed by a "generalissimo" (Shogun). Under the Tokugawa Shogunate, (1615-1868) the Shogun's "royal demesne" (tenryo lands) included about 20% of the country. There were several hundred feudal lords (daimyo), who owned and governed fiefs (han). and who retained trained warriors known as bushi or samurai. During the Tokugawa period, the samurai were eventually absorbed into bureaucracies which constituted the real administrative governments of the han. Although, trade and cultural contact with the outside world was prohibited, the Tokugawa period was marked by a "commercial revolution" based on Japan's large internal market. There was extensive monetization of agriculture (about 50%), and extensive cultivation of cash crops such as cotton, indigo, sugar, tea and tobacco. Although the Japanese bourgeoisie (chonin) occupied a low place in the Japan's formal class structure (shinokosho), they controlled the bulk of Japan's wealth. One of the reasons for this "commercial revolution" was the sakin kotai system developed by the Bakufu in order to establish centralized control over the country. This system obligated the daimyo to maintain elaborate residences in the capital city of Edo and to leave family members in Edo as hostages to the Bakufu. The large outlays needed to construct and maintain these residences and the outlays needed to finance the travel to and from Edo of the daimyos and their retainers provided a large part of the economic stimulus for Japan's commercial revolution. In other words, the manufacturing and commercial sector, because it had arisen in the interstices of Japanese feudal society prior to the centralization attempts of the Tokugawa shogunate, was, therefore, strengthened not weakened by the Tokugawa "centralization process", even without the benefits of external trade and despite the fact that Confucian culture held the merchant class in low esteem. However, by the beginning of the 19th century the enormous growth in luxury spending was creating a severe financial crisis for the daimyo and the Bakufu. Exacerbated by crop failures, this crisis was accompanied by debasement of the currency, famines and peasant upheavals. After the opening of Japan by Admiral Perry in 1854, this crisis became terminal. Unequal trade agreements, forced on Japan by the Western powers, precipitated massive currency devaluations, massive inflation and widespread internal disorder. Had the bakufu been the only source of political cohesion in Japan, the result could have been a slide into backwardness and colonial dependency. However, in Japan's southwest, there were han known as "outside" (tozama) han. These han were historically antagonistic to the Bakufu. They had been involved in illegal foreign trade and had knowledge of outside affairs. They had witnessed the destructive effects of European intervention on China, and were alarmed at the impotence of the Bakufu in the face of European pressure. They smuggled samurai abroad and assimilated Western military, scientific and industrial techniques. In 1868, the tozama han of Satsuma, Choshu and Tosa launched a successful coup against the Bakufu. Using "emperor worship" as a "ruling ideology" (tennoism), they established a capitalist state along Prussian lines.

Like the European feudal system, the Japanese feudal system had a large degree of "fault tolerance" and "redundancy" built in. Therefore, when it went into crisis in the early 19th century, the result was not collapse, but advance, as the collapsing Bakufu gave way to the "modernizing han". Japan's feudal structure made it an unappetizing target for the colonial powers. It was difficult for the colonial powers to coopt or manipulate a society like Japan's with a complex partially decentralized power structure. In fact, Britain finally ended up supporting the "modernizing han".

This, in brief, was the history of Japan and the West. The history of the rest of the world, is essentially the history of the impact of 500 years of Western colonization on that world. An overstatement to be sure, but the fact is that there is no society in the world today whose history and present condition would be at all comprehensible apart from its relations with the West. This is why the "multiculturalists" are wrong when they downplay the importance of Western society. If one wants to understand the present state of the world, including the non-Western world, the only place to start is with Western society. Let's examine this assertion briefly. In what might seem like a paradoxical, upside down analogy, L. S. Stavrianos (1976) draws some striking parallels between today's world and the West's dark ages. Specifically, Western society was formed by the Barbarian invasions of Rome. Present day global society was formed by the Western "invasion" of the rest of the world. The Barbarian invasions of Rome were followed by a period of "Roman/Barbarian dualism", (enclaves of Barbarian society surrounded by large areas of Latin society coexisting under separate political structures). The European expansion into the rest of the world has been followed by a period of "developed/underdeveloped" dualism. World society today consists of a "developed enclave" (known as the "North", the "Center", or the "developed economies") surrounded by a far larger area of underdevelopment" (known as the "South", the "periphery" or the "underdeveloped economies"). In turn, each of the underdeveloped economies in the "South" consists of a developed "enclave" which is itself surrounded by a far larger area of underdevelopment. (Dualism on a global scale is mirrored by dualism on a national scale) Each of these "developed enclaves", in turn, was created by some form or another of Western economic penetration of the non-Western world; administrative alliances with local elites (as in India or Egypt), use of tax systems to monetize peasant agriculture (as in Africa) direct construction of mines, oil wells, and plantations (as in Indonesia or Africa), economic alliances with rural oligarchies (as in Latin America), and the "treaty port" system to penetrate large pre-capitalist markets (as in China). (In the latter case, Western economic penetration led to a capitalist zone in the coastal areas of China which expanded to become the rapidly developing "enclave" known as the "Pacific rim economies".)

It's important to stress that the present day capitalist system, in contrast to the previous tributary forms, is a truly global system. This is why it is wrong to refer to an underdeveloped region as "feudal" or "pre-capitalist". Even where "pre-capitalist, feudal activities", such crop-sharing, corvee' labor, debt bondage, peasant agriculture, handicraft manufacture, subsistence agriculture or slavery, exist, these activities are nonetheless linked to the world capitalist system. For example, in many cases, these "backward sectors" of Third World economies subsidize the "advanced sectors", which are, in turn, dependent on the outside world economy for markets, financing and intermediate inputs. In other cases, these "backward sectors" are, themselves, subsidized by remittances from workers in advanced countries or advanced sectors. Thus, there isn't a region in the world today that isn't, to a greater or lesser extent, and, for better or worse, economically and culturally linked to the world, capitalist system; the world's first truly global social system.

Like the Barbarian invasions of Rome, the Western "invasion" of the rest of the world was extremely traumatic. The catastrophes visited on South American and African societies by the Spanish conquests and the trans-atlantic slave trade have been well described. Even when European penetration was more neutral, it still administered a tremendous shock to societies that were, in any case, experiencing severe internal difficulties as well.

"A typical third world economy with settled, rather than shifting agriculture, before contact with European capitalism would be almost entirely agrarian. The development of productive forces in such an economy would take the form of acquisition of new skills and use of new techniques for the cultivation of crops or production of goods without any great increase in the use of fixed capital. However, such an economy would be characterized by a centralized state . . . Most of these economies would be endowed with a handicraft sector which would produce the simple tools and consumer goods needed by the peasantry . . . Viewed from outside such an ecnonomy may appear to have considerable slack in it . . , The fact that landlords or noblemen have a large number of retainers or that considerable resources are devoted to social ceremonies or that vast amounts of land are used as pasture may be taken as evidence of such slack. But, in many cases, this 'surplus' . . . turns out to be illusory: the employment of retainers is essential to the maintenance and smooth functioning of a landlord dominated society, the expenditure of resources in social ceremonies is often an essential part of redistribution within the society, and the reservation of vast amounts of land as pasture or cultivable waste is necessary to maintain the fertility of the soil and the productivity and number of the domestic animals . . . When European capitalists burst on the scene as conquerers . . . the balance of this economy was upset. The Europeans apppeared with a demand . . . for particular types of goods, it had to be met by changing the structure of production. The change in the structure of production could not be effected without upsetting the existing social relationshsips, for (a) the economy was not geared to the production of commodities for the market, except as a subsidiary activity, and (b) where demand was for tribute, it could not be met without depriving some sectors of the population of their earlier earnings. Thus, the impact was rarely, if ever, a costless adjustment to an increased monetary demand." A. K. Bagchi, 1982

Now What?

Did the traumatic impact of the West on the non-Western world block this world from experiencing its own, indigenous "industrial revolution". In other words, would the industrial revolution have occurred elsewhere had it not occurred in the West? Some historians think not. They maintain that so many events had to happen at just the right time, and under just the right circumstances, to produce these revolutions, that to talk about these events occurring elsewhere is pointless. (D. Landes, 1969, P. Crone, 1989). Other historians think otherwise. They maintain that the forces leading to industrial capitalism were global in nature and not purely European. Eventually, according to this view, Western levels of scientific and economic advance would, by the sheer passage of time, inevitably have been reached somewhere; if not in the West, then elsewhere. (See J. L. Abu-lughod, 1989, S. Amin, 1980, 1989, E. L. Jones, 1988, and E. L. Jones et al, 1993). However, these kinds of "counterfactual" historical speculations ("What would have happened if?") are ultimately beyond the scope of this chapter whose primary concern is with the questions "What happened?", "Why did it happen?", and "Now what?".

To address this latter question, what does Amin's formulation have to say about the present state of world society and its possible future? In Amin's formulation, world society consists of a developed Center (North) and an underdeveloped Periphery (South). It operates under the capitalist mode, which is a global mode. Global capitalism, in turn, is divided into Central capitalism and Peripheral capitalism. Peripheral capitalism bears the same relationship to Central capitalism that feudalism bore to the tributory mode, namely Peripheral capitalism is an incomplete, not yet fully formed version of the capitalist mode. It is for this reason, Amin speculates, that any potential barriers to world economic growth, while they would be far more traumatic to the populations of the Periphery than to the populations of the Center, might also be far more readily transcended in the Periphery than in the Center, precisely because the Periphery operates under an incomplete, and, thus, more flexible, version of the capitalist mode. Thus, Amin's formulation puts "North/South relations" at the center of all socioeconomic and political trends, problems and crises in the world today. In fact, many analysts are coming to the conclusion that developments in the South will, for reasons of demography alone, play an increasingly important role in all aspects of life everywhere. The *World Bank Development Report* of 1991 puts it as follows:

"In the time that it takes to read this paragraph, roughly a hundred children will be born—six in industrial countries and ninety-four in developing countries, Here lies the global challenge. No matter what the outlook in the industrial countries, the world's long-term prosperity and security—by sheer force of numbers—depends on LDC development."

In other words, there's no question that, if the populations of the underdeveloped world "weigh in" at anything approaching their relative numbers, it is inevitable that the influence of the South on the North can only grow over time. It is for this reason, we believe, that much of the widespread confusion over future trends stems precisely from an inability to adequately conceptualize North-South relations. For example, here's a common misconception; the belief that the North differs from the South by a time gap; that Asia, is decades behind the West, Africa centuries behind the West, and so on; This "time gap" misconception is essentially the belief that the North is the South's future, and that the South is the North's past. To be sure, both the North and the South have evolved enormously over the past 500 years, but this evolution has taken the South as far away from the ages of feudalism or antiquity as it has taken the North. A country like Somalia, for instance, where warlords fight with rocket propelled grenades and armored vehicles, and, where this fighting is televised, is as far away from the feudal ages as is any country in Western Europe. As far as the future is concerned, it could just as well be said that the South is the North's future. Just as the dark ages of "Barbarian/Roman dualism" evolved into a "Barbarian/Roman synthesis" which, in turn, evolved into Western society, so will the present period of "North/ South dualism" evolve into a "North/South" synthesis which, in turn, will evolve, for better or worse, into a new global society. Because of the rapid pace of technical and demographic advance, this "synthesis" will take place on an enormous scale, and in decades rather than centuries, and its repercussions will impact business planning and decision-making everywhere.

To elucidate this in more detail, we will quote from ourselves:

"Let's look at human society, as it were, 'from outer space' with no preconceptions. What would we see? We would see human society as 'islands of development in a sea of underdevelopment'. The 'islands of development' would include the developed countries and the developed enclaves in the underdeveloped countries. The 'sea of underdevelopment' would contain approximately 80% of the world's population. . . . We would see the primary social system on the planet, the system by which human activity is coordinated and regulated, namely the capitalist, free-market system, spreading into more and more areas of global society formerly not under its sway, into the service sectors through the industrialization and globalization of the financial sectors through the use of digital technology, into the eastern bloc through private sectors loans and internal structural reforms, and finally, and we believe most importantly, into the underdeveloped, pre-capitalist 'peripheral' areas of global society, namely the less developed countries, precipitating unprecedentedly rapid growth in some of them, turmoil and upheaval in others, collapse and catastrophe in still others, but transforming all of them. We would also see enormous social and institutional barriers to the worldwide geographical expansion of the capitalist system. In the less developed world, these barriers would include the lack of an entrepreneurial class, the lack of free, competitive markets, in land, labor and capital, the inequality of land and income distribution, the feudal, oligarchic and bureaucratic restrictions on economic development, the 'hollow' and dependent nature of the economies, the backwardness of agriculture, overpopulation and maldistribution of population (particularly in Africa), the unrepresentative nature of the political processes (particularly in the Middle East). In the West, these barriers would include the saturation of consumer markets in many countries, and hostility towards the less developed world and fear that it might repeat the Japanese success. In the Eastern bloc these barriers would include the firmly entrenched bureaucratic, black market and barter economies, and the antiquated, hopelessly uncompetitive nature of much of the capital stock. The 'shock waves and interference patterns' generated when the expansion of the global capitalist system runs up against the barriers to expansion mentioned above constitute nothing less than the economic and political history of the last 20 years, the oil shocks, the debt problems, the trade imbalances, the drug problems, the rise of the Israeli right, the Palestinian intifada, the rise of religious fundamentalisms, the spread of democracy, the upheavals in the Eastern bloc, Iran and China. To give a brief example of the above assertion, American and global economic policy over the past ten years has essentially consisted of responses to crises in 'North/South' economic relationships, crisis caused by the turbulent expansion of the capitalist system into the less developed world. For example, in 1979 at the IMF conference in Belgrade there were calls for long-term LDC development bonds to be issued to sop up excess 'petrodollars', relieve global inflation and convert short-term and rapidly growing LDC debt into long-term development bonds, Since the U.S. was not remotely ready for such a proposal, Paul Volcker flew back from Belgrade to Washington and imposed the tight money policy of 1979. When this began to precipitate an extremely serious LDC debt crisis in 1982, the Reagan administration politically, unable to deal with the situation directly (in was only in 1989 that the U.S, with the 'Brady plan') instituted a policy of using the U.S. deficit as an 'engine of growth' for the global economy and of tolerating a large trade imbalance to give the debtor LDC's a place to which to export in order to be able to make the interest payments on their debt. This began to precipitate a fairly sizable amount of 'industrial redployment' from the U.S. to the developing world (without solving the debt crisis). In the mid-80's this began to generate an intense upsurge of protectionist sentiment. This 'protectionist crisis' led to the 'G7 agreement' to force down the value of the dollar. This in turn precipitated a flood of dollars from abroad into the U.S. asset markets, leading to the wave of mergers, the 'junk bond' phenomenon, the upsurge in real estate prices, the 'homeless crisis' in the U.S. and the 1987 turbulence in the global stock markets." from a 1989, Cambridge Forecast Group paper, presented at the <u>Symposium on Global Change held by the Energy Research Institute of the Japanese Ministry of International Trade and Investment.</u>

We will explain this in more detail in chapter 5, but, for now, we now will turn our attention to the Eastern bloc. For purposes of brevity we will confine our attention to Russia, since Russia is the most economically, demographically and politically significant country of the region. We deal with Russia now, because, to some extent, Russia doesn't quite fit into the above formulation.

The Uniqueness of Russia

"No one denies that Russia is unique.", writes David Fairlamb of "Institutional Investor". Of course, every country is unique, but Russia is "more unique" than any other country. To be sure, Russia has a great many cultural similarities with the West; a very high literacy rate, a large skills base, an advanced scientific and technological sector, and an extensive common artistic heritage. However, Russia has a very different history from that of the West. Russia was never part of the civilization of antiquity. It was never part of the West European German-Roman synthesis. It was never colonized by the West, and it was never integrated into the Western global economic system to the extent that the rest of the world has been. From a social and institutional point of view, Asia and the Third World are actually closer to the West than is Russia. This is why Western descriptions of Russia tend to rely on metaphor; "the new Byzantium", "a Third World country with rockets", "an industrial Asiatic despotism", "an industrial feudalism", and so on.

"The idea that Russia's historical destiny was essentially different from that of Central and Western Europe had a considerable ancestry. It was the central theme in the famous debate between Slavophils and Westerners in the early nineteenth century; and it ran through the discussion as to whether feudalism in the Western sense had ever existed in Russia; or whether the system of land holding and of social obligations in earlier centuries represented something unique so far as European development was concerned." (M. Dobb, 1948). One of the debates between Slavophils and Westernizers concerned the significance of Russia's origins as a Scandinavian colony. Many Westernizers believed that such an origin made Russia an essentially Western country whose destiny lay with Europe. The Slavophiles believed that early Russian society evolved from indigenous Slavic society and that the Viking colonizers of the 9th century had a neglible impact. In fact, there isn't any episode of Russian history, from Viking colonization in the 9th century to IMF stabilization in the 1990's, that isn't the subject of intense debate. There are debates about the impact of Mongol occupation, about the vast peasant flights that occurred under Ivan IV, about the origins and significance of the village commune or Mir, about whether the agrarian reforms of 1861 left Russia with a capitalist or feudal agriculture, about whether the Stolypin reforms of 1906 could have averted revolution had the first world war not supervened, about whether the democratic provisional government could have survived had it ended the war and redistributed the land, about whether Russia could have survived the German onslaught of 1941 without the forced industrialization of the 1930's, about whether the slave labor camps aided or impeded this forced industrialization, about the reasons for the collapse of communism and the implications of this collapse for the future, and, finally, about whether the IMF/World Bank stabilization, privatization and structural adjustment programs designed for Western and Third World economies can work in Russia.

Perhaps one could say that Russian history contains a unique combination of Western and non-Western influences. As M. Cherniavsky (1971) points out, the whole debate over Russia's "Scandinavian origins" is largely beside the point. The Scandinavian (Norman) conquerers who installed England's feudal government were Danish settlers in France who had assimilated European social structures and institutions. In contrast, the Scandinavians (Varangian Swedes) who plied the north-south rivers of the Donetz basin to trade with Byzantium (and who supposedly started the early Russian state (the Kievan State)) were un-Christianized slave traders and not really "Western" in the Norman sense. The earliest Russian source materials are the Early Russian Chronicles, which were systematized at the beginning of the 11th century and record events going back to the 9th century. Prior to that, there is source material from non-Russian societies (such as Constantinople) and from archaelogical investigations. The recent tendency among historians is to stress the similarities between indigenous Celtic, Germanic and Slavic societies. It was only in the course of time that these societies diverged radically; the Celts and Germans were influenced by Western Roman society, and the eastern Slavs by Turkic steppe society. In the latter half of the last millennium, Russian society evolved a class structure, possibly under Varangian influence. At the top of the social hierarchy, was a sort of military caste, the Druzhina, and, at the bottom, were debt peons and slaves (Kholopy). The Druzhina devolved into two classes, a landed merchant nobility (Boyars) and a class of warrior princes (Knyazi). As this was taking place, Russian society was also under the influence of Byzantium, which was a large market for Russia's exports (furs, slaves, bees wax, wood and honey). When Byzantium went into decline, the political and demographic center of Russian society shifted to the Northeast. Possible causes for this shift were a flight of population to escape the political conflicts and peasant enserfments which followed the decline of trade with Byzantium: a demographic explosion in the northeast possibly caused by assimilation of the Finno-Ungrian people of the area; a flight of population to the forests to escape from the nomadic invasions that periodically swept over Russia and continously set back its economic development (the Pechenegs in the 11th century, the Kipchak Turks in the 12th century and finally the Mongols in the 13th century)

Russia was actually part of the Mongol empire for a time, and began its centralization process under the "Mongol yoke". In fact, some historians maintain that the Mongol state was the basis for the Tsarist autocracy. that the early Russian Tsars were successors to the Khans, but this has always been a matter of controversy. Suffice it to say that when Russia's centralization process began, under Mongol tutelage, the dense network of commercial, manufacturing, and scholastic autonomies, which had characterized western feudal Europe, didn't exist in Russia; Russia's economy had been devastated by the Mongol invasions and its recovery from the invasions "stunted" by Mongol enslavement of skilled craftman and Mongol monopolization of foreign commerce. Therefore, the centralization process, which, in Europe, was to lead to the "states system", was to take a very different path in Russia.

Briefly, the Russian Tsarist autocracy was created by Ivan III, Vassily III and Ivan IV (Ivan the Terrible). Ivan III refused

tribute to the Mongol Khans, conquered the northestern
Principality of Novgorod and used the lands aquired thereby
to finance (by means of small land grants called "knights
fees" or pomesti) a new class of military retainers (called
pomestchiki) as a counterweight to the Boyars. Ivan IV
expropriated lands from the Boyars and use them to finance
the creation of a royal guard corps known as the oprichniki
which became an instrument of state terror. He also created
a permanent infantry and broke the military power of the
Mongol Khanates. Starting from a radius of 250 miles
around Moscow, the Russian Tsarist state, partly because of
its acquisistion of heavy artillery and partly because of the
internal disintegration of the Khanates, was eventually to
become heir to the vast Mongol Empire, thus achieiving its
enormous size.

The decades immediately following the liberation from
the "Mongol Yoke" were a period of rapid economic,
agricultural, and commercial advance. However, this was
not to last. Starting with the disastrous Livonian wars, under
Ivan IV, the exactions of the Tsarist autocracy on Russian
society were accompanied by (and contributed to) a series
of catastrophies, which, over the next two centuries, were
to strengthen the Russian autocracy, and weaken all other
sectors of society, to a degree which was unprecedented in
European history. After a long period of disastrous wars,
epidemics, crop failures, famines, outside invasions, civil
chaos, massive peasant flights and massive peasant uprisings,
the upper strata of Russian society banded together under
the aegis of the central state, and against the peasantry. The
peasants were bound to the land and then to their lords; the
landed nobility, the towns, the merchants and the clergy
were all bound to the autocracy. Entrepreneurial energies

were diverted away from commerce and into climbing the bureaucratic and military hierarchies, so that when Russia began to industrialize in the 19th century, it was under the impetus of the Tsarist state rather than the bourgeosie.

In short, even after Russia's successful assimilation of western science, technology and commercial techniques and, even after the agrarian reforms and industrialization of the 19th and early 20th century, Russia was still closer, in many ways, to a pre-European "tributary form", than to a western European state. By the early 20th century, Russia "was both a major industrial country and a technologically backward medieval peasant economy; an imperial power and a semi-colony; a society whose intellectual and cultural achievements were more than a match for the most advanced culture and intellect of the western world, and one whose peasant soldiers in 1904-1905 gaped at the modernity of their Japanese captors." (E. Hobsbawm, 1987).

Both Russia and Japan represent "borderline cases" in the history of industrialization. Feudal Japan was culturally non-western but socially western, whereas Russia was culturally western but socially non-western, (features which have enormous imnplications for present day Japan and Russia).

To sum up, immediately prior to the outbreak of World War I, Russian economic growth was impressive. However, this economic growth was taking place in the context of an increasingly antiquated and decrepid socio-political structure, similar in many (though not in all) respects to a pre-capitalist "tributary form". What would have happened had World War I not supervened is a question that we will leave to one side. Suffice it to say that when Rusian entered the "on ramp" to industrialization, the external environmental was uniquely unfavorable. The world capitalist system was undergoing a period of severe and catastrophic contraction, a breakdown in international trade, severe depressions, the rise of anti-capitalist ideologies such as communism and fascism, and the two world wars. This had a drastic impact on the form Russian development was to take; an autarkic, forced industrialization "superimposed" on a collapsed, largely pre-capitalist, bureaucratic, "tributory" structure. The Soviet economy, prior to Gorbachev, consisted, first of all, of a centralized, bureaucratic sector, a sort of industrial version of the Czarist agrarian economy. This sector consisted of isolated, uncoordinated, (but very vertically integrated) industrial units dependent on distant bureaucracies for management and coordination, This "official sector" was complemented by a complex, partially market-driven, "off the books" sector, the dynamics of which no one, to this day, really understands. The Gobachev reforms led to the partial collapse of the former economy and the expansion of the latter.

So much has been written about the reasons for the collapse of communism and the end of the cold war that there is us to dwell on it. Certainly, the causes of these events were, to a large extent, internal to the Soviet Union. None the less, their timing was not unrelated to the general global trends that we discussed earlier. To illustrate this point, we will quote from the same source as before.

"There are many indirect ways that overall global trends affect the Soviet Union. For example, the upheavals caused by the turbulent and uneven capitalist expansion into the

Islamic world, the Islamic resurgence, the Iranian upheaval, the rise of a militarily aggressive Israeli right in response to Palestinian diplomatic successes, all of these occuring close to Russia's southern border, led, at first, to an increase in superpower tensions in the early 80's, and then put enormous pressure on both superpowers to end the cold war. It is no accident, for example, that the sudden 'arms reduction' summit in Reykjavik Iceland occurred during the same week that the Israeli Prime Ministerhip passed from Labor's Shimon Peres to the right-wing Shamir. One can be sure that the Middle East was discussed at that summit (and that both Russia and the U.S. are engaged in 'behind the scenes' coordination in the Middle East and Eastern Europe.) In addition, the rapid advances in digital technology precipitated by the industrialization and globalization of the financial and service economies and by the intense competition in global markets confronted Russia with the specter of an unwinnable arms race in the application of digital techniques to weapons, and with the specter of its industrial products falling more and more behind world standards. Also, Lenin's theory of 'imperialism', while not absolutely disproved by the post-war prosperity in West, was absolutely disproved by instances of successful capitalist development in the Third World. One can imagine that, not only the reformers, but also many of the conservatives within the nomenklatura must have taken note of the increased Western pre-occupation with the Third World as a source of new markets. They must have been thinking, 'We're white, we're European. If the West needs new areas of capitalist growth why not us? And if the Asians can do it, why can't we?'" from a 1989, Cambridge Forecast Group paper, presented at the <u>Symposium on Global Change held</u>

by the Energy Research Institute of the Japanese Ministry of International Trade and Investment.

What about the future? From the same source as above:

"The Japanese fears of a self-sufficient, 'white' sector of the global economy, which is able to dispense with Asia and the Third World, are illusory. Obviously, the Eastern bloc, because of its proximity to the Common Market countries in the west and to Japan in the East, because of its close cultural of some of its member countries to Western Europe, . . . will offer a large number of opportunities for profitable joint ventures and industrial redeployment. However, the 'white centrist' image of the Eastern bloc as a long-term 'white' engine of growth for the global capitalist economy as a whole, is, in our opinion, mistaken. To exaplain briefly, the 'marketization' of the Eastern bloc (to an extent large enought to be a global engince of growth) raises an 'infinite complexity' of social, economic, institutional and legal questions, questions which, in practise can only be answered by the penetration of outside capital, i.e. by the integration of the eastern bloc into the global capitalist market. Thus, the successful 'marketization' of the eastern bloc requires its successful integration into the global market. And, the amount of outside capital and aid that would be required to bring the bulk of eastern bloc industry up to the very competitive standards of the global capitalist market, without, at the same time, precipitating an unsustainable drop in the real standard of living, would be astronomical, unless this global market is expanded. Thus, the successful integration of the eastern bloc into the global capitalist market will ultimately require the expansion of the markets in the less developed world. And the looming issues of east/west economic integration will again bring to the fore the overriding question of North/South relations." from a 1989, Cambridge Forecast Group paper, presented at the <u>Symposium on Global Change held by the Energy Research Institute of the Japanese Ministry of International Trade and Investment.</u>

Or to explain this in another way:

"The Soviet Union's attempts to transform itself into a market economy can be compared to an organism trying to grow a new nervous system. It's not that easy to do. The alternative is to link up with the nervous system that already exists, namely the global capitalist market. But, in order for that to happen, the global capitalist market itself has to be geographically expanded by means of successful economic expansion in Asia and other parts of the Third World. Thus, the opinion that the events in the eastern bloc will somehow render the less developed world irrelevant could not be further from the truth." from a talk given by the Cambridge Forecast Group at the Other Economic Summit at Houston, Texas, July 1990.

THE WORLD ECONOMY FROM CHARLEMAGNE TO CLINTON

[1] With the exception of parts of South East Asia and the south tip of India.
[2] Quote taken from P. Anderson, 1974.
[3] Quote taken from B. Moore, 1968.
[4] Quote taken from P. Anderson, 1974.

During the 18th century, there was also a great deal of "Sinophilia" among certain European intellectuals, such as Voltaire and Leibnitz, as well as a vogue of "Chinoiserie" in art and household furnishings. (J. K. Fairbank 1983:157)

Chinese mathematics was primarily algebraic rather than geometrical. During the Song and Yuan periods, the Chinese led the world in the solution of algebraic equations. (J. Needham 1981:10)

The drought resistant rice was a fast growing breed of Vietnamese Champa rice. Aquaculture provided soil fertility and opened up large areas for agricultural cultivation by controlling malaria, although the Chinese didn't make the connection. (W. Eberhard 1985:255)

J. L. Abu-Lughod suggests that, had the Ming court supported the maritime activities of South China, Portuquese colonization of the East-West maritime trade routes could have been blocked by China. (J. L. Abu-Lughod 1989:322)

The Su Song astronomical clock was destroyed or abandoned, the use of pound locks was relinquished, (M. Elvin 1973:179) and the water-powered spinning machines were given up. (E. L. Jones et. al 1993:31) In fact, from the 15th century onwards, (M. Elvin 1988:103) most of the major technological progress in pre-modern China was due primarily to "a flow of. improvements and importations from outside". Examples of the latter are wind-driven pumps, the flywheel cotton gin and reading glasses. One cannot conclude from this, however, that major technological and scientific advance would not have resumed in China, at some point, even in the absence of Western influence.

This was marked by an increase in regional economic specialization, and a widespread growth of "market towns" in the countryside. (M. Elvin 1973:269-284) including the introduction of new crops such as sweet potatoes and maize from America.

One of the reasons for the enormous growth of population in the Qing dynasty was the relative absence of civil and military conflict during the Qing period.

W. McNeill (1963) maintains that the initial Arab conquests were "a reassertion of very ancient lines of cultural demarcation", that they essentially "stayed within . . . territories that had once belonged to. ancient. Persia and Carthage."

The Islamic world came close to a "scientific revolution" at the end of the last millenium, and China came very close to an "industrial revolution" at the beginning of this one. Both civilizations seemed to draw back, however, "at the last minute", as though afraid of crossing some sort of threshold. This has raised the question of "why?". Most histories of these regions take a stab at this question, usually offering an "Asiatic despotism" type of analysis. with population and economic output "spiraling ever upward" over time. and to concentrate on the region between the Nile and the Oxus, the so-called "Islamic heartland".

A. G. Frank and B. K. Gills 1993:158

The authors call them "world-historical" cycles.

These empires, the Roman, Parthian Persian, Central Asian Kushan and Han Chinese empires, comprising the "center" of the civilized world, formed a broad "strip" (called the oekumene) extending along the silk route from the Pacific to the Mediterranean, and from there to the Atlantic. Interestingly enough, it was the "outliers" of this strip (Europe and Japan) which first advanced to industrial capitalism.

Political structures are sometimes divided into city states, nation states and universal empires (such as China or the Ottoman, Persian or Byzantine empires). In Amin's, terminology, a tributory form would be an advanced universal empire, and the modern nation state would be characteristic of the capitalist form, the successor to the tributory form. If we were to divide the pre-modern civilized world into three parts; (1) Asia, (2) the Indian subcontinent, and (3) the Hellenistic world (Alexander's empire) plus Europe, then (1) the primary world-view of Asia would be Confucianism, (2) the primary world view of the Indian subcontinent would be Hinduism, and (3) the primary world view of the Hellenistic world plus Europe would be the "medieval construct".

See M. Lombard, 1975.

For two contrasting views on the role of technology in the evolution of feudal society see L. White (1962, 1969) and R. H. Hilton and P. H. Sawyer (1963).

The failure of a large Eurasian empire, such as Rome, to reconstitute itself, in some form or another, after a barbarian invasion was the exception and not the norm (See C. Wickham, 1985 and E. L. Jones, 1988) and, thus, seems to require an explantion. a system of production, moreover, which had been superimposed on a very backward geographical region.

In contrast to the eastern Roman empire which had been superimposed on a preexisting Hellenistic society.

During the 12th century, Europe experienced an "educational revolution" which saw the formation of autonomous universities modeled after the craft guilds.

Or, in other words, looked at from the point of view of a tributory society, Europe's development has yet to be completed. (P. Crone 1989:169)

As early as 1268, Roger Bacon wrote about experiments by Robert Grosseste to use lenses for magnification. He also speculated about using mirrors to "cause the sun, moon and stars, in appearance, to descend here below". (R. Bacon, *The Opus Majus*).

There are accounts of the 13th century German emperor, Frederick II, locking a man in a wine cask to prove the non-existence of the soul (i.e. that the cask didn't lose weight when the man died) and bringing children up in isolation to see if language ability was innate, and, if so, which language; Hebrew, Greek, Latin or German? (C. H. Haskins 1927:334)

Nor did Copernicus's theory make much sense on scriptural grounds, since, after all, Joshua had "ordered the sun, not the earth, to stand still".

This crisis was of concern mainly to scholars and theologians. Most of the people in 16th and 17th century Europe had other things to worry about.

Although Newton himself continued to believe that divine action might be necessary to correct minor perturbations in the orbits of planets. (H. Kearney 1971: 192)

Much of it influenced by the same Hermetic corpus that played so important a role in the western scientific revolution. (M. G. S. Hodgeson 1977:239)

Discrepancies and anomalies which were uncovered because the Western Christian version of the "medieval construct" had less resistance to empiricism.

In fact, Andrew Tanzer ("The Bamboo Network", Forbes, 7/18/94) does both things in one and the same article.

Some historians (P. Crone 1989:172) maintain that cultural developments, the caste system, Confucian values, Sunni orthodoxy, etc., are, to a large extent, the "solutions" to the problem of "civilization building". Because the non-Western civilizations, in contrast to the West, developed "stable solutions" to these problems, they had no incentive to undergo an industrial and scientific revolution. Other historians maintain that there are no permanent "stable solutions" to the problems of civilization building. There are always disequilibria which eventually lead to economic and scientific advance.

For example, Islamic science and Chinese technology might have come together somewhere other than in Europe, in Japan perhaps, (or in the Americas, once they were colonized by old world societies) with the same fortuitous results.

"will impact" could be changed to "is impacting".

The role of nomadic steppe society in world history is hard to evaluate because there is no modern analogue. Because of their mobility, the nomadic steppe tribes could, under the guidance of talented chieftains, form enormous tribal confederations quickly, confederations which, until the advent of modern weaponry, formed the most effective fighting forces the world had ever seen. Because of their ability to live off the land and off plunder, they could put most of the male population on horseback, could communicate rapidly across continents, and could coordinate military maneuvers across hundreds of miles. This gave them an advantage over the settled agricultural societies, which could only provision an army to the extent that they could generate an economic surplus, and usually dealt with the nomadic tribes by a combination of military suppression, tribute, diplomacy and cultural conversion. Economic weakness obviously made a society more vulnerable to nomadic invasions, but a large enough invasion, which had absorbed the latest military technology, was literally unstoppable. The Mongol invasions of the 13th century came very close to conquering the entire eastern hemisphere, against opponents that were by no means weak.

The Mongols assimilated the military use of iron, and then went on to master the use of siege technology and naval technology as well. There is no intention here to suggest a "nomad theory of history". With the possible exception of Persia, the nomadic invasions were only one in a very large number of factors influencing the long term development of the different regions of the globe. Nonetheless, nomadic steppe society played a very important role in the political centralization process of most of Eurasia, either by direct conquest, or by external military pressure, or by the internal "coup d etat's" of military slave castes. Two exceptions to this pattern, interestly enough, are the West and Japan, where it was the commercial sectors (merchants, pirates, bankers) that played the critical roles in the centralization process.

To given an interesting example of the "power of history", C. Keydar (1987) outlines the economic differences between the western Roman empire and the eastern Roman empire (Byzantium), and shows how those differences are still present in contemporary Latin America and Turkey.

To give some more recent examples, P. A. David discusses the role of individual entrepreneurs in the the evolution of technology. He addresses the following question: "When do specific actions, taken purposively and implemented by identifiable agents (say entrepreneurs), have the power to significantly alter the course of technological history?" (P. A. David 1991:52)

D. H. Fischer (1970) discusses the topic of historical fallacies. Two such fallacies are the metaphysical fallacy and the Baconian fallacy. The metaphysical fallacy is asking the question "why". A "why" question is ultimately unanswerable, and it distracts a historian's attention from more managable and productive questions such as "what was the standard of living in such and such a region at such and such a time."

The Baconian fallacy consists in learning as many details as possible in an attempt to discern an overall pattern in the details. It consists of "gathering facts like nuts and berries, until (one) has enough to make a general truth".

This is a doomed effort because there are an infinite number of facts. It's impossible to learn them all. A historical scholar needs a hypothesis, a paradigm, a presumption, or a preconception that is potentially refutable by the available facts, in order to know how to go about gathering facts. (In other words, the attempt to know "everything about everything" or even "something about everything" is a doomed attempt.)

As is evidenced by out introduction to this chapter, we agree with Fischer's analysis. Thus, the reader of this book might be surprised to find that a much of our argumentation turns out to make a heavy use of both of the above two fallacies. The reason for this is that we are not interested in learning scholarly truths about the past, but in making inspired quesses about the future. There are two procedures that we have found useful in that regard. One of these procedures is to learn a mind-numbing number of facts about a mind-numbing number of subjects, to put all of these facts onto the oija board, and to stare at them, clearing from one's mind (to the greatest extent possible) all hypotheses, paradigms, prejudices, preconceptions and presumptions, in order to try to discern some sort of "macro-pattern" in the confused jumble of information. Another procedure is to ask the question "why" about the past even if the question has no objective answer.

Quote taken from P. Anderson, 1974.

K. A. Witfogel (1957) maintains that Chinese civilization arose in response to the problems of flood control, as opposed to the ancient civilizations in middle east which arose in response to the problems of irrigation in an environment which was getting dryer.

The White Lotus rebellion.

Pronounced "Soong".

W. Eberhard speculates that the far ranging Chinese naval expeditions of the early 15th century were sponsored by the Muslim eunuch Zheng He with the intention of forming an alliance between China and the Middle Eastern Muslims against the Mongol leader Timur who was planning to invade China at the time. After Timur died and his empire disintegrated, according to this theory, the Chinese naval expeditions were stopped because they were no longer needed. (W. Eberhard 1977:268) E. J. Jones says that trade by sea was banned in order to stop Japanese smuggling, piracy and bribing of Chinese officials. (E. L. Jones 1981:204) J. L. Abu-Lughod suggests that an economic slump together with widespread epidemics caused the Ming empire to turn inward. (J. L. Abu-Lughod 1989:344). It has also been suggested (A. Cotterell 1990:197) that the restoration of the Grand Canal, and the relocation of the capital from Nanjing to Beijing, reduced the need for sea transport of the grain tribute and, thus, reduced interest in naval technology.

Pronounced "Ching".

The dark ages, the agricultural revolution of 900-1300, the crisis of the 14th and early 15th centuries, the discoveries, the commercial revolution, the religious wars, the scientific revolution, a second agricultural revolution in the 18th century, and the industrial revolution of the 18th and 19th centuries.

An important claim to political legitimacy during the Caliphate period was a claim to genealogical descent from a relative of Muhammad.

The concept of property in the medieval Islamic world was different than the modern western concept and, thus, so was the concept of slavery. Mamluk would be better translated as "permanent military servile retainer." The Eqyptian Mamluks were a military slave caste whose members were recruited as boys outside the empire, often from the nomadic tribes of Central Asia. One of them would be chosen as Sultan and the rest would remain slaves. This institution was developed further developed under the Ottoman empire, into the *devshirme* or "child tax", imposed on Christian Balkan subjects of the empire. In the Ottoman empire, these slaves were called Janissaries and formed an administrative and military caste. Being a slave to the Sultan didn't necessarily imply a low social status because, theoretically, the Sultan "owned" everything.

In contrast to China, where the ancient agricultural infrastructure has been maintained over the centuries, the Middle Eastern agricultural infrastructures, in Mesopotamia and Persia, despite periods of recovery under the Arab Abbassid dynasty and Mongol Ilkhanid dynasty, were eroded through tax farming, nomadic invasions and neglect.

For a description of Eqypt's abortive early 19th century attempt to industrialize, see D. S. Landes, 1980, and P. Gran, 1979.

This survey of the theory of "Asiatic despotism" and the history of the various regions of the world essentially follows P. Anderson (1974), although it also has material and quotes from other authors. For a comparative survey of the history of the various regions of the world, (together with inspired speculation as to "underlying causes") it's hard to do better than P. Anderson (1974). The only problem with Anderson's survey is that it's very difficult reading. For a more readable survey of the same history, with conjectures as to causal explanations, see E. L. Jones (1981) and (1988). See also J. Baechler et al (1988) for an analysis of the different "trajectories" of Europe, China, the Islamic world and India. For a long term history of the world global trade routes, see J. A. Abu-Lughod (1989). And, of course the two classics in the field of comparative long term history are Arnold Toynbee's "A Study of History" (1946) and William McNeill's, "The Rise of The West" (1963).

E. I. Jones (1988) approaches this problem from a different angle. He divides the European transformation from 1600-1900 into its "constituent parts"; namely the scientific revolution, the industrial revolution, the development of capitalism, and initiation of intensive economic growth (growth in per capita economic output by means of technical, agricultural, organizational and commercial innovation). Jones (1988) concentrates on the latter. He postulates three (and possibly four) independently occurring instances of intensive growth; in Europe during the industrial revolution, in Song China, in Tokogawa Japan (and possibly in the Abbasid Caliphate). This yields three "data points" to study rather than one. Jones postulates that all societies have an innate potential for rapid intensive growth. This is because human beings everywhere have a natural propensity for innovation, tinkering, learning, and cooperation with others for mutual gain and a natural desire to escape from poverty. The question then becomes: if the vast majority of people everywhere, and at all times, want to escape from griding poverty, then "what's stopping them?" (See E. L. Jones, 1992.) Why hasn't this natural human desire to be rich translated intself into a rising standard of living in more places, and at more times, during the course of human history. The answer to this question is that a certain level of technical development, and a certain configuration of political, social and institutional forces, must be present in order for this innate propensity for intensive growth to manifest itself. Jones (1988) studies Europe, Song China and Tokugawa Japan in order to analyze and generalize about the political and social factors that enable and inhibit intensive growth. He speculates that in China a continuous progress in technological innvovation might have led to a "scientific revolution" based on empirical observation, and from there to an independent discovery of Western mathematics and deductive logic. The basic point that Jones makes is that there were periods of intense, "European-like" economic dynamism in both China and Japan prior to the

European industrial revolution. There is a considerable degree of overlap between Jones (1988) and the S. Amin approach that we present in this chapter.

For an analysis of the impact of changing world trading patterns on Europe's rise to dominance over the rest of the world, see I. Wallerstein (1974), J. L. Abu-Lughod (1989) and A. G. Frank (1993).

Amin's approach to historical theorizing, by embracing all history, avoids the problem of an "infinite regression of prior causes". For example, in his fascinating book, The Medieval Machine, J. Gimpel (1977) attributes Europe's industrial revolution to an earlier European industrial revolution in the Middle Ages (which saw spectacular advances in the construction of clockwork mechanisms). This however immediately leads to the question of what caused the earlier industrial revolution, and so on.

It is important to stress that a modern European nation-state, even a pre-industrial nation-state, was a much stronger entity than a non-Western "tributory form" (a form of government which E. L. Jones referred to as a "lethargic state"). (E. L. Jones 1988:130-146) For example, the bureaucracies of the advanced "tributary forms" were very thin layers on the surface of peasant societies. It is wrong to think of them as analogous to modern bureaucracies. In Manchu China, for example, there were approximately 40,000 men of "geniune official status . . . ruling over a country of 200 million which grew to 400 million by the middle of the nineteenth century" (J. K. Fairbank 1983:115). In fact, one could say, that, as the West advanced towards the industrial revolution and world domination, non-Western society was evolving political structures, which, although geographically large, were nonetheless easily manipulable and controllable by Western colonial powers. In India, the British took over much of the revenue collection system of the defunct Mughal empire. In China, the British inserted themselves into the Chinese "imperial tribute system" that had historically been used by Chinese dynasties to deal with the "barbarians", and then, after the Opium Wars, the British expanded their priviledges into the "treaty port system", a form of "joint Sino-foreign administration" similar to that used by the previous Mongol and Manchu conquerers of China. (J. K. Fairbank, 1967:204-231). It was only after it had assimilated western technology, western weaponry and western political forms (nationalism) that the non-Western world was able to throw off its Western colonizers.

Hellenistic thought (sometimes called Neo-Platonism) is more than just Greek geometry and Aristotle's physics. It is a complete, all embracing system of thought encompassing the afterlife, the soul, the supreme being, the origin of space and time, and so on. It was systematized in the 3rd century AD by the Egyptian philosopher Plotinus. Plotinus's thought had an enormous influence on the Christian worldview, the Islamic worldview, and on the modern scientific worldview as well. S. Amin (!987:21-22) sums it up as follows:

"(Plotinus) asserted that it was possible to attain to absolute truth through exclusive reliance on deductive reason, without falling back upon particularist mythologies. Secondly he held that this absolute truth necessarily implied the recognition of the soul as an individualized, immortal entity, the subject and object of moral activism universal in its nature. Thirdly, he urged that search for truth through dialectical reasoning be supplemented with an adherence to ascetic practices. Such an appeal to intuitive feelings, an import brought from distant India by the Persians in the time of Alexander, might have cast doubt on the supposedly infinite power of human reason. Plotinus, however, merely gave it a supplementary status. He argued that the ascetic exercises would help the soul to liberate itself from corporal and mundane encumbrances thus purifying reason and rendering it more lucid . . . Fourthly, Plotinus bowed to the fashionable attachment to Chaldean cosmogonic systems, making do with the borrowed Chaldean cosmogony . . . It's hard to judge whether this grand synthesis represented an advance on the thinking of antiquity, or a backward slide therefrom."

Whether an advance or a retrogression, Plotinus's "grand synthesis" represents the way in which a "tributary world view" tends to evolve; i.e, in the direction of completeness and universality. Plotinus's synthesis also continues to have a strong influence on contemporary Western thinking. Both contemporary, popular astrology and contemporary accounts of "near death experiences" derive from ideas presented in Plotinus's Enneads. The Neoplatonic belief that reality is describable mathematically (there has always been a very close relation between mathematics and mysticism) is one of the inspirations for modern economics, particularly the neoclassical and "new classical" varieties.

A "world view" has three aspects; (1) an explanation of "final causes" and "ultimate meanings" (i.e. "Why does anything exist?"); an explanation of nature; (3) and an explanation of social relations between people (i.e., kinship, "mandate of heaven" of imperial rule, primogeniture, etc.). In contrast to the "tributory world view", the modern world view addresses these three aspects separately. The first is dealt with by religion, the second by the scientific method, and the third by economics. If you were to ask someone in America to name the most important long-term determinants of their life in society, the answer would most likely be "supply and demand", "economics" (the job market and/or the housing market, etc.)

The Merovingian dynasty (named after a Frankish king Merovech) was started by Clovis I (465-511AD), a Frankish king who united the Franks by force, took over the Roman tax collection system, and converted from Arianism (a Christian heresy which postulated Christ as a lesser deity than God) to Catholicism, thus getting the backing of the Catholic Church. The Carolingian dynasty (named after Charles Martel the man who supposedly "invented feudalism") was started by administrators (Mayors of the Palace) to the Merovingians kings. These administrators, in alliance with the landed magnates, eventually came to rule in their own name. The first such ruler was Peppin III who deposed the last Merovingian king in 751AD. His son, the emperor Charlemagne (Carolus Magnus or Charles the Elder), was coronated by Pope Leo in 800AD. Charlemagne's abortive attempt to construct a European central government, in alliance with the Papacy, devolved into the Holy Roman Empire, a line of German emperors, which was finally ended by Napoleon in 1806.

Thus, the development of feudalism was also influenced by two technological factors, the stirrup and a larger, more powerful, breed of horse, both of which made mounted armor possible.

See above.

For a compendium of the meager source material on Mediterranean trade in early medieval times see *Medieval Trade in the Mediterranean World*, 1970, W. T. H. Jackson editor. The Jews were an extremely important factor in early medieval European trade, having almost a trade monopoly in the interior provinces of France and Germany. A. Leon (1970) uses this fact to extend the Pirenne thesis into a theory of European anti-Semitism. According to Leon, the indispensable commercial role of European Jewry offered them some degree of protection against the exterminist attitude, adopted, after the Crusades, by Christian Europe towards non-Christians (Pagans) and Christian heretics (Albigensians). When the European commercial revolution rendered their commercial role redundant, the European Jews were swept successively from one western European country after another into Turkey, Eastern Europe and Russia.

M. Cipolla dates the diffusion of the water mill from the 6th century, the heavy plough from the 7th century, the three field system from the 8th century, and the horseshoe and the tandem harness from the 9th century. (C. M. Cipolla 1976:168) By the 13th century, at the latest, these innovations were having a decisive impact on European agricultural productivity, although what happened in the interim is not clear. (G. Duby 1976:103) For an analysis of the chronological and geographic distribution of source material about feudal European agriculture (estate records, farming leases, farming manuals, written settlements of land disputes, land contour patterns) see G. Duby 1976. In any case, most scholars agree that the period from 900-1300 constitutes a genuine "agricultural revolution" the surplus of which made the rapid growth of commerce and manufacturing possible. Gimpel (1976) maintains that feudal Europe underwent a sort of "industrial revolution" as well. "The Middle Ages introduced machinery into Europe on scale no civilization had previously known. This was to be one of the main factors that led to the dominance of the Western hemisphere over the rest of the world. Machines were known in the classical world, of course, but their use in industry was limited. Cogs and gears were employed only for creating toys or automata. In medieval society, however, machinery was made to do what previously had been done only by manual, and often, hard labor." The motives behind feudal European agricultural innovation are unclear. P. Anderson (1979) following K. Marx (*Capital*, Volume I) maintains that the long term stability of feudal rents gave the peasants an incentive to maximize output on their plots. A great deal of land reclamation was done by the Cistercian monks who had a longer "time horizon" than estate owners. These monks also advocated the application of scholarly learning to agricultural improvements. Of course, ecclesiastical institutions were far more likely than other land owners to keep records of their activities, so it's impossible to identify them as the main driving force behind agricultural innovation and extension. Some historians (See R. S. Lopez, 1976) identify the underpopulation of early feudal Europe as a spur to the utilization of labor saving technologies, such as wind mills, water mills, the tandem harness, and so on.

In non-European "tributary forms", political power could be fragmented and decentralized for long periods of time. Nonetheless there was always a sort of economic, political, institutional or cultural "template", so to speak, on which centralized power could be reconstituted, or on which competition between centralized and regionalized power structures could take place. To take a very extreme example, pre-colonial India was a country of enormous geographical, linguistic and ethnic diversity. For much of its history, it was very politically fragmented; an enormous array of rapidly shifting "states" and "micro-states". India's diverse geography made centralized empire building very difficult. To some extent, the caste system and local village organization substituted for centralized power (R. Thapar 1968:91). Despite India's geographical diversity, it did not develop a system of stable regional states along European lines (E. L. Jones 1981:194). Instead it tended to oscillate between periods of centralization and longer periods of extreme fagmentation. Three times the tendency towards a centralized tributory form asserted itself over India's geographical diversity; the Maurya dynasty, 321BC-185BC, (a period in which the principles of Indian government were codified), the Gupta dynasty, 340AD-520AD (a period of cultural and intellectual development, which included the crystallization of Hindu metaphysics, advances in astronomy, and the invention of decimal arithmetic), and the Mughal dynasty, 1526AD-1707AD.

To take an another example, closer to the West, let's compare the feudal European fief with the Arab Abbasid military land grant known as the Iqta (which was to evolve into the Timar in the Ottoman empire and the Jagir in the Mughal empire). Iqta's were not automatically inheritable. They could be revoked or altered by the ruler at will. Peasants were not subjects of the iqta-holder, but of the state. Political decentralization in the Middle East "entailed no fundamental institutional changes and could, in changed circumstances, be reversed." (I. M. Lapidus 1988:151)

In the collapsed Western Roman empire, on the other hand, there was no "template" on which centralized power could quickly reconstitute itself. The Western Roman slave system was superimposed on, what from a social point of view, was "virgin territory". There was no pre-existing social system and no pre-existing economy to undergird it. The collapse of the western Roman empire was more than a dynastic collapse, it was the collapse of an entire "system of economic production". There was no way to reconstitute it, because, without the Roman empire, the slave economy was not viable. A new economic and political system had to be built "ex nihilo". When political centralization took place, it was forced to take place "from the ground up" so to speak, and it led to a totally new "organism", the western nation-state.

It has been said that, in Germany, all the constituent parts of the European nation-state came into being, but in the wrong way, at the wrong times, and in the wrong sequence, with results that were disappointing in some cases, such as German unification, and catastrophic in others, such as the investiture wars, the 30 years war, and the world wars. This is probably a better explanation than Rosa Luxemburg's for the catastrophies of the 20th century. Tribal elements were very strong in early Germany, together with the overlay of the abortive Carolingian empire. German feudalism developed belatedly under the impact of the investiture wars between the empire and the Papacy. Unlike France, where feudalism developed first, and was then gradually brought under the control of a centralizing monarchy, or England, where a monarchy and a feudal system were installed "whole cloth" by the Norman conquerers, German feudalism developed in opposition to the German monarchs. The advent of firearms accelerated the centralization process in Europe in the 17th century, but, at this point, Germany was rent by the 30 years war. In Italy, the vestiges of urban Roman society were strong, and the emergence of strong city-states suppressed the centralization process (even though the Italian city-states developed many of the techniques of European statecraft). Nation-building required the right balance between urban dynamism and (in an era when most wealth was still agricultural) feudal, rural power.

This crisis began with population pressure on the land, then there was exploitation of marginal lands, soil exhaustion, soil erosion and flooding, famines, the bubonic plague, depopulation, the hundred years war, civil wars, labor shortages, seignoral brigandage, plunder and greater pressure on peasants to make up for these shortages, the flight of peasants to the towns, violent peasant upheavals such as the Jaquerie, the decline in the terms of trade against agriculture (the "so-called agricultural depression"), and, in general, the weakening of the "manorial system" and the increased dependence of the landed nobility on the monarchies. See B.H.S. Van Bath, (1963), P. Anderson (1971).

J. L. Abu-Lughod (1989) describes the European crisis of the 14th century as part of a "world crisis". This "world crisis" involved the spread of the plague to China, the Islamic world and Europe, the collapse of the overland Mongol trading routes, and an economic contraction in all three areas. In later centuries, the world "recovered" from the crisis. The Middle East and China saw the growth of militarily stronger, more extensive, more stable, more effectively administered (and more ossified) "tributary forms", namely the Ottoman empire, the Mughal empire and the Qing dynasty. The Ottoman Turks and the Tungusic Manchu's promoted a return to orthodox Islamic and Confucian belief systems and embarked on a program of geographical expansion, colliding at certain points with an expanding Russia. For its part, Europe also recovered from the crisis of the 14th century. However, Europe's recovery gave rise to capitalism, the nation-state system, the industrial and scientific revolutions and, ultimately, the "Europeanization" of the rest of the world. The 15th century is identified as the period in which Europe decisively overtook the rest of the world, if not in standard of living, or military stength, then at least in dynamism and expansiveness.

For a comparison with China's transition from feudalism to "absolutism", see W. Eberhard (1987:47-59). As in Europe, competition between the Chinese "warring states" (500-250BC) led to rapid technological and economic advance, and also led to geographical expansion via colonization (because of an outflow of refugees from the wars). The critical difference between Europe and China was this: Europe's period of centralization, occurred 2000 years later than China's. Europe was heir to an additional 2000 years of global technological and social advance. Thus, whereas China's "late start" (its iron age began in 500BC) enabled it to develop a particularly successful and durable form of the "tributary mode", Europe's "late start", 2000 years later, enabled it to transcend the "tributary mode" altogether.

The way in which this happened is, of course, the history of Western society. It was a bewilderingly complex process, different in every part of Europe. In many cases, the drop in the terms of trade against agriculture induced landed nobles to turn serfs into rent paying tenants, or to convert to cash crops, such as wool or industrial crops. Thus, agriculture was significantly monetized. The monarchs broke the power of the guilds, restricted the activity of highwaymen and robber barons, and instituted the right of inalienable private property, thus strengthening the bourgeosie. This is because, promotion of trade and commerce and the strengthening of the bourgeosie, allowed monarchs to maintain armies not dependent on the loyalties of the nobility or the peasantry. The reappropriation of Greek and Roman knowledge, idea systems, and institutions during the renaissance also played an important role in the commercial, industrial and scientific revolutions which followed. In the Italy and some parts of Germany the strength of the urban sectors, blocked the centralization process entirely, while in Russia the weakness of the urban sectors led to Europe's most rigid autocracy, one which had many features in comman with a classical "tributory form". (See P. Anderson, 1978, 1979, R. Bendix, 1980, E. I. Jones, 1981, 1988). It has been suggested (E. L. Jones 1981:105) that the decentralized geographical distribution within Europe of regions of "high arable potential under plough agriculture" played a role in the subsequent evolution of the decentralized European "states system". It has also been suggested that the location of Europe (and Japan) on the "periphery" of Eurasia allowed these societies to remain decentralized while an autonomous commercial and artisanal sector evolved. In the Eurasian heartland, in contrast, the enormous and continual warfare between the nomadic societies of the north and the settled agricultural societies of the south led to the centralization, rigidification and ossification of the latter, so that the emergence of an autonomous commercial sector was suppressed. (E. L. Jones 1988:110-115; P. Anderson 1978:214-216) In fact, one could say that the "nomadic element" played as important a role—either as direct conquerers, sources of external pressure or as military slaves (Mamluks, Janisseries)—in the centralization process of China, India and the Islamic world, as did the "commercial element"—merchants, artisans, bankers, pirates—in the centralization process of Western Europe and Japan.

In assessing the impact of nomadic invasions on China, M. Elvin (1973:91-110) discusses the military incentives and disincentives for technical innovation in late medieval Europe and post-Mongol China. The Song period in China was a period of rapid techological and industrial advance. However, this era of "industrial revolution" was followed by nomadic invasions which mobilized China's spectacular technological advances against it. The Jurchen conquerers of the Northern Song mastered the use of mounted armor and siege warfare, and the Mongol conquerers of the Southern Song mastered the use of gunpowder and naval warfare. One suspects that the attitude of the succeeding Ming-Qing dynasties towards technological innovation must have been affected by this trauma. According to M. Elvin (1973:91-110), the Ming dynasty preferred to rely on logistical superiority in its military confrontations, rather than on technical superiority, which could always be appropriated by the enemy (invading nomads (barbarians) or internal insurrectionists (bandits)). Medieval China, like contemporary America, was faced, not with the threat of technological competition, but with the threat of technological proliferation. Nobody in Ming China, or anywhere else in the world, for that matter, could possibly have foreseen Europe's industrial revolution and its subsequent colonization of the world. The main danger of European technology had to be seen, therefore, as its destabilizing effects within China, which could be warded off by keeping European influence at arms length. As late as the 19th century a Qing official expressed these fears about European technology to an English diplomat.

"I asked him what we ought to do if bandits use the trains to invade us. (He) answered that . . . while the bandits can take the trains, they cannot occupy the whole railway. If the railway is cut, the train cannot run. I said that . . . (barring the total destruction of the railway) . . . the bandits could easily fix things up to transport their own soldiers." (R. W. Huenemann 1984:40)

Post-feudal Europe, on the other hand, was faced with an entirely different configuration of military pressures. The chances of a European peasant somewhere declaring himself head of the Holy Roman Empire and taking over Europe (ala Zhu Yuanzhang's rebellion against the Yuan dynasty) were remote to say the least. Equally remote was the conquest of Europe by Mongol horsemen. European governments faced the pressures of competitive military innovation from adjacent states more or less equally able to innovate. Suppression or neglect of technological advance was obviously not an appropriate response to this situation.

This is not to say that inter-state military rivalry was the demiurge of Western technological progress. Nor is it to say that post-Mongol China had settled into a pattern of permanent technological stagnation that could only have been ended by Europe's influence. It is to say that the reason why feudal Europe's technological advances perpetuated themselves, while Song China's petered out, was that Europe's technological advances occurred during Europe's period of formation, before European society had "crystallized" into a "tributory form". Therefore, the logic of technical advance became "embedded" in Europe's development process, and interacted with it in a way that fostered technological innovation and ultimately debouched into capitalism.

The Hermetica was wrongly believed to be very ancient. It was attributed to a mysterious Eqyptian writer, Hermes Trismegistus, who was alledged to have been the recipient of a divine revelation about the physical world, in the same way that Moses was the recipient of a divine revelation of about the moral world. The Hermetica became available to the West after the fall of Constantinople in 1453. Later on, the classic scholar Isaac Casaubon (1559-1614) proved that the Hermetica was Neo-Platonist in origin. Another mystical text, with Neo-Platonic influences, which influenced Renaissance thinking was the Jewish Cabbala. (H. Kearney 1971:37)

In formulating his program of discovering a larger and larger body of partial truths about nature through scientific experimentation, Francis Bacon made two mistakes. First of all, he drastically underestimated the amount of time it would take to do this. Secondly, he discouraged purely mental speculation as the kind of mental wool gathering that led nowhere and that modern researchers should avoid. In this, he underestimated the role of purely mental constructs in the formation of the hypotheses needed to design experiments in the first place. One of the most important of these purely mental constructs was the concept of "rectilinear motion in a vacuum", a construct which played a critical role in the development of Newtonian-Galilean mechanics, and a concept which, to some extent, was a Western Christian addition to Aristotelian cosmology, though it also had some Stoic origins. (D. C. Lindberg 1992:248). The notion of rectilinear motion in a vacuum was necessary in order to allow God to take a planet and move it beyond the periphery of the spherical Aristotelian universe, should he choose to do so. Aristotle himself assumed that there was nothing, not even empty space, outside the universe, an assumption which limited God's ability to push heavenly bodies out of the universe. Many of the theories and hypotheses which led to the scientific revolution had their origin in Hellenistic thought. H. Kearny divides these notions into three "traditions"; the organic, mechanistic and magical traditions. (H. Kearney 1971:22) In the organic tradition, nature was explained by analogy to a living organism. The chief inspiration behind this tradition was Aristotle. According to Aristotle, for example, a falling stone moved towards the earth, because this was the "natural" thing for it to do; it had an "affinity" for the earth because it had a lot of "earth" in its makeup. In the mechanistic tradition, the natural world was compared to an elaborate machine. This tradition had its origin in the speculations of Hellenistic philosophers known as "atomists" and in the work of Archimedes. A scientist in the mechanist tradition was Descartes, who, believed, for example, that animals were machines and that the universe was filled with a swirling substance whose motions drove the movable heavenly bodies. Another scientist in the mechanistic tradition was Galileo. The magical tradition was essentially Neo-Platonism. The key feature of this tradition (leaving aside the mystical elements) was the belief that God had given the natural world a mathematical structure. Examples of scientists in the magical tradition are Copernicus, Kepler and Newton. (Gravity or "action at a distance" was regarded by many contemporary scholars as an "occult force".) The important point is that the conflicts between these traditions were decided not simply by decree or by argumentation but, ultimately, by controlled, reproducible experiments. For example, the significance of Galileo's experiment of dropping two unequal weights and timing their descent was not that he was the first scholar to do this. In fact, it had been done a thousand years before by a Byzantine scholar, John Philoponus, who came to much the same conclusions. The significance of Galileo's experiment was that it was performed over and over by different researchers "in a battle between two paradigms, the organic (which held that the heavier weight should fall faster) and the mechanistic". (H. Kearney 1971:69)

Quote taken from D. C. Lindberg (1992)

Both Islamic and Western Christian thought eventually encountered "the limits of rational metaphysics". At this point they diverged. Western Christian thought evolved into modern science. Modern science is the discovery that natural phenomena can be "taken out of context" and forced to behave in the same way over and over again in response to the same initial conditions (experiments), and that this can be done in order to prove or disprove purely mental speculations about nature (theories). This makes it possible to design a scientific experiment in such a way that everything—everything either known or unknown, everything in this world or in some other, entirely supernatural, totally unimaginable world—everything, in short, external to the experiment can be "left to one side". It is not necessary, for example, to worry that the experiment is being affected by the improper performance of some religious rite somewhere, or by some totally unknown phenomenon in some totally unknown realm. In the natural sciences, at least, it is not necessary (as it sometimes seems to be in the social sciences) to know everything about everything in order to know something about something. It is not necessary to have the final, ultimate truth about everything, nor is it necessary to apprehend everything "at one fell swoop", as in some mystical vision. A larger and larger body of partial truths can be built up, partial truths which will be universally acccepted, because they are demonstrable and useful. This, essentially, is the key addition of Western thought to Hellenistic thought. It's important to stress that this insight was not logically self-evident, given the evidence at the time, and was essentially a "discovery". It was this "discovery" that formed the basis for the "modern world view".

Thus, there are essentially two outgrowths from Hellenistic rational metaphysics. They are (1) modern science, and (2) theosophy. In modern science, a (sometimes private) mental construct (a theory) is tested by publicly observable, controlled, reproducible experiments. In theosophy, "ultimate reality" is apprehended directly and personally (dhawq) by meditation, but this meditation has to be controlled and disciplined by a public metaphysics (faylsafah). (M. G. S. Hodgeson 1977:237) One notion, of Neo-Platonic origin, that occurs again and again in medieval thought, is the notion that the basis of everything is light. The 11th century Sufi philosopher, Yahya Sukrawardi, developed this notion into an elaborate "theory of everything" called illuminationism (Ishraqi). Suhrawardi's treatise, Hikmat Al-Ishraqi (The Wisdom of Illumination) covers such diverse topics as natural science, physics, optics, deductive logic, space, time, consciousness, and eternity. According to Suhrawardi, "the divine essence was pure light, and the reality of all other things was derived from the supreme light. Degrees of light were associated with degrees of knowledge and self-awareness . . . the emanation of light from the primary being established a hierarchy of angelic substances standing between God and the world . . . the vertical order of angels gave rise to the celestial spheres; the horizontal order of angels constituted the world of Platonic forms and archtypes, and gave rise to the angels that governed human souls . . . The hierarchy of being was a ladder of illumination along which the purified soul could return from the material world to the world of archtypes." (I. M. Lapidus 1988:213) Both Suhrawardi and later Sufi philosophers, such as Ibn Al-Arabi, designed extremely sophisticated mental constructs somewhat reminiscent of modern set theory. The 13th century English theologian, Robert Grosseteste, also accepted the notion that light was the basis of everything. He developed a metaphysics which was, in some respects, a more primitive version of illuminationism, and had the same Neo-Platonic inspirations. According to Grosseteste, in the beginning, God created a single, dimensionless point of matter, and a single dimensionless point of light. The light expanded outward into a large sphere drawing the matter with it. Matter provided the "substance" of the universe. Light provided the "dimensions" and "corporeal forms". Grosseteste accepted the idea of a "world soul", but then retreated from it. He believed that the study of optics was the key to understanding the world. He suggested the use of a magnifying lens to aid in the observation of objects that were far away or very small. (J. Gimpel 1976:185)

"For (the study of optics) shows us how to make things very far off seem very close at hand . . . to make distant objects appear as large as we choose . . . or to count sand, or grain, or grass, or any other minute object."

J. Gimpel (1976) speculates that the invention of eyeglasses in Italy in 1280 may have been stimulated by Grosseteste's writings. In any case, it is easy to see how his writings presage the invention of the telescope and microscope. Thus, it was the "underdeveloped nature" of Western scholasticism which permitted it to develop in the direction of empiricism and, ultimately, in the direction of modern, reductivist science.

Much of pre-modern Western cosmology derives, in essence, from Babylonian (Chaldean) astrology. This astrology held that "predictable celestial events foreshadowed terrestrial occurrences". (W. McNeill 1963:292). In particular, it held that the exact position of the movable heavenly bodies at the moment of a person's birth determined the course of the person's life. This made it tremendously important to be able to calculate and forecast the exact movements of the heavenly bodies. Even minor anomalies became very significant. For example, the astronomical observations of Tycho Brahe (which led to Kepler's discoveries) were motivated by precisely this type of astrology. (H. Kearney 1971:133) Kepler, in turn, persisted in spite of repeated failures, in his attempt to discover the mathematical rules of planetary motion, because of his intense faith (derived ultimately from Chaldean cosmogony) that such rules existed. (Ibid) Chinese cosmology, on the other hand, held that the "driving force" of all phenomena, whether terrestrial or celestial, was, not celestial mechanics, but human social activity. (J. K. Fairbank 1967:39) Natural anomalies, including celestial anomalies, could be symptoms of maladministration by the state. ("Our experience in governing has been (brief), so that we (have made mistakes), hence on January 5, . . . there was an eclipse of the sun . . . We are dismayed." Han Shu.) (S. Nakayama 69:45) In other words, "the Mandate of Heaven" did not depend on mathematical rules, but on the behavior of the dynasty. This necessarily implied a certain amount of indeterminacy in the mechanics of celestial motion. This, in turn, tended to make less likely the linking of mathematical model building with empirical observation, and thus to disccourage a "scientific revolution" of the Newtonian-Galilean type. Neo-Confucian cosmology attempted at one point to construct a crude theory of three dimensional planetary motion. However, "the most striking characteristic (of Chinese astronomy) is the lack of conceptual schemes" (S. Nakayama 1969:151). As Nakayama points out, the advantage of a conceptual scheme is "that discrepancies between it and actual observations can be clearly recognized. Such recognition isolates variations of a smaller magnitude, which call for a more complex scheme based on more accurate observations." Thus, the importance of astronomical conceptual schemes to the Western world view tended to promote astronomical advances, and the lack of Chinese "scheme consciousness" tended to retard them. A description of the ways in which the pre-modern Chinese world view influenced the development of Chinese science and mathematics is way beyond the scope of this book. For those who are interested, Mark Elvin's book The

Pattern of the Chinese Past (1973) and Joseph Needham's book Science in Traditional China (1981), both give a readable introduction to this question. We'll give a very brief synopsis of this topic here. The Chinese Daoists had a "theory of nature", albeit a mystical one, and J. Needham suggests that Daoist cosmology played an important role in the development of Chinese chemistry, including the development of gunpowder. (J. Needham 1981:54) In northern Chinea, during the Yuan (Mongol) dynasty and the preceding Jin (Jurchen) dynasty, the Chinese made impressive advances in univariate and multivariate polynomial algrebra, and the driving force behind these advances was likewise Daoist mysticism. Polynomials were represented by a positional array. Powers of x were represented by position in the array and coefficients were represented by the number of counting rods placed at each position. Up to four unknowns, designated "heaven", "earth", "man" and "things" were handled. However these mathematical advances did not penetrate into the mainstream Chinese world view, and, by Ming times "there was no one left who could understand the more advanced positional algebra". (M. Elvin 1973:193) The 17th century Chinese scientist Fang I-Zhi (1611-1671) developed a scientific research methodology somewhat similar to the process of learning a motor skill until it becomes "second nature". The point, according to Fang I-Zhi, was to investigate all "the objects of existence" in the natural world, whatever they might be, and to build up an "intuitive feel "for how nature, as a whole, works. The human mind and senses are structured to perceive things in a certain way, so that there's no point in asking what's "really" out there. One can, at most, perceive only "shadows and echoes". In effect, the "laws of nature are simply another way of referring to the laws of the mind", knowable by introspection. There is no question here of combining rigorous conceptual schema with empirical observations, but rather of combining empirical observations with a form of "holistic awareness" of the patterns of natural phenomena. (M. Elvin 1973:230) During Song times, Chinese Confucian scholars did attempt to construct a cosmological scheme which stressed the reality and knowability of the external, natural world. They attempted to look at society as part of a larger natural cosmos, and to locate, within this cosmos, the source of human "social morality" (finally the most important issue in the Chinese world view). The cosmos was divided into li ("principle" which included—among other things—those qualities, such as benevolence, sacrificial spirit, righteousness, and so on, which make for social cohesion), material force (qi) and raw matter (zhi). Inanimate objects admitted no principle. Lower life forms, such as animals, "are born with material force containing an extremely dense level of blockage and there are places where no principle can penetrate it. Even the cases of the benevolence of the tiger and wolf, the sacrificial spirit of the wild dog, and the righteousness of the bee and ant are ones in which there has been only a small amount of penetration, comparable to . . . a single shaft of light entering a crack." Virtuous individuals were very "clear" and admitted a great deal of "light". (D. J. Wyatt 1990:53). In the Ming period, however, philosophers sought morality solely within human thought, a point of view known as "moral intuitionism". (M. Elvin 1973:226) To be sure, a great deal of Chinese metaphysics (perhaps all of it) is lost in translation (A. C. Graham 1964:55), but our brief description of it should demonstrate the profound differences between the Chinese world view, on the one hand, and the Western/Byzantine/Islamic world view on the other. All of which is not to imply that industrial progress in pre-modern China was blocked by deficiencies in scientific theory. By Song times, Chinese industry had all the science it needed to advance much further than it actually did. (M. Elvin 1973:298).

This is the standard Confucian four class structure, scholars, farmers, artisans and merchants.

C. Totman (1981) maintains that late Tokugawa Japan was approaching Malthusian limits because of population growth and the prohibition of foreign trade. S. Hanley (1983) maintains that the economy of late Tokugawa Japan had a high standard of living by pre-modern standards. Susan B. Hanley (1983).

Obviously, these quotes from ourselves represent our own opinion, and are not necessarily the viewpoint of any of the other authors quoted in this book.

This does not necessarily imply a stable functional relationship between exchange rates and foreign investment. (See V. G. Stevens 1993.)

By which we mean the former Russian empire.

Two years later, President Bush was to say that all the money in the world couldn't solve the problems of Russia.

"Literally, since the imposition of the 'Tartar Yoke', the political economy of the CIS has been a centralized one, a feature which of course was vastly intensified by the 70 years of communist rule. For a region as centralized as the CIS to develop an internal private sector market is like an organism trying to grow a new nervous system. It's not that easy to do. The alternative is to link up with the nervous system that already exists, namely the global market, i.e. integration with the global market. But the global market which now exists is simply too tight and competitive to accommodate the CIS. This market has to be expanded It has to be expanded by addressing the problems of Third World development. To elaborate, take the problem of bringing the CIS into the world monetary and financial system. One way to do this is to expand the world financial system to accommodate the CIS, the 'Marshall Plan' or 'grand bargain' approach of massive Western financial and monetary aid. But the CIS is simply too big for this, the world financial system would be strained to the breaking point (the so-called 'global capital shortage'.) Another approach would be to shrink the economy of the CIS to accommodate a 'hard ruble'. But this would involve shutting down much of the CIS.

One way to get around this dilemma would be aid in the form of facilitating computerized barter and countertrade among the republics of the CIS and between the republics of the CIS and the debt-burdened NIC's (newly industrializing countries). The usual objections to barter are (1) it is oligopolistic, and (2) that the transaction costs are high. However, barter on a global scale need not be that oligopolistic and the new techniques of communication and information storage and processing would certainly lower the transaction costs. Furthermore, aid in this form would not send shock waves through the financial systems of the G7 countries as would a 'Marshall Plan' or 'grand bargain'." from *Cambridge Forecast Report*, February, 1992.

CHAPTER 5

SINCE THE REAGAN REVOLUTION

In this chapter, we will describe, in detail, how the trends and processes described in chapter 3 have shaped economic and political events since the "Reagan revolution" of 1981. To oversimplify somewhat, we will describe how global rich/poor relations have been the "demiurge" of historical change from the "Reagan revolution" to the present.

To begin with, we would like to clear up a possible misconception. This chapter will be **about the recent past, not about the next century,** when, according to many commentators, global rich/poor relations will **certainly** be a key factor in global change. After all, most of the world's enormous population growth is in the poor regions of the world; regions which therefore, by sheer weight of numbers, must eventually come to have an all pervasive influence on economics and politics everywhere, including economics and politics in the rich regions of the world. Three mechanisms are generally postulated for this influence. First of all, the rich regions of the world could potentially be overwhelmed by migrants from the poor regions of the world. Secondly, upheavals caused by population pressures in the poor regions of the world could touch off global military conflagrations. Thirdly, the populations of the poor regions of the world could exceed the "carrying capacity of the earth", and thus precipitate "global environmental crises", which would embroil the rich regions of the world as well. This could happen whether or not the poor regions of the world industrialize successfully. If they do industrialize successfully, then "it is inconceivable that the earth can sustain a population of 10 billion people devouring resources at the rate enjoyed by richer societies of today—or at even half that rate". (P. Kennedy, 1993). If they don't industrialize successfully, then the earth's environment will be overwhelmed by massive increases in slash and burn agriculture, overgrazing, deforestation, and desertification. In fact, the world's poor, once they reach a certain demographic size, can do nothing at all that doesn't destroy the earth's environment. Wood gathering produces deforestation. Rice paddies produce methane which worsens the greenhouse effect. Livestock herds produce the same result through animal flatulence. In other words, if the poor populations of the world "so much as fart upwards", as the saying goes, they could fatally tip the earth's environmental balance to the detriment of the rich populations as well. Therefore, "the greatest test for human society as it confronts the twenty first century is how to use 'the power of technology' to meet the demands thrown up by the 'power of population'; that is, how to find effective global solutions to free the poorer three quarters of humankind from the growing Malthusian trap of malnutrition, starvation, resource depletion, unrest, enforced migrations, and armed conflict—developments that will also endanger the richer nations." (P. Kennedy, 1993).

All of the above is precisely what chapter 5 will not be about. First of all, what is the the "carrying capacity" of the earth ? Is it ten billion people? Twenty billion? Thirty billion? Has it, in fact, already been exceeded?[1] Secondly, what does "the greatest test for human society" have to do with day-to-day, individual decision making? What does it have to do with interest rates, taxes, inflation jitters, health care reforms, budget agreements, hiring quotas, consumer confidence, banking regulations, exchange rates, and so on. After all, this book is addressed to individual decision makers, who are concerned precisely with these kinds of minutiae, and not to national governments, international organizations, or humankind as a whole.

Short Term Minutiae

And, on the face of it, the issue which engaged the world's rich minority, in the period under discussion, did not seem all that relevant to the human race as a whole, nor to the world's long term future. Issues such as Christian fundamentalism, tax cuts, the black/Jewish conflict, the "Reagan recovery", US/Israeli relations, deficits, drugs, industrial competitiveness, the "renewal of America", the "decline of America", sexual harassment in the work place, gays in the military, health care reform, the "gender gap", takeover artists, junk bond felons, homelessness, political correctness, pitbulls, date rape, the "new world order", hypodermic needles washing up on beaches, the "forgotten middle class", the underclass, gridlock, child abuse, the "new populism", and so on, came and went with no seeming rhyme or reason. One got the impression, that, in the developed world, in the majority of cases, politics and economics were literally decoupled from the needs of the majority of the world's people and from the world's long term future.

This impression is illusory however. During this period, the day to day and month to month political and economic changes in this country and around the world were, to a greater extent than at any time previously, and to a greater extent than one might have thought possible, "generated" and "driven" by "North/South" relations.

Now this statement might sound farfetched. After all, if there was a "driving force" of the recent past, wouldn't that "driving force" have to be the fall of communism and the end of the cold war? For one thing, these events drastically reduced the likelihood of a nuclear holocaust, and, if that likelihood was never large, then it was never zero either, and the possibility of a sudden end to the human race, certainly had an all pervasive impact on the global politics everywhere. In fact, some of the gloom that pervaded the American political mood after the end of the cold war was probably due to the fact that the human race was now perceived to have a future, and that the needs of many future generations now had to be taken into account. There were also more mundane ways in which the fall of communism and the end of the cold war shaped the political and economic events of the past several years. The capital needs of the former communist countries, the costs of German reunification, and the defense cutbacks in the West, were all important causes of the current global economic slowdown. Many analysts have called these factors "political shocks", analogous to the 1970's "oil shocks" in their depressive effects on the world economy. World politics was also signifantly changed by the ending of the cold war. The superpowers were able achieve a resolution of the Iran/Iraq conflict and to end their involvement in the Afghan civil war. This ended Iraq's geo-political importance to the West, and, thus, ended Iraq's ability to attract the open handed post-war financing it was expecting; financing that might have enabled it to avert a post-war economic crisis. It was the possibility of such a crisis that led us, in January 1990, to predict a political upheaval in Iraq, and it was to ward off such a upheaval, that Saddam invaded Kuwait. Conversely, one of Bush's reasons for going to war against Iraq, rather than relying on sanctions or air strikes, was his (accurate) anticipation of unpredictable future changes in the (then) Soviet Union, and a consequent desire to resolve the Gulf crisis quickly before it was subsumed by a larger and potentially far more dangerous crisis. One can also be sure that the intended audience for the Gulf war's elaborate techno-military display was not "would be Saddams" in the Third World, but hardliners within the Soviet military-industrial complex. It is for these reasons that the Gulf war could justly be called "the last battle of the cold war". Closer to home, it was fear of post-communist Russian and eastern European economic competition that led Salinas of Mexico to propose the North American Free Trade Agreement (NAFTA) which played so prominent a part in U.S. political debates. The ending of the cold war also changed the political equation in Israel and America. The upsurge in Russian Jewish immigration to Israel emboldened Shamir's Likud party to scrap the Labor/Likud alliance, accelerate the settlements activity in the occupied territories, scrap the "Shamir peace plan", and try to push a $10 billion loan guarantee through the US Congress in the Fall of 1991 in order to finance the absorption of the Russian immigrants (without cutting back the settlement activity). The resulting conflict between the Bush administration and Israel's supporters in Congress (and elsewhere) weakened Bush politically and contributed to his electoral defeat in 1992. To take an example from the more recent past, President Clinton's political problems in the spring of 1993 began after he advocated military action against the Bosnian Serbs and then backed off in the face of Boris Yelstin's opposition (deciding, obviously, that nothing in the Balkans was worth weakening Yelstin's position in Russia). That incident was to some extent, Clinton's "bay of pigs", and left him struggling with the image of being weak and inept. One could go on forever giving examples of how the end of the cold war and the fall of communism have influenced politics and economics everywhere. Suffice it to say, that these events have to be regarded as seminal.

And yet, in a larger sense, couldn't one say that it was America that was the "driving force" behind the events of the last 13 years? After all, America is certainly the one country in the world whose actions most affect the rest of the world, and whose internal affairs are the least affected by the outside world. In fact, according to many observers, it was America that "won" the cold war, by its 1980's arms buildup, and by its insistence on human rights as a prerequisite of detente. In addition, D. P. Calleo (1982) makes the point that the so-called "external economic shocks" of the 1970's, the post-Vietnam inflation, the breakdown of the Bretton-Woods monetary system, the flood of "stateless" US dollars, the raw materials price rises and the "oil shocks", all of which were supposed to presage American loss of control over the global economy, were, in reality, the direct consequences of US monetary policy. After that policy was changed, under Volcker, raw material and oil price inflation ended, and the flood of "stateless dollars" was brought back under control.

In fact, the oil price collapse, brought about by Volcker's tight money policy, played a not insignificant role in the Soviet economic crisis which was one of the factors behind the collapse of communism.

Furthermore, American influence over world politics and economics has, if anything, increased, not decreased, as the years have gone by. In the 1950's and 1960's, for example, Third World Asian countries, with Russia's backing, were able to fight the United States to a military standstill. Now America is the world's unchallenged superpower, and no other country, or combination of countries, even comes close to matching it. In the 1960's, non-western values and cultures became faddish among America's youth, leading to many of the features of the so called "hippie culture". Now it is American values and culture that are permeating the rest of the world.

"It is America that today is the genuinely catalytic nation—the object of admiration, resentment, imitation, and—even more dramatic—of immediate and intimate impact on the social mores of other nations. America dominates the global chatter, the global perceptions, and the global educational interactions. At any point more than five hundred thousand foreign students . . . Foreign imitation of America is now a worldwide phenomenon. This is not only a matter of cultural fashions, social styles or patterns of consumption. It also manifests itself in politics both on the serious and trivial levels. The growing worldwide sensitivity to human rights although in part the inevitable consequence of global political awakening, has been intensified by America's emphasis on the issue." Z. Bzrezinski, 1993.

The Third World in the Mind of America

So how can we maintain that the underdeveloped world, the world's "poor majority", was the "driving force" of the last 13 years. Wasn't it precisely this "poor majority" that was more and more marginalized in the last 13 years?

The current chapter will be the answer to these questions. For the present we would like simply to refine what we are saying. The main "driving force" for change over the last 13 years has been the interaction between American politics, American policy and North/South relations, or, as we put it in our 1987 book The Trade Backlash Against Japan, "how the political situation in America is wrapping itself around the North-South question and vica versa."

In order to explain this, we are going to begin with a concept which might seem rather nebulous, so we ask you to bear with us. This concept relates to what we believe is one of the most important feature underlying American political life over the past 13 years. This feature is not a political movement, not a political party, not political strategy, not a political worldview, not a political theory and not a political agenda. It is a rather a mood, a feeling, an underlying anxiety, in many cases, a subconscious anxiety, but one whose effects on American and world politics are enormous. It is very related to recent advances in communication which have made the planet a "global village".

"The most important political effect of technological innovation has been to create social intimacy on the global scale—overcoming time and distance. But that new intimacy both combines and collides at the same time. In much of the world, the daily struggle for survival by the acutely impoverished masses now occurs in the context of an intense awareness of a totally contrasting life style on the part of its own elites as well as of the cornucopian West." Z. Bzrezinski, 1993

In fact, this intimacy works both ways. As we put it in our 1987 book, The Trade Backlash Against Japan: "Simply stated, Americans in the 1980's have the following anxiety: if you hook up my destiny and the destiny of the non-Western world, if you connect the Western future to the Third World—what happens to my primordial assets. You turn on the radio in America and listen to a talk show. You hear a union leader and he says: 'Look you can't compare me to a French or Japanese worker. Where will this stop? Why not compare me to a worker in Sri Lanka? What does he make, 30 cents a day? Should I compete with him for 20 cents?' You switch on your TV. Jimmy Swaggart, the fundamentalist preacher, says about a Pro-UN Reagan speech: 'The devil entered the White House.' You begin to see the reflection, the indicator which tells you what is really going on. The real issue is the North/South problem, the relation of the West to the Third World, the developed countries to the less developed countries. The fear, loathing, anxiety, mental paralysis in the American mind is: if it takes $50000 to keep me 'on the road' and $1000 to keep a Guatamalan campesino 'on the road', if you connect me to him, what happens? Do we divide $50000 and $1000 by two? Do we trade places? Who decides this?"

The sentiment that we are referring to is a sort of "LDC phobia", a fear of the "vast hungry masses out there" that could somehow "take what we have". In our Japanese books and articles, we used the term nativism to refer to this sentiment. In fact, nativism is not a completely accurate term. Navitism refers to anti-foreign sentiment in general, and the sentiment we are describing is directed primarily against the poor countries. Samir Amin's term "pan-occidentalism" would probably be more accurate, but it's too much of a mouthful, so we'll stick with the term nativism. Nativism, as we use it, does not necessarily imply any position on the range of so-called "North/South issues" that come up in the international forums, issues such as intellectual property rights, debt forgiveness, minerals rights on the sea bed, commodity price stabilization agreements, trade in services, Multi-Fibre arrangements, and so on. It's hardly likely that many Americans even know what these issues are, much less have a position on them, one way or another. Nativism does not necessarily imply liberalism or conservatism, being for or against free trade, or being a Republican or a Democrat. Nonetheless, nativism is one of the most significant domestic political phenomema in past 13 years. In the 80's, it took the form of a "Rambo-like" belligerence, an attitude brought about by the US defeat in Vietnam, the two OPEC oil shocks, and the Iranian hostage taking. Carter was seen as a "liberal wimp" who was letting the US be pushed around by Iran and price gouged by OPEC. In the 1992 election, OPEC had been busted, communism had fallen, Iraq had been crushed, and most Third World countries were adopting free market economics and trying to ingratiate themselves with the US. In this kind of environment, nativism took the form of isolationism, protectionism and self pity. Bush was seen as an "out of touch" conservative, so in love with free market economics that he was allowing, indeed encouraging, American factories to relocate American jobs to "slave wage" Third World countries. He was also seen as a "gung ho militarist" who was always sending the marines to help some Third World people, the Kuwaitis, the Kurds, the Bangladeshis and the Somalis, while ignoring Americans who were "hurting" from unfair competition with low wage Third World countries.

The influence of nativism is not confined simply to Presidential elections. In fact, it's pervasive. It influences analyses both in the popular and business press and in the electronic media. Most importantly of all, from the point of view of planning, it influences and distorts analyses of the future and thus influences swings in investor and consumer moods. For example (Cambridge Forecast Group, Science and Technology Today, 1985), "during the height of the second oil shock in 1980, there was an explosion of investor interest in biotechnology, particularly in the use of gene splicing techniques to produce cheap oil and petrochemicals. In this case, 'bacteria that produce oil' became a substitute for Arab countries that produce oil and were seen as a way of 'getting away from the Third World'. Two years later, when the price of oil began to drop, so did investor interest in biotechnology particularly in the U.S. (though logically the possible future commercial prospects of possible revolutionary advances in biotechnology would not be affected by marginal drops in the price of oil). At the present time, when many Americans feel threatened by cheap manufactured imports from low-wage LDC's there has been an explosion of interest in 'artificial intelligence' and 'intelligent robots'. In this case, 'intelligent robots' are seen as a substitute for cheap Third World labor and as a way of 'getting away from the Third World'." Of course, true artificial intelligence and the production of oil and petrochemicals from biotechnology are "techno-hype", nowhere to be seen on the commercial horizon. Yet "techno-hype" doesn't occur in a vacuum. In the truculent atmosphere of the 1980's, many Americans tended to think of Arabs as "bacteria that produce oil" and Asians as "intelligent robots", and were looking for artifical replacements.

Nativism was also an important reason for the "death of liberalism" in the seventies and eighties.

"In the early seventies, Third World demands for an international income redistribution constituted a sort of moral offensive. A great many European and American scholars took claims for a 'New International Economic Order' seriously. Many American liberal intellectuals suffered considerable discomfort. Third World claims inconveniently pushed liberal ideas to their logical conclusions. An integrating liberal world, like an integrating liberal nation and state, presumably implied a bond of brotherhood and, somewhere in the distance, a common standard of welfare." P. Calleo, 1982.

Living in "an outrageously rich society in a hungry, restless and straitened world", the interests of very few Americans "lay with radical world income redistribution." Thus, many of the constituents of New Deal liberalism, who saw themselves as benefitting from liberalism (redistributionism and egalitarianism) within the nation, definitely did not see themselves as benefitting from liberalism on a global scale, with result that, for many Americans, liberalism itself went out of favor.

As paradoxical as it might seem, nativism was also an important reason for the "resurgence of liberalism" in the early nineties. After the fall of communism and the end of the cold war, there was a widespread perception, inaccurate to the point of absurdity, but influential nonetheless, that the outside world was now somehow less important to America's destiny. With the "realm of political perception" thus confined to the domestic arena, redistribution began to seem politically palatable again. Clinton's "soak the rich" message touched a political chord with many of the "Reagan Democrats". (This was particularly the case since many of the rich were expressing an increasing interest in trade with and investment in the Third World.)

It's important to realize that it's not merely global redistributionism that makes Americans nervous. It's any linking of "our destiny" with "their destiny". Thus, it's no wonder that the most controversial, and divisive issues in American political life usually have a very large "North/South" component.

In the 1980's and early 1990's, these issues have generally fallen into two main categories; trade issues and Middle Eastern issues, particularly the Arab/Israeli dispute. In fact, prior to the fall of the Likud government, at times of tension between the U.S. and the Israel, the Arab/Israeli dispute became a paradigm for the North/South conflict in general.

"Israel with its strategic importance and the ties that link it with the first-(world) nations, presents the world with the spectacle of a first-(world) population directly confronting a second—and third—(world) combination of enemies.

251

Power relationships that are usually mercifully disguised by distance appear in sharp relief on the West Bank of the Jordan river . . . Israel is a mirror in which Europe and America see themselves" W. R. Mead, 1987

The Israeli cause commanded a widespread popular sympathy in the developed countries, particularly in the U.S. and Britain, and the Palestinian cause commanded a widespead popular sympathy in the underdeveloped countries. The Israelis, in a sense, "represented" the developed North, the Palestinians "represented" the underdeveloped South. This fact, moreover, played a very important role in the way in which these issues were presented to the American public. ("The Middle East is not the Middle West". "Israel is in the Middle East, but not of the Middle East". "Israel is a good country, in a bad neighborhood", "Israel made the desert bloom. The Palestinians didn't make the desert bloom.") To the extent that Israel, with U.S. acquiescence, took a hardline stance on the Palestinian issue, this became a signal that the Palestinians "don't count", and, by implication, that the Muslim world and the Third World "don't count". This tended to placate American "Third World phobia". On the other hand, if the U.S. pressured Israel to be less hawkish, this became a signal that the "Third World counts", and American "Third World phobia" tended to increase. It is no accident that, in the same week that Bush pressed for a delay on the 10 billion dollars in loan guarantees to Israel and attacked "the Jewish lobby", his approval rating in the polls began to plummet, and consumer confidence in the American economy began to plummet:

"The free fall in consumer confidence exceeds anything that can be explained by economic variables." R. Brinner, DRI/MacGraw-Hill, 11/91

Why did this happen? Was it because Americans opposed Bush's position on the loan guarantees? Not at all. Polls taken at the time showed that Americans supported Bush's position by a margin of 3 to 1. Was it because of the "all powerful", Svengali-like Israeli lobby which could manipulate public opinion at will (as Bush himself implied in his "one lonely little guy" speech)? Again no. The Israeli lobby is neither as united or powerful as is generally believed. In fact, there was a sort of "coup d' etat" within AIPAC directed against members who had sided with Shamir in the Bush/Shamir fight.

American confidence fell because the American public could not understand why Bush (if he thought the Israeli lobby was so all-powerful) was squandering his post-Gulf-war popularity in a fight with it, in an election year, in a recession, when there were so many pressing American domestic problems, and on an issue that most Americans (wrongly) regarded as "marginal". After all, what did "land for peace" mean? The Arabs were no military threat to Israel without Russian support. Arab oil power had been neutralized by the precedent of American military intervention to guarantee the flow of oil, and, in any case, the Palestinians had antagonized the their wealthy Gulf State benefactors by siding with Saddam. So what did it matter if Israel settled the Palestinian issue once and for all by simply colonizing the West Bank and foreclosing any possibility of a territorial compromise? If America was the world's only superpower, then what could the Palestinians possibly do? Surely, Bush (known for his hard headed, pro-American approach to foreign policy) wasn't proposing to fix all the world's inequities before turning to address America's pressing economic needs? Surely, there wasn't any sort of connection, God forbid, between the world's inequities and America's pressing economic needs?

In short, something didn't "add up". Either Bush was a "foreign policy junkie" who "didn't care" about the important domestic problems that were "hurting" Americans, or (and this was too disturbing to admit) the Third World was more important than Americans had been led to believe. It was for this reason that Bush began to come under intense criticism that he was "paying too much attention to foreigners like the Palestinians, the Bangladesh flood victims, and the Kurds and not enough to the American middle class", and both his popularity ratings and faith in his economic management began to drop.

The general economic climate of the early nineties also contributed to nativist anxieties. Over the past ten years, the IMF and the World Bank have been urging the less developed countries to imitate the "Asian tigers". The less developed countries have been urged to implement market oriented reforms, to attract outside capital, and to strive to become competitive in the markets of the developed economies. After a period of resistance, many of the LDC's began to take the this advice. As the Third World investment climate improved (and in reaction to the disappointing results of the Eastern Bloc's economic reforms), American investors began to develop an interest in Third World economies. Chinese and Latin American stock markets began to boom. Flight capital that had fled Latin America in the 80's began to return. The higher echelons of the American business sector began to develop a more favorable attitude towards the Third World in general. For example, when asked about the long term stagnation in the American standard of living, Donald V. Fines, Chairman of Caterpillar Tractors said, "There should be a narrowing of the gap between the average American income and that of the Mexicans. As a human being I think that what is going on (redeployment of American industry to Mexico) is positive. I don't think it is realistic for 250 million Americans to control so much of the world's G.N.P." All this engendered a fear in the American public of an alliance between the business elites above them and the impoverished Third World masses below them. Many Americans began to feel simultaneously victimized by a perceived loss of economic status, and, at the same time, demoralized and guilty about the truly desperate economic needs of the Third World.

These contradictory feelings led to an attitude which could perhaps be called "liberal nativism", a longing for an "egalitarianism which stopped at the waters edge". One of the manifestations of "liberal nativism" was "Japan bashing". Japan, being the only non-Western country to join the "rich man's club", became a target for anti-Third World economic anxieties, (especially for the anti-Third World economic anxieties of liberal Democrats.) Bashing an economically powerful country like Japan justified a sense of "victimization" which would hardly be possible when bashing a poor, underdeveloped country.

Another manifestations of "liberal nativism" was victimology, the attempt by groups in American society to portray themselves as "victims", and vie for the sympathy of the political leadership, (as though they wanted to coopt

Third World "victim status".) Tapping onto this mood, Clinton scored big in the Presidential debates by assuring the American viewers that he "felt their economic pain", whereas Bush got clobbered when he was unable to come up with an instance of personal economic trauma, and, thus, could not portray himself as a "fellow victim".

Liberal nativism came to a climax during the NAFTA debate of late 1993, a debate which generated an astounding amount of hysteria in an American public usually bored stiff by trade agreements. Commentators, at the time, wondered why a trade agreement between the United State and a country like Mexico with an economy the size of Los Angeles should touch off such passions, especially since the much more significant global GATT negotiations were attracting so little public attention. In fact, this mystery has to be understood, not on the level of substance, but on the level of symbolism. Like Israel/Palestine, the United States/Mexico constituted a symbol for the North/South question as a whole. This is because the United States, in addition to being the world's leading industrial power, is the only major industrial power physically adjacent to a Third World country. Thus, it was the physical proximity of Mexico that led to the intensity of Americans' economic anxieties about economic integration with Mexico. Mexico, because it shares a border with the United States, and because it was a low-wage Third World country, was seen as being able to absorb a large part of the American job market in an enormous "sucking sound". It was for this reason that "America/Mexico" replaced "Israel/ Palestine" as the paradigm of the North/South question, and NAFTA replaced Arafat as the focus of anti-Third World anxieties. Thus, even as Israeli Prime Minister Rabin shook hands with Arafat and admitted that there was no way in hell the PLO could pose a threat to Israel, Clinton and most of the country's economists were trying to convince a sceptical American public that Mexico would not bring the U.S. economy to its knees. Mexico (the only Third World country that is physically contiguous with the United States) had become the target for the whole range of pent up anxieties about economic competition from the Third World.

To avoid any misunderstandings, we are not, in this chapter, saying that all, or even that most, of the political positions taken on Middle Eastern or trade issues were necessarily motivated by nativism. In fact, our analysis, at this point, is not about political positions at all (if by "political position" one means a well thought out, firmly held, commitment one way or another), but about moods and anxieties.

Nor are we implying that the American public was at a high pitch of xenophobia most of the time. On the contrary, Americans were probably more tolerant of foreigners than are most other nationalities.

Furthermore, the level of nativist sentiment in America has tended to fluctuate wildly over time. For example, in the late 80's, when global environmental fears about the ozone layer and the greenhouse effect began to surface, nativist sentiment waned. One began to see sympathetic articles in the popular American press about the need to close the global "rich/poor gap". Global poverty was portrayed as a threat to the global environment, and, thus, as a threat to the populations of the North and the populations of the South. In response to this perceived environmental threat, American sympathy for the Third World increased, and nativist sentiment decreased. Nativist sentiment also decreased in early 1994 when the passage of NAFTA was followed, not by a drain of U.S. jobs southward, but by an increase in U.S. employment.

Nativist sentiment is certainly not a result of political obtuseness on the part of the American leadership. In fact, every American administration, since the Carter administration, has been intensely aware of this sentiment, either upon taking office (Bush), or several years after taking office (Reagan), or several months after taking office (Clinton), or in the last few months of office (Carter). Of course, every American President, since Roosevelt, has faced the basic dilemma of having to be both 'President of the world' and President of the U.S. simultaneously, but, in the late 70's and early 80's, this dilemma became particularly acute, when the economic interdependence between the developed and underdeveloped world, (an interdependence which had always provoked political backlashes among Third World populations) began to ignite hostility and anxiety in the American electorate, and, even worse, began to evolve in a way that was extremely confusing to the Western political and economic leadership. Reagan responded to this dilemma by theatrics, media manipulation and public "mood manipulation". Bush responded to this dilemma by secrecy (the so-called "stealth Presidency), and then by military triumphalism (the "new world order"). Clinton responded to this dilemma by "slickness", "waffling", "glibness", and then, in early 1994, by Japan-bashing.
We are now almost ready to begin our history. Since, in this history, we will be quoting extensively from ourselves, and. since, many of the quotes were written several months to several years before the events they describe took place, there

will be certain inaccuracies in the quotes from ourselves.
We will point out these inaccuracies, and will analyze the
deviations from our predictions and the actual events they
predicted.

We want to stress that, in this history, we will not be
expressing approval or disapproval of any particular leader,
policy, position, or theory. We don't have any one particular
point of view, but will try, as much as possible, but as
succinctly as possible, to describe things simultaneously
from all points of view.

The Reagan Revolution

When President Reagan took office in January 1981, there
was a mood of economic and political pessimism in the
country.

"In 1980, the nation was in the grip of the greatest
economic crisis it has faced since the Great Depression. The
United States had endured a decade of chronic economic
disappointment accompanied by a series of acute political
shocks, from the defeat in Vietnam to the OPEC oil crises.
Not since the Depression had the American economy
seemed so fundamentally flawed, or had so many Americans
questioned our ability to control our own economic
destiny. It was not uncommon to hear economists and
political leaders arguing that we were doomed to declining
standards of living, that we had entered an era of limits." L.
B. Lindsey, 1990

And yet the dire predictions of "another 1929" which had
become increasing commonplace since 1973 (the breakdown

of the world monetary system) had failed to materialize. The world economy was proving surprisingly resilient to the monetary chaos and the oil price shocks of the 70's. One of the main reasons for this resilience was the quantum leap in communication and information processing technology that was beginning to make itself felt in the early 1970's. This new technology was making it possible for businesses to operate in a climate of extreme monetary, financial and price volatility. In fact, the monetary and price upheavals of the 70's were proving stimulatory to many sectors of the global economy. New financial instruments proliferated to enable businesses cope with the economic volatility. The information processing industry boomed as businesses sought more extensive and more up-to-date information in order to keep track of constantly shifting market conditions. Robotic technology improved as labor costs grew. Commodity price booms generated increasing economic activity in many Third World countries, even as heavy industry in the West stagnated.

In fact, more alarming than economic anxieties was the feeling that the world political system was spinning dangerously out of control. In 1979, a revolutionary government gained power in Iran, took the American embassy staff hostage, and was threatening to spread chaos throughout the Middle East. A Marxist government in Afghanistan tried to push through an insane land reform program, touched off a civil war, and then itself disintegrated into warring factions. This brought a massive Soviet military invasion, the first Soviet invasion of a non Warsaw Pact country since World War II, which, together with Russia 1970's arms buildup, reignited the cold war between the superpowers.

Candidate Reagan was seen by his supporters as a tough, belligerent, no-nonsense leader who could bring the world political situation back under control. However, whereas Reagan was primarily anti-Soviet, many of his strongest supporters were primarily anti-Third-World. For example, in 1980, the conservative economist Milton Freedman wrote an editorial in which he expressed the opinion that a Soviet takeover of the Middle Eastern oil fields might not be such a bad thing, because the Soviets would be more reliable suppliers of oil that the crazy Arabs and Iranians. To take another example, the conservative commentator William Buckley, in an interview with Reagan, asked whether the United States would not be justified in invading the Middle Eastern oil fields, if OPEC raised the price of oil to a level which seriously threatened the American economy. To which Reagan replied, "No. That would be imperialism." Buckley was dumbfounded. All he could stammer out was, "What?". Reagan corrected himself. "You know. I mean gunboat diplomacy." This exchange was symptomatic of a tension between Reagan and his supporters that would manifest itself continuously during the next eight years. Whereas many of Reagan's supporters were counting on Reagan to put "the Third World gremlins" back into their box, Reagan himself was primarily concerned with the U.S.-Soviet conflict. In fact, the tension between Reagan's anti-Sovietism and his supporters anti-Third-World-ism was to form a constant undertone to the Reagan administration (culminating finally in Irangate).

Of less dire human impact than the world's political crises, but important nonetheless for the purposes of this discussion, was the crisis taking place in economic theory. The economic orthodoxy in the United States since 1945 had been Keynesian economics. Since, as is usual in economic matters, there remains a continuing controversy as to exactly what actually constitutes Keysnesian economics, we will use the definition of one of the former members of Reagan's Council Of Economic Advisors, supply side economist Lawrence B. Lindsey:

"The Keynesians, whose views had been forged in the Great Depression, with its catastrophic contraction in the supply of money and credit, believed that government could most effectively manage the economy by managing the demand for goods and services. The government could do this through fiscal policy, primarily by increasing or diminishing government debt through changes in tax and spending policies. In times of economic contraction the government would spend more, thus increasing demand directly, thereby boosting the income of consumers and boosting demand indirectly. The increase in demand for goods and services would stimulate new production and employment and the economy would expand. Under the opposite economic conditions the government would reduce its spending or raise taxes to keep the economy from overheating and prices from rising . . . By 1980, this set of policy prescriptions had reached both its practical and theoretical limits . . . The Keynesians had no solution for the combination of rising prices (which to them indicated excess demand) and a falling economy with high unemployment (which to them indicated to little demand). The Keynesians were accustomed to using government fiscal policy to smooth out the booms and busts of the business cycle. But, by the late 70's, the business cycle had twisted into a diabolic double helix, in which unemployment and inflation rose together." L. B. Lindsay, 1990.

In fact, in 1980, one could say that, despite the widespread economic uncertainties, many of the world's economies were performing better than most of the world's economic theories. By the late 70's, two new economic theories had arisen to challenge the Keynesian orthodoxy. The first of these, extremely influential with the Reagan coalition, was supply-side economics. According to supply-side economics, tax cuts can be the cure for both inflation and recession. To state it simply, tax cuts, by increasing the rewards to economic activity, stimulate both production and consumption, and, therefore, stimulate supply as well as demand. The increased aggregate supply cures inflation, and the increased aggregate demand cures recession. For a readable account of supply-side economics, see The Great Experiment (1990) by Lawrence B. Lindsey. Less well known by non-specialists, but taken more seriously by most professional economists, is rational expectations economics, a formidable challenge to the technical underpinnings of Keynesian economics. Like the new growth theories, rational expectations economics is difficult to describe in non-technical terms. Basically, it criticizes Keynesian economics for failing to model the ways in which consumers, workers, and investors form expectations about the future. Therefore, according to rational expectations, Keynesian economics has no way of knowing how the participants in an economy will respond to changes in government policy. Rational expectations also criticizes Keynesian economics for dropping the pre-Keynesian assumption of "market clearing", because dropping this assumption makes the mathematics of modeling individual economic behavior impossibly difficult (although rational expectations mathematics is hairy enough). Rational expectation theory, while not well known among non-specialists, has come to have a great influence on economic theory in general, and, thus, indirectly on global economic policy.

The incoming Reagan administration consisted of many political factions with a wide divergence of beliefs. There were internationalist "Wall Street" Republicans, parochial "Main Street" Republicans, cold warriors, monetarists, supply-siders, Christian Evangelicals, the Moral Majority, State Department "Arabists", and Neoconservative partisans of Israel. At many times, these various factions were at daggers drawn. However, all of them (or most of them) were united by support for two fundamental policies, (1) distrust of the welfare state, and support for free market solutions to America's chronic problem of stagflation, and (2) a hardline stance toward the Soviet Union as a solution to America's weakened influence on world politics.

Soon after taking office, the administration guided through Congress a massive series of tax cuts (the ERTA or Economic Recovery Tax Act) and a massive increase in defense spending. However, commensurate cutbacks in government spending to balance the massive tax cuts were stymied by "gridlock" between liberals who wanted cutbacks in military spending and conservatives who wanted cutbacks in social spending. The Federal Reserve was keeping interest rates astronomically high to pressure the administration and the liberal congress to agree on spending reductions. This was precipitating a "global liquidity shortage". In early 82, in an article entitled Reagan Watching and George Gilder's Wealth and Poverty, we characterized the American political situation as follows:"

"It is well known the two policies most associated with the Reagan administration are:

- the tight money policy of restraining the growth of the money supply:
- the 'supply side' policy of reducing both government social expenditures and taxes.

These two policies which were forced on the U.S. by the world economy would have been implemented by whatever political administration was in power, had, in addition, also long been advocated by all of the main factions of the 'Reagan coalition' namely the supply siders, the corporate community, the 'neoconservatives', the moral majority, the "cold warriors", the conservative Republicans. The fact that these policies which had long been advocated were in the process of 'implementing themselves' gave a feeling of inevitability to the Reagan victory which led people to talk of the 'Reagan revolution' and to predict a unified, decisive and effective administration. In fact, the story of the next two years was the story of the fragmentation of the Reagan coalition.

To see why this was so we have to go back to our first newsletter '*Cambridge Forecast Reports*,' Vol. I, June 1979, in which we stated:

'Political activity in the industrialized countries in the 1980's and beyond will be of three types: (I) nativist, blue collar, populist, petit-bourgeosie, anti-Third World, (II) establishment, pro-business, pro-Third World (III), young, anti-business, pro-Third World.'

The Reagan coalition is divided between political tendencies I and II above. For example, the 'neoconservatives' and the 'moral majority' are essentially Jewish and Christian populist movements respectively which support position I, whereas many of the "cold warriors" such as the Secretary of Defense Weinberger would tend to support position II. As the past two years have shown, any event which tends to polarize the U.S. around North/South issues, and which brings to the fore tendencies I, and II described above, also tends to fracture the Reagan coalition. To take some quick examples:

- The Israeli intervention in the Lebanese civil war (This referred to the limited military actions prior to the 82 invasion) led to the fight between the neocons in the National Security Council (Position I) and the 'Arabists' in the State Department and the CIA. (Position II);
- The revolution in Central America intensified the fight between the 'Atlanticists' in the State Department such as Haig (position I) and the 'cold warriors' in the Defense Department (position II) who advocated negotiations with the revels to lure them away from Marxism;
- The war between Britain and Argentina led to the fight between the 'Latin colonel sympathizers' and the 'Eurocentrists' in the Reagan administration, in particular to the fight between Jeanne Kirkpatrick and Haig.

The above perspective allows us to make sense of George Gilder's brilliant polemical book 'Wealth & Poverty' which became the bible of the Reagan administration and which must seem mysterious to Japanese readers with its bizarre combination of insights and evasions. Gilder's book became the bible of the Reagan administration because it celebrated those economic, political and social trends which brought the Reagan coalition to power while at the same time evading and obscuring those economic, political and social trends which eventually split the coalition.

Our perspective is that there are two main routes by which the American economy will recover from its present economic crises. One of these is the industrialization and privatization of the service economy partially through the use of the latest digital technology. For the short to the medium term, this will be the main avenue of economic growth. (For the longer term, the necessary precondition for American and Western economic growth is Third World economic development.) To oversimplify enormously, one can say that 'Reaganomics', 'Supply-side economics', the 'Reagan revolution' or whatever is the political and economic ideology called forth the the industrialization and privatization of the American service economy and George Gilder's 'Wealth & Poverty' is its main political manifesto. For example, in the chapter 'The Productivity of Services', Gilder gives a layman's description of the growth of the service economy under the stimulus of government social spending and its current future industrialization and privatization by the use of electronic techniques. In other chapters, he criticizes the public sector for stifling the private sector through taxes and regulation, for competing for its markets, and for raising the cost of its labor inputs by welfare and other social subsidies.

However, the most significant fact about the book and the reason for its popularity lies in the way it deals with the issues of global economics and the issues of long-term world economic growht. Obviously, to go too deeply into either of these tow issues brings one immediately into North/South issues, precisely the issues on which the Reagan coalition is hopelessly divided. Gilder gets around the first of these issues, the issue of global and trade politics, by simply not discussing it at all. He deals with the second of these two issues, the issue of long-term global economic development and growth by saying that it is essentially a very complex 'random walk problem' which is not amenable to rational discussion. To illustrate by some quotes:

'The dynamics of economic growth consists of a largely spontaneous and mostly unpredictable flow of increasing diversity and differentiation of new modes of production.'

'Rationalistic calculation for all its appeal can never suffice in a world where events are shaped by millions of men acting unknowably in a fathomless interplay of complexity.'

Implicit in these quotes is the possibility that future technical progress will allow the world and American economies to resume their upward growth while at the same time avoiding the painful and devisive global and North/South issues which lie in wait for the Reagan administration and the western economies in general.

Our own studies indicate that many of the people in the American business community who read Gilder's book came away with the impression that rapid American growth was possible without massive public, protectionist involvement in investment decisions (position I above) and without getting commercially involved with alien cultures and nations (position II above). Thus, there need be no conflict betwen the two positions. As is becoming increasingly clear, the story of American life in the 1980's and beyond will be the story of precisely such as conflict." CFG Reports, 4/82.

And what were "the painful and devisive global and North/South issues which . . . (lay) in wait for the Reagan administration and the western economies in general."? To answer this question, let's go back to the Chapter 2 discussion of global economic growth.

"Businesses hire workers to produce economic output. Part of this output is consumed by the workforce and part is invested by businesses in order to create more economic capacity. This greater capacity is, in turn, used to hire more workers, which are used to produce an expanded amount of output, part of which is consumed by the expanded workforce and part of which is invested to create still more economic capacity to hire still more workers, and so on, the only limiting constraint being the size of the potential workforce. Given the billions of people outside the industrial market economies, such a growth model would certainly seem to have a lot of potential. The Malthusians often look at the burgeoning populations of the underdeveloped world as an unmitigated disaster. But to many investors, the enormous amount of talent, resourcefulness, ingenuity and drive for material betterment that must be present among so large a number of people, is often seen as an opportunity for unbounded economic expansion. The economist Milton Freedman (1992) has compared it to 'the equivalent of a second industrial revolution'".

Now obviously such a pattern of economic growth, requires at least one of three things: (i) population growth in developed regions, (ii) labor migration from underdeveloped to developed regions, or (iii) capital transfers from developed to underdeveloped regions. Since, the developed world (unlike the uderdeveloped world) is demographically stable, and, since (as is becoming increasingly obvious) there is a limit to the amount of immigration that the developed world can absorb from the underdeveloped world, it should be apparent that, if the growth pattern described above is what is "on the agenda" in the future, then, what is also "on the agenda", is an ever increasing amount of capital flow from the developed to the underdeveloped world.

R. Lucas (1988) (See Chapter 2 of this book) analyzes the failure of this latter phenomenon to occur (to the extent that would be predicted by standard economic growth theory). However, Lucas' arguments apply only to private investment. In addition to private capital investment, there were other sources of North/South capital transfer. These sources were both chaotic and turbulent but massive nonetheless. One such source (during the 50's and 60's) was U.S. cold war foreign aid, and massive U.S. war spending in Asia during the Korean and Vietnam wars (an important cause of the "Asian economic miracle"). Other sources, (in the 70's) were inflationary surges in LDC commodity prices, and bank recycling of surplus OPEC petrodollars (both highly unstable sources).

In the 1979 and 1980, there were various proposals to formalize the latter form of North/South capital transfer. One such proposal was the Willy Brandt Report, North-South, which advocated a sort of "global Keynesianism", international public spending in the poor regions of the world to stimulate the world economy as a whole. In 1979, at the IMF conference in Belgrade, there were calls for long-term LDC development bonds to be issued to sop up excess "petrodollars", relieve global inflation and convert short-term and rapidly growing LDC debt into long-term development bonds, The list of reasons why this was politically impossible would fill a library. Paul Volcker flew back from Belgrade to Washington and imposed the tight money policy of 1979. While it was obvious that simply a U.S. tight monetary policy in the absence of anything else would inevitably precipitate a Third World debt crisis, reestablishing unilateral U.S. control over its money supply was seen as the more immediate problem.

Nonetheless, there had been a great deal of discussion, both public and private, about the need for Western/OPEC cooperation, and, in consequence, about the need for a solution to the Israeli/Palestinian problem. Furthermore, these calls for Western/OPEC cooperation were coming not from wild eyed radicals but from major heads of state. For example, in June of 1980, leaders of the industrialized countries supported the idea of a "summit conference" between representatives of the industrialized countries, the oil producing countries and the developing countries. This kind of talk was making both Israel and its supporters in the United States very nervous. In fact, one of the motives for the 1982 Israeli invasion of Lebanon was precisely to ward off such international pressure for a territorial compromise. For example, in early 1981, both the Pentagon and the CIA were pressing for a U.S. recognition of the PLO, while some advisors in the National Security Council were urging U.S. permission for an Israeli invasion of Lebanon to root out the PLO. When Israeli Prime Minister Begin told U.S. Secretary of State Haig at Sadat's funeral that he was planning the latter course of action, Haig responded, "If you move, you move alone." In June of 82 Israel invaded Lebanon and laid siege to Beirut. In August of 82 the Mexican debt crisis erupted.

These then were "the painful and devisive global and North/South issues which . . . (lay) in wait for the Reagan administration and the western economies in general", namely the Third World debt crisis and a crisis in American/Israeli relations.

The American political and economic response to these two crises was the "Reagan recovery", and, it was the Reagan recovery which led to the current state of world politics and world economics (including, by the way, the collapse of communism and the end of the cold war). In early 1983, in our article The Limits of Recoveryism (which, in retrospect, should have been entitled How Congressional Gridlock Was Transformed into North/South Development Strategy) we characterized the Reagan recovery as follows:

"Towards the end of 1981 and the beginning of 1982, the U.S. central bank had put, what might be called, an 'embargo' on dollars. This 'embargo' together with a fall in the price of oil tended to drain liquidity out of the world financial system and, ultimately, to precipitate the 'Third World Debt Crisis' of the late 1982 and early 1983. At this point, whether by accident of design, a new U.S. (and, to some extent, Trilateral) policy was put into effect, which can best be described as a 'cartel on hard currency'. This policy was marked a large reflation in the U.S. (and to a lesser extent in Germany) together with a widespread wave of LDC debt reschedulings most of which carried very steep interest rate terms and austerity requirements. In other words, the U.S. was providing the liquidity necessary to head off a possible world banking crisis, but it was charging a very steep 'tax' on these dollars, the tax coming in the form of LDC austerity requirements and rescheduling fee and interest rate terms. In addition, the liquidity which being drained out of the system by the reshcedulings and 'semi-defaults' was keeping dollars scarce in spite of the large U.S. reflation.

This led to a model of growth which might best be called the 'deflationary' or 'hard currency' model of growth. This model of growth (stated briefly), says that the U.S. because of the world 'money shortage' is now in the position of exporting a very valuable and scarce commodity, namely dollars and it can achieve very favorable 'terms of trade' on this 'export, especially with the LDC's and the peripheral European countries. These favorable 'terms of trade' together with of global investors to hoard 'hard currency' will allow the U.S. to finance increasing levels of consumer spending and government spending without generating inflationary pressures. Thus, a U.S. 'consumer led recovery' can be generated which is 'funded from outside' by favorable terms of trade and the propensity of foreign investors to hoard U.S. dollars (dollar denominated debt). Thus, according to this model of growth, the trade deficit can be used to bail out the budget deficit.

To render this model of growth viable, the maximum possible level of austerity must be imposed on the debtor countries in order to reign in their imports from the developed economies in order to 'make room' for consumer spending in the U.S. so that U.S. consumer spending can be vastly increased without generating inflationary pressure. Thus, we have observed that the world economic and political establishment, particularly in the Reagan administration, and the IMF, which at the beginning of the debt crisis in the summer of 82, were speaking of the need for preserving LDC markets for western exports have been taking an increasingly 'tough' stance on LDC austerity requirements as U.S. consumer spending has picked up . . .

The important fact to observe about the 'hard currency' or 'deflationary' model of growth it is not a model of permanent world economic expansion and not intended to be one. It is rather intended to 'last until the U.S. elections'. The importance of generating a favorable economic climate in the U.S . . . has been stressed by many economic analysts such as Alan Greenspan and Helmut Schmidt and others. Obviously, the U.S. is the most important country in the formation of world economic policy and, thus, the U.S. electorate is one of the most 'destabilizing' elements in world economic policy since it has the ability to potentially seize control of this policy and turn it in a purely nationalistic direction. Reagan's increasingly protectionist stance is an example of this potential. Thus, the importance of preserving a favorable U.S. domestic economic climate is not only felt by the Reagan administration but also by many of the Trilateral policy makers.

The (up until now) ebullient mood of the U.S. consumers also deserves mention. The importance of dealing with the U.S. budget deficit and the dangers of Third World debt have been stressed by many U.S. policy makers such as Paul Volcker, Donald Regan, and Martin Feldstein without (up until now) putting a dent in the 'festive' mood of American consumers. The message that the American consumers have been getting from American policy makers (whether intended or not) can be summed up as follows: 'The recovery is exceeding anybody's expectations. But it will eventually run into budget deficit problems and Third World debt always remains a danger. But, who knows, we've been wrong before, nobody really understands how the world economy works anyway. Maybe the world economic crisis will simply vanish as suddenly as it came on and for equally inexplicable reasons."

Certainly, the extent to which consumers have run down savings in the face of high unemployment and cutbacks in the 'social safety net' is not a phenomenon that one could explain solely on the basis of individual economic rationality such as 'pent up demand' to find housing and replace worn-out automobiles. There has also been a tremendous increase in 'impulse buying'. In fact, all the 'horror stories' about Third World debt and economic privation seemed to improve the consumer mood rather than worsen it. A possible explanation for the phenomenon is as follows: In early 1983, the LDC's at the non-aligned conference took a political position which maintained that the Third World debt crisis showed the dependence of western and even American economic growth on the expansion of LDC markets for western exports. In other words, they were attempting to use the debt crisis as a wedge to open up a dialogue on North/South economic issues . . . The Reagan administration took up this line in asking for increases in IMF reserves (Donald Reagan's editorial in February 3, 1983 edition of the Wall Street Journal). In taking this line, both the Third World and the Reagan administration seriously underestimated the intensity of the populist, nativist, anti-LDC sentiment among large sectors of the American electorate (sentiment which played a large part in Reagan's 1980 electoral victory although he probably wasn't aware of this factor until the Falklands, Lebanon and LDC debt crises). The nativist counterattack to the relatively 'pro-Third World' line of the Reagan administration was not long in coming and this caused the Reagan administration to do an 'about face' and simply stress the 'recovery'

To sum up, the American consumers were very threatened by the whole idea of American dependence on Third World markets, (or, for that matter, on Third World anything) and decided to eliminate this dependence by increasing their levels of consumption . . .

However, this policy of increasing consumer spending in the U.S. while reducing the pace of development in the LDC's is a solution the world economic problem in the same way that Israeli colonization of the West Bank is a 'solution' to the Palestinian problem. Namely, consumer spending is expropriating the credit and purchasing power that the LDC's need to develop, and the only way around this dilemma is either U.S. budget cutbacks or inflation.

Thus, the 'hard currency 'model of growth has a finite life expectancy. If the U.S. attempts to solve the budget and debt problems simply by rescheduling and constantly injecting reserves to 'cover' the rescheduling and wash away the deficits then the result will inevitably be inflation. In other words, the amount of liquidity necessary to fund the U.S. budget deficit, finance increased consumer spending and capital investment in the U.S. and simultaneously fund LDC imports at a level which avoids a 'social calamity' in the LDC's would also eventually be enough liquidity to re-ignite inflation . . . However, the 'hard currency' model of growth could fail for political reasons long before inflationary pressure is generated.

Obviously, a political upheaval in one of the large debtor LDC's would be a significant impediment to the 'hard currency' model of growth. But, leaving LDC politics to one side, American politics (could) . . . also play a significant role, (in halting this model of growth) less because the level of American economic hardship is that bad (it isn't even for most of the unemployed) but simply because of the enormous political leverage of the American consumer. Namely, the 'hard currency' model of growth was intended to placate the . . . nativist, protectionist, anti-LDC sentiment within the American political scene. It has, in fact, served to materially strengthen this political tendency, and also to embolden it. That is, this tendency now has a great deal of 'space' to advance its demands, such as (for example):

- increased protectionism;
- Congressional control of the Fed;
- restrictions of international bank lending;
- industrial policies."

In fact the "Reagan recovery" was never meant to be a perpetual engine of global economic growth. As we said in Political Aspects of the Reagan Recovery, in early 1983:

"The Reagan administration was alarmed at the speed with which North/South economic and political issues began to enter into public consciousness after the Israeli invasion of Lebanon and the emergency global debt negotiations. Neither the Reagan administration nor other factions in the American political establishment . . . have as yet staked out a position on these issues and they don't want to see a public debate on these crucial issues develop in wayas that are uncontollable or unpredictable . . . Thus, the 'recovery' is not seen as a solution to global economic problems, but as a means of buying time to prepare a solution."

Let's elucidate the above quotes (with the benefits of 20/20 hindsight). The Third World debt crisis and the debacle in Lebanon provided an "education" in North/South political and economic issues for the Reagan administration.

In order to cope with the Third World debt crisis, which threatened the global banking system, the administration knew that it would have to address itself to the problems of Third World development, about which it knew little. As a result, it turned for advice to the International Monetary Fund and the World Bank, whose role during the 80's expanded from trade balance financing (IMF) and project lending (the World Bank) to "Third World development management", and who enshrined export-led growth from the South to the North as the cardinal principle of LDC development (setting the stage for the protectionist backlash of the early 90's).

The administration became aware of the intense, anti-Third, World nativist sentiment in the United States, a sentiment which had played a big role in Reagan's defeat of Carter, and a sentiment which would obviously make it very difficult for the administration to deal with the Third World's economic needs. As Reagan's Treasury Secretary, Don Regan, mused at one point, "How can we give the Third World a break on its loans and explain such a policy to the American voter who is paying an astronomical interest rate on his mortgage?" How indeed? When Reagan formed an alliance with liberal Democrats to pass a U.S. increase in IMF funding to deal with the Third World debt crisis, one of Reagan's well known Christian Evangelical supporters said, "The Devil has entered the White House".

The administration also became aware that it had an "Israel problem", which we will explain below.

In the early 90's, there was a spate of books about U.S./Israeli relations purporting to show Israeli "duplicity" towards the U.S. Two notable examples of this genre were The Sampson Option by Seymour Hersch (Random House, 1991), and Dangerous Liaisons by Andrew and Leslie Cockburn (Harper-Collins, 1991). How much of this material is true, how much fantasy, and how much disinformation, is certainly very hard to say. However, the appearance of these books certainly demonstrates one thing: there was a great deal of tension between the Israeli government and the American administration during the Reagan/Bush era. Furthermore, this tension didn't start with the Bush/ Shamir fight of 1991, but was present almost from the very beginning.

The conventional view of Reagan's attitude towards Israel is expressed by G. W. Ball and D. B. Ball in their 1992 book, The Passionate Attachment:

"Because the cold war supplied the coordinates by which Ronald Reagan charted all aspects of foreign policy, he warmly embraced the doctrine that Israel was an important U.S. 'strategic asset', a bastion blocking the encroachment

of Soviet power into the Middle East. He had expressed
that view during his 1980 campaign that Israel 'was perhaps
the only remaining strategic asset in the region on which
the United States can truly rely . . . Finally, he announced
that he would use the full panoply of U.S. influence to
'insure that the PLO has no voice or role as a participant
in future peace negotiations with Israel'. Reagan was thus
clearly the most partisan of Israel's supporters, just when
in 1981 Israel's Arab neighbors seemed prepared to make
peace with Israel."

All this is certainly true, but it is not the whole story.
The fact is that the Begin government in Israel was very
distrustful of the incoming Reagan administration. All the
talk, during the 70's, about the need for Western/OPEC
cooperation, about the need for North/South cooperation
in general, and the increasing sympathy among the OECD
countries and the transnational business community for
Palestinian rights, were making the Israeli government
very nervous indeed. The Israelis feared that once the
Reagan people learned about the importance of Western/
OPEC economic cooperation and the importance of
North/South economic cooperation (and the upcoming
Third World debt crisis might be just the thing to teach
them), their attitude towards the Israeli/Palestinian conflict
would change. Thus, from the very beginning, the Begin
government began a strident policy of confrontation with
the incoming Reagan administration. For its own part,
after the Israeli and invasion of Lebanon and the American
debacle in Lebanon, the Reagan administration certainly
did not see the Begin government as a strategic asset, but
as a strategic liability. Furthermore, the administration had
become well aware that the Israeli right was able to mobilize

enormous support from the anti-Third World "nativists" within the U.S., within the "Reagan coalition", and within the Reagan administration itself, particularly among the cold war neo-conservatives, the military, and the Christian fundamentalists. Thus, after the events of 82, the Reagan administration was very loath to be seen putting public pressure on Israel, interfering in Israeli politics, or coming between the American Jewish community and Israel. (This is particularly the case since the administration needed both the Israeli lobby and Israel's supporters in Congress to support its approach to the world economic problems.)

All of the above determined the Reagan approach to the Third World debt crisis. Any thought of "North/South" capital transfers or Western/OPEC cooperation, ala the Brandt Commission Report, was of course, out of the question. Instead, the standard IMF/World Bank prescriptions were to be followed to the Third World debt crisis, namely the Third World countries were to contract their imports and export their way out of the crisis. This raised an obvious "fallacy of composition. To wit: "if everyone is exporting who is importing?". The answer to this question was to be—the United States! That is, the Reagan strategy was to have the United States be the "importer and borrower of last resort" (as David Hale of Kemper Financial Services put it). The U.S. budget deficit was to be a "Keynesian stimulus", if you will, for the world economy, and was to replace Third World markets that were lost owing to the IMF austerity programs. The U.S., furthermore, was deliberately to run a large trade deficit, in order to give the debtor countries someplace to export to. Surplus countries, such as Japan were, in turn, to use their dollar holdings to help finance the U.S. budget deficit. The depressed nature of much of the world economy and the role of the dollar as "safe haven" made this possible. In essence, the U.S. deliberately generated a large trade deficit in order to bail out the budget deficit. (As far as the "Israel problem" was concerned, the approach of the Reagan administration was to put the Arab/Israeli dispute "on hold" and pray for the Israeli labor party to get in.)

As can be expected, the world's finance ministers regarded this strategy of "debt-led" global economic growth as hair raising, but, in the absence of an alternative, they went along with it. In his 1992 book Changing Fortunes, former Federal Reserve Chairman, Paul Volcker, describes a conference of the world's finance ministers.

"(Then Secy of the Treasury Don Regan) aggressively delivered a speech telling his foreign counterparts that they had it wrong and we had it right . . . I happened to walk into the room in the middle of it all, with Regan in full flight, almost shouting. It was immediately apparent that this was not a high point for the niceties of international diplomacy . . . But Regan did have an important point. Their economies and those of the rest of the world were being substantially buoyed by the United States, quite directly by our rapidly expanding imports. The administration might in foreign eyes have seemed totally ideological in its tax, its budget and its exchange rate policies . . . But that same ideology was doggedly resisting protectionism and promoting more open markets around the world in the common interest".

As former Japanese Finance Minister, Toyoo Gyohten, put it:

". . . if the United States were to cut its deficit and slow its economy who would replace it as the engine of growth? So let me say there was a certain amount of mutual aquiescence in the crimes of another, because we were all sinners to some extent." Ibid.

From both a geopolitical and domestic political point of view, the Reagan strategy of "debt-led" growth certainly had a lot of advantages. First of all, it put the control of the world economy squarely back into the hand of the U.S. The OPEC petrodollar surpluses vanished, so the whole dreaded issue of "Western/OPEC" cooperation vanished as well. The U.S. also gained an enormous amount of political leverage over the rest of the world. After all, the U.S. was now the world's "importer of last resort" and nobody wants to argue with a good customer. Finally, the downward pressure on oil prices deprived the Soviet Union of hard currency and certainly hastened the collapse of "the evil empire". The tax cuts together with the drop in inflation certainly pleased the American consumer. Finally, for reasons that we will explain below, the Reagan strategy of "debt-led" growth ameliorated (but did not end) the conflict between the globalist and nativist factions within the Reagan coalition.

Nonetheless, throughout the 80's, the Reagan administration was far more pre-occupied with Third World development issues than it was letting on. In fact, at the end of 1984, when Reagan was asked what achievement he was most proud of, he said, "getting through one more year of the Third World debt crisis." Nonetheless, the Reagan administration (like the succeeding Bush administration) was very reluctant to get into public discussions of global economic issues, particularly North/South economic issues, (which is one of the reasons why the American public now feels that it's not being "leveled with" about economic matters). Instead, the main approach of the administration was to play up the "miraculous Reagan recovery" generated by "supply side" tax cuts, and to explain the battering that American industries were taking (because of the high dollar, surging imports, the collapse of the Latin market for American exports, the diversion of investment capital to the financial and service sectors), by saying that the U.S. was "entering the age of information".

This does not mean that the Reagan administration was keeping its anxieties about North/South issues a state secret. In fact, the Reagan administration was far more candid about the North/South problems it was facing than was the succeeding Bush administration. (although the Bush administration, aided by the end of the cold war, went much further in implementing actual "solutions" such as the Brady plan, the NAFTA, the Baker Middle East peace plan). The administration's official statement on the LDC debt problem in 82, entitled National Security Directive 3, was classified and then leaked. It said that a U.S. economic recovery would solve the global debt problems without inflation. There was also a dissenting opinion which said the opposite. This was probably a device to send one message to the domestic audience and another message to the trilateral partners prior to the upcoming economic summit conference. Later on, the question of aid to the LDC's was discussed in *The Carlucci Commission Report*, a sort of "cold war Brandt report".

The 1985 book Third World Development, a three volume encyclopedia of commercially oriented articles on Third

World development, published by Grosvenor Press, featured articles by Ronald Reagan, George Schultz and Caspar Weinberger. These articles stressed free trade, privatization, free market liberalization, and carefully controlled social and agrarian reform, which "avoided chaos and disorder". The literature put out by the International Center for Economic Growth, started by Casper Weinberger after he left the administration, gives a good idea of the kind of thinking about Third World development questions that was taking place in the Reagan White House in the mid-80's. In fact, we found some (lower level) Reagan appointees to the Agency for International Development and the Department of Commerce quite enthusiastic about promotion of Third World development and the benefits it would have for the U.S. economy.

However, the Reagan administration, as a whole, certainly preferred that the American public think about something other than Third World development.

"The last thing the administration wants is to have its policies subject to a blast of rhetoric by articulate anti-Third World spokesmen (of whom there are many) for which it would have no good answers." CFG 10/83

The main tactics used by Reagan to distract the public from global economic issues were theatrics, media manipulation and public mood manipulation, examples of which will be given later in the chapter.

To continue, the Reagan "debt-led" model of growth was designed to last "until the elections" of 1984. In fact, it ran into political difficulties several months prior to the elections.

"Since IMF policy required suppression of imports, (LDC) exports had to be expanded, and since many European countries were also undergoing austerity, the only place to do this was to the U.S. market. Thus, the U.S. became the 'borrower and consumer of last resort' (in the worlds of David Hale) of the entire world economy, and the debt crisis was converted into an 'import crisis' . . . This vitiated the 'recovery euphoria' which was being experienced by many parts of the American public, and led to all sorts of strange analyses that 'those foreign exporters are stealing our recovery'. The vision of the Third World as an economic threat (also came to the fore, because) . . . the Third World as military threat' anxieties were being reduced by Reagan's move towards dialogue with Russia." CFG 1/84

As the U.S. trade deficit began to balloon, anti-Third World, nativist sentiment which had, in the 70's, been concerned with the defeat in Vietnam, the OPEC cartel, the Iranian hostage taking, and the enhanced diplomatic status of the Palestinians, began, in the mid-80's, to become alarmed at the foreign products which were flooding into the U.S. market. One of Reagan's appeals to the American voter in the 1980 election was that he was seen as a "Third World basher", as someone who would "bring America back", "make America first again", as someone who would make up for the humiliations of the Vietnam defeat and the Khomeini hostage taking. In 1984, the Democrats began using Reagan's "America first" image against him. If Reagan was going to make America "number one" again, the Democrats asked, then why was he "giving away" so much of American industry to other countries, especially low wage, Third World countries? When Reagan, in response to a terrorist incident, said, "America is a friendly old man with a spine of steel" the Democrats countered that the spine was increasingly being made of Korean steel. For his part, Reagan knew that the flood of foreign imports into the U.S. economy was tarnishing his "America first" image, and he did bow to protectionist pressure to some extent. However, there was a definite limit to how far he could go in that direction. The Reagan "debt-led" model of growth in the early 80's depended completely and absolutely on America's ability to import from the rest of the world. If this ability were to be choked off by protectionist legislation, then the foreign market for U.S. debt would vanish, much of the Third World debt would have to be be written off as uncollectable, U.S. money center banks would take enormous losses, and the world economy would begin to unravel. In fact, one could say, that the main problem on the mind of the Reagan administration in the mid-80's was how to combat protectionist sentiment without directly discussing global economic issues with an American public that didn't want to hear about them. One of the approaches of the administration to this problem was the use of distractions and "theatrics". Political debates would be started with the purpose of distracting people from trade issues. For example, in the 1984 Presidential campaign Reagan said something about America being a Christian nation, a statement which provoked Mondale into devoting a lot of attention to the separation of church and state, an issue which very few voters cared about, and a welcome diversion from trade issues. In fact, distractions, theatrics, mood manipulation and media manipulation became important features of governance during the middle years of the Reagan administration.

"The American fear (of the Third World) . . . in (a) . . . vague and inchoate way does grasp the basic diagnosis: The future will be decided by the changing relations between the West and the Third World . . . Ronald Reagan came in in 1980 after the Iran hostage crisis. The American public wanted an anti-Third World kabuki with an aragoto Danjoru, namely Ronald Reagan. They waited for his Kabuki style 'nirami' (tough stare) against the Third World, which was the bombing of Libya . . . The American far-right National Security Council provides a kind of nagauta in the backgroup. It is absolutely false to argue that . . . Reagan = The opposite of Carter. This is true . . . to an extent, i.e. Reagan's aragoto versus Carter's wagoto. However, both were primarily occupied with the North-South problem. Ironically, if you look at the recent book Third World Development with essays by Reagan and Schultz you see that Reagan is . . . in favor of Third World development and not 'anti-Third World' as he keeps implying by his 'nirami' which is (used as a tranquilizer) for the American mind." CFG book, 1987.

Although Reagan did, by these methods, succeed in deflecting nativist criticism of the American debacles in Lebanon, protectionist sentiment continued to grow, and, by the end of 1984, the Reagan administration knew that it had a serious problem that needed more than media wizardry to solve.

"As it turned out, the administration had real difficulty with the protectionist onslaught in Congress and is now seriously rethinking its economic policy. To expand on this latter point, the administration is now pressing for a general North/South trade conference to formalize a North/South industrial redeployment strategy (our high-tech and services for their raw materials, agricultural products, and manufactures)." CFG 11/84

It was at this point that the "Reagan revolution" came up with the concept that was to dominate global development strategy for the next decade (and beyond). In order to explain this concept. it is important to observe that the "Reagan revolution" was not so much a revolution as it was a continuation and intensification of long standing U.S. policy towards global economic growth. Since 1945, the US had historically run budget and trade deficits in order to act as "an engine of growth" for the rest of the world economy. (See D. P. Calleo, 1982.) The Reagan debt-led model of growth simply put this strategy into "full throttle" by an "order of magnitude" increase in the U.S. budget and trade deficits, and, in order to ward off inflation, financed the deficits by debt creation rather than by monetary creation.

The Reagan debt-led model of global growth, however unpalatable it might have seemed from a bookkeeping point of view, was in fact a bold and decisive strategy. For several years, it put the U.S. squarely back in charge of the world economy. and allowed the U.S. to break the international OPEC/West/LDC "gridlock" on global economic strategy. The world's most important commodity was now, not oil, but the U.S. dollar. Commodity prices plunged. Large parts of the global economy were turned into a "global distress sale" and U.S. growth was financed from the "proceeds". A significant portion of the Third World's consumer markets were shut down and replaced by the U.S. consumer market. The world's financial power and "market" power which had been dispersed between the U.S., Europe, Japan and OPEC was now pulled firmly back into the hands of the U.S. In short, Reagan's response in 1982 to ten years of Western, OPEC and Third World bickering was: "You'll do it my way. Even if I'm not quite sure what my way is yet.".

In other words, the U.S. was now able to set the agenda for discussions of global development strategy for the next decade.

The strategy towards North/South development that ultimately emerged from this U.S. dominance was the so-called neoliberal strategy. Its most important feature was the initiation, in 1986, of a new round of global trade negotiations, the Uruguay Round, of the General Agreement on Trade and Tariffs (GATT). To give some background, the origins of the General Agreement on Tariffs and Trade (and of its stillborn predecessor, the International Trade Organization (ITO)) go back to American-British wartime discussions concerning the shape of the post-war world economy. Despite vigorous efforts by developing countries (in the Havana negotiations of 1947) the draft ITO Charter only "paid lip service to development concerns". The GATT, a separate temporary agreement negotiated by 23 countries (which became permanent when ITO was never ratified), was even less receptive to the needs of the developing countries. Tariffs on trade in manufactures between developed countries were reduced substantially under the auspices of GATT, but products in which the developing world had a comparative advantage (such as textiles or agricultural products) received much less favorable treatment. In addition, when the developing countries diversified into industrial exports, they faced a proliferation of new discriminatory non-tariff trade restrictions directed specifically at them (see notes).

The basic thrust of the Uruguay Round was as follows: It had been estimated that the above restrictions on LDC exports to the West cost the Third World 500 billions dollars each year. The West would agree to abolish those restrictions, thus providing 500 billion dollars worth of economic benefit to the Third World. In return, the Third World would agree to:

- open up their service economies to imports;
- give wide automony to outside investment;
- agree to strengthen their patent protection of western technologies, (thus, according to some critics, "locking in" western advantage in these technologies).

According to the neoliberal strategy, such an agreement, and even the promise of such an agreement, would bring about a massive North/South capital transfer. This capital would be lured by the promise of access to Western markets, by cheap labor, and by a favorable climate for Western investment brought about by deregulation in the LDC's. This flood of capital investment would, in turn, "jump start" the Third World economies, lead to a rising standard of living and open up markets for Western exports. The Third World would follow the path of the dynamic Asian LDC's and would simultaneously break the cycle of slow growth, trade imbalances and fiscal deficits in the West. In the meantime, the West's increased access to LDC service sector and high-tech markets, brought about by the GATT agreement, would reduce protectionist sentiment in the West.

"Cheap labor is drawing investment and production away from the industrial countries. Plentiful goods and materials are crowding the world markets, and annual exports from developing to industrialized nations have risen by $100 billion since 1989. A new economic order is being born. Eventually, the entire world should share the bounty of this new order. As nations develop, their need for imported goods rises, and worldwide demand grows. Multinationals expect the developing countries to become vast new markets by the end of the decade (for Western high tech, capital equipment and services, ala GATT) as productivity and incomes climb worldwide. History is on the side of the optimists." (Editorial from Business Week, 8/2/93.)

Could it really be this simple? Of course not. In the early 90's, there was a flurry of criticism, from both the right and the left, of the global growth strategy described above. For example, environmental and consumer groups criticized the GATT on the grounds that to subject local and national environmental, safety, health, and patent legislation to the control of global and regional trade agreements would be to put local and national governments in an impossible strait jacket and make it very difficult to adjust local policies to local conditions. Some Third World critics called GATT an offer of "market access (but) with draconian reciprocity". There was also "left wing" criticism of the "global underconsumptionist" sort which went as follows: Because of widespread global poverty and underdevelopment, global consumer markets are too narrow to allow sustainable global economic growth. The strategy of using Western consumer markets and LDC cheap labor to "bootstap" the global economy won't work. It will run into a brick wall of Western protectionism and underconsumption long before LDC standards of living rise enough to relieve Western markets of the pressure of cheap imports. Therefore, some sort of "global Keysnesianism" is needed to enlarge LDC consumer markets. For an example of such criticism see Walter Russell Mead's article *The New Global Marketplace, from Changing America, Blueprints for the New Administration*, 1992.

Actually, many of the supporters of the "GATT approach" to the North/South question, including many officials in the Reagan and Bush administrations, knew very well that a lot more was needed in the way of global economic policy than simply global trade agreements. Like "the Reagan recovery", GATT, and the promise of GATT, was seen as a "holding action", in this case a long term holding action as opposed to a short term holding action. If one had to paraphrase Reagan and Bush thinking, one would say, "The world economy is globalizing and changing in ways that are aren't entirely understood. The best thing to do is to free up national and international restrictions to the movement of knowledge, goods, liquidity and capital and see what happens. Besides, free trade and free markets are like 'motherhood and apple pie'. Keynesianism has been descredited as unworkable on a national level. GATT is an established, entrenched global institution. If countries can't agree on a trade agreement, then how the hell are they going to agree on 'global Keysnesianism'?"

Another goal of the Reagan/Bush global development strategy—both in its short term form (the "Reagan recovery" and in its long term form (GATT, structural adjustment and NAFTA)—was to unite the globalist and nativist factions of the Reagan coalition. And here, let it be repeated that the term "nativism", as we use it, does not refer to a political position, a political belief or a political worldview. It refers to a sentiment, a sentiment, moreover, which can be experienced by the same individual at some times and not others, and for some reasons and not others. Thus, there are many different kinds of nativism. There is—among other forms—race nativism (fear of non-white countries with economic, political or military power), flag nativism (fear of the Third World as a military threat to the West, or fear of Third World criticism which might make the U.S. "look bad"), and wage nativism (fear of low wage economic competition from the Third World). For example, in the 1984 Presidential election, Reagan used flag nativism to distract the Reagan Democrats from wage nativism. In the 1992 Vice Presidential debate, candidate Al Gore used wage nativism against the Republicans (by criticizing an Agency for International Development program which resulted in a relocation of U.S. businesses to Central America) in order to distract attention from his advocacy of a "Marshall Plan" for the Third World. With the exception of the blue collar Reagan Democrats, the nativists in the Reagan coalition tended to fear the Third World more as a military, cultural, or ideological threat (or as a threat to Israel) than as an economic threat. A pattern of global economic growth in which military, political, market, financial and "cultural" power remained with the West, even as parts of the Third World achieved industrial success within Western markets, was, in general, acceptable to the nativist wing of the Reagan coalition. After all, "the customer is king". As long as the Third World remained largely dependent on western markets, then the Third

World would have to adjust to western values, western culture, western needs and western world views, if it wanted to sell its products, so that, even as Third World products invaded the American market, American culture and values would reach out to inundate the Third World. Eventually, "they" would become more and more like "us", a state of affairs more or less acceptable to the nativists in the Reagan coalition. Thus, from the early 1980's to the early 1990's, the Jewish neoconservative right and the Christian right were to make a transition from nativism to globalism. For example, in 1984, the neoconservative Ben Wattenberg was invited to accompany a Reagan administration team to a U.N. population conference in Mexico. The position taken by the Reagan team at the conference was that development, and not abortion, was the solution to the problems of Third World overpopulation. The conference's Third World participants agreed, and this indeed was the position taken by the conference. However, the final statement also included a condemnation of Israeli settlements on the West Bank. This soured Ben Wattenberg on Third World population growth. He was soon to come out with a book entitled the The Birth Dearth. In the Birth Dearth, Wattenberg bemoaned the fact that most of the world's population growth was concentrated in the non-Western regions of the world, regions whose non-Western values and culture made them unlikely candidates for sustainable economic growth. In the meantime, the developed Western regions of the world were experiencing a "birth dearth" which would deprive them of the population increase needed to sustain economic growth. In the late 1980's, however, Wattenberg had come to the conclusion that American culture and values were spreading to the rest of the world, and expressed a far more sanguine view of the world's prospects in The World's First Universal Nation.

Let's get back to out history. In his book, *Changing Fortunes*, Paul Volcker divides the history of Reagan/Bush era into four periods; "The Latin American Debt Crisis", "Bringing Down Superdollar", "More Experiments in Economic Management", and "The New World Order". (To which we add a fifth period, "Nativist Backlash to the New World Order".) The seminal period of this history, in our perspective, and the cause of all the succeeding ones, was the Latin American debt crisis. We will explain this below.

In late 1984, the Reagan debt-led model of growth was running into severe difficulties. When asked, at the time, what achievement he was proudest of, Reagan said, "getting through one more year of the Third World debt crisis". And, indeed, the Third World debt crisis was no longer an imminent threat to the world financial system. In fact, since 1983, the commercial banks had been receiving more in debt-service payments from the heavily indebted developing countries than they were extending to them in new loans. An enormous net resource transfer from the debtor countries to the American economy was taking place. The Reagan debt-led model of growth, while stimulating economic growth in the export-oriented Asian LDC's, was suppressing it in the Latin LDC's, threatening chaos and upheaval on America's doorstep, and leading to a surge in Latin immigration to the U.S. (and the growth of the Latin drug trade). In addition, the American trade deficit was generating a protectionist backlash in the U.S., and the increasing U.S. budget deficit was causing alarm in many sectors of U.S. business community.

In 1985, the U.S. sought the help of the other G5 countries in dealing with this situation. The result was the G5 meeting in the Plaza Hotel on September 22, 1985 for coordinated intervention to bring down the value of the dollar (called the Plaza agreement). The purpose of this dollar devaluation was to make U.S. goods more competitive on world markets in order to allow the U.S. to work down its trade deficit. According to P. Volcker (1992), the Plaza agreement was "the most aggressive and persistent effort to guide exchange rates on both a transatlantic and transpacific scale since floating had begun more than a decade earlier". The principal architect of this policy was the new Treasury Secretary James Baker. Many other members of the Reagan administration had been very nervous about a devaluation of the dollar. Their fears were expressed in a scenario called "the hard landing scenario". According to "the hard landing scenario" a fall in the dollar exchange rate would cause foreign investors, fearing an exchange rate loss, to shy away from dollar investments, thus, choking off the inflow of foreign capital that was allowing the U.S. to finance its budget deficit. In fact, this did not happen. The foreign capital, which had been flowing into U.S. debt, now flooded into the U.S. asset markets, into stocks, into real estate and corporate acquisitions. This, in turn, generated the so-called "junk bond market" to finance the buying of U.S. conglomerates to be "unbundled" and sold off to foreign investors. Investors, both foreign and domestic, continued to pour capital into the U.S. economy, leading to the "go-go" years of the late 80's. The commercial real estate boom precipitated by the tax provisions of ERTA, continued in many regions of the country. Despite increasing volatility, the financial markets continued to provide employment, generate profits, and stimulate economic activity in the burgeoning service economy. Both the U.S. trade deficit and the U.S. budget deficit began to decline, and economic optimism increased.

However, even as the growth of federal debt slowed down, both private and corporate debt continued to soar. Consumers borrowed to finance the purchase of goods and the purchase of residential real estate. Corporations were acquired by means of "leveraged buyouts" and resisted takeover by means of "poisoned pill" borrowing. Commercial real estate borrowing continued to grow.

To sum up this period (and to oversimplify enormously both for rhetorical purposes and purposes of brevity) we can say that the Third World debt had been "resolved", and Third World debt "neutralized", as follows: problematic and risky Third World debt had been dwarfed by a stupendous rise in First World debt, with the result that, by the late 80's and early 90's, the the Third World debt crisis was no longer a threat to the U.S. banking system. That role was to be played by the First World Debt crisis; the savings and loan debacle, the surge of corporate and personal bankruptcies, the massive amount of non-performing real estate loans.

However, there are three points that must be made about the First World debt crisis. First of all, it was a lot more manageable than the Third World debt crisis. It was a lot more manageable because it did not span the North/South divide and, thus, did not raise the specter of a nativist backlash. Imagine, for example—given the uproar over NAFTA—the political feasibility of applying a savings and loan type bailout to Latin America.

Secondly, (and this was very important to the Reagan administration), borrowing kept the American import and consumer market going, thus, providing both domestic political support and political leverage over the rest of the world. Even though the U.S. needed the help of its Trilateral partners to manage the world economy, it still "called the shots", because every country in the world (with the possible exception of North Korea) wanted access to its lucrative market.

Finally, the buildup of First World debt had financed a pattern of world economic growth in which IMF conditionality and World Bank structural adjustment made sense in the aggregate. America "borrowed to import", and, in so doing, provided an "import engine", which rendered a strategy of export-led growth for the Third World as a whole least vaguely plausible.

In other words, many of the economic problems of the late 80's the debt problems, the "bubble economy", the market instability, the protectionist pressures, the unemployment problems, the corporate bankruptcies, etc. were, to a large extent, the consequences of a global economic strategy whose genesis lay with the Third World debt crisis, the Israeli/Palestinian conflict, and widespread American anxieties about the underdeveloped world. The economic and political problems of the 80's were, in effect, manifestations of an enduring crisis in North/South economic and political relations. As S. Amin (1990) puts it:

"For more than 15 years the world economic system has been in an enduring structural crisis. This is a world crisis marked by the collapse of growth in productive investment, a notable fall in profitability (very unequally distributed in sectors and companies) and persistent disorder in international relations . . . The current crisis is therefore most apparent in the field of world relations. North/South relations and the conflicts around them constitute the central axis of the current crisis. . . . In circumstances (such as the 1930's) the Keynesian policies of redistribution of income might have been a solution to the crisis. By contrast, (the present crisis) comes after a long period of full employment, the rule of the welfare state,etc. Today's deficient demand is essentially deficient demand in the periphery . . . In other words, only a redistribution at the international level in favor of the South would permit a fresh start for the world. The obvious question is 'under whose aegis' will . . . this be carried out?"

One of the purposes of the Reagan debt-led model of growth was precisely to buy time to formulate an answer to this latter question (while simultaneously keeping it from becoming a subject of public debate and nativist anxieties). However, when Bush became president, the Reagan debt-led model of growth had begun to slow down.

The Stealth Presidency

Nothing could be further from the truth than the belief that Bush was a "do nothing president". It might be more accurate to say that he was a "tell nothing president". Like Reagan, he was not terribly anxious to get into a public debate about global economic development and "North/South structural crises". However, his attempts to distract people with attempts at Reaganesque charismatic theatrics came across as forced and patronizing. To a large extent, his main method of distracting voters from touchy global economic and political issues was simply not to talk about them, and not to be seen dealing with them. He would conduct his foreign policy, including his foreign economic policy, as quietly as possible, often by means of secret meetings and personal communication with world leaders. At the June 1992 North/South environmental summit, he agreed to very little, and told everyone to convene the conference again after the U.S. and Israeli elections were over. In addition, (and we're not saying that this was a conscious strategy) Bush's abrasive domestic political style, his "Willy Horton" campaigning, his liberal bashing, his woman baiting, and so on, had the effect of taking American hostility towards the outside world and redirecting it into into internal, domestic animosities, animosity between liberals and conservatives, blacks and whites, Jews and Christians, men and women, religious and secular and gays and straights. Strident, "in your face" group identity politics drowned out discussion of global affairs. After the Gulf war, Bush tried to use military triumphalism to get Americans enthusiastic about U.S. involvement in global issues, the so-called "New World Order". This attempt failed dismally. One year after the Gulf victory, Americans were accusing Bush of "being more interested in Kurds and Palestinians than Americans". Domestic intergroup hostilities, hostilities which, to some extent, Bush had helped foment, were now being directed against Bush, who, like Carter before him, had become the scapegoat for everything Americans feared about the outside world. Expressing a common misconception about the Bush administration, the economist Rudiger Dornbusch said:

"At the end of the Gulf, war Mr. Bush enjoyed uniquely high approval ratings. He could have asked for anything and Congress would have gone along; strikingly he did absolutely nothing except sit on his polls."

Bush had indeed built up a great deal of political capital after the Gulf victory. Many Americans thought Bush had done what Carter should have done to Iran in 1979 and what Nixon should have done to OPEC in 1974. However, Bush was to use all of this political capital (and then some) in stopping Israel's breakneck settlements drive. In the fall of 1991, he asked Congress to make the proposed $10 billion Israeli loan guarantees dependent on a settlements freeze. He knew that the Shamir government would never accept a settlements freeze, and that, therefore, there would be heavy pressure on the Israeli electorate to vote Shamir out. Congress, under the threat of a presidential veto, did indeed go along with Bush, but, after the fracas, Bush's popularity had vanished, and his domestic political base had shrunk to almost nothing.

When Bush left office in 1993, Shamir had been replaced by Rabin, Arab/Israeli peace talks were under way, the U.S. economy, after the rapid growth of the 80's, had been successfully guided to a "soft landing", and, for the first time since the 1970's, the developing world was growing faster than the West, with the consequence that investors, for the first time in decades, were beginning to talk about the Third World as an opportunity for the U.S. rather than as a threat to American interests, or as a global slum, doomed to poverty and famine. All this was, to a large extent, the result of Reagan/Bush policies of debt-led global growth. For all the global problems these policies failed to address, much less solve, the Reagan/Bush policies had, by the early 90's, shown that Third World countries could undergo rapid economic growth, even in a context of Western economic sluggishness. These policies had also converted a sizable number of previously sceptical Third World leaders to a pro-American, democratic and free market point of view. Ironically, it was the very perception that the Third World was now having more "economic success" than the West that contributed to the backlash against Bush in 1992. Bush, despite all his right wing theatrics and strident liberal bashing, had, like Carter in the 70s, become stigmatized as "pro-Third World".

"In 1988, George Bush said, 'We're going to create 30 million new jobs.' What he didn't tell us was that they would be in Guangdong Province, Yokohama, and Mexico." Pat Buchanan, 1992

When Bush campaigned for the presidency in 1988, he maintained that the U.S. budget deficit could be signicantly lowered by economic growth. In fact, the exact opposite turned out to be the case. Under Bush, the budget deficit was to be, not lowered, but once again put to political and economic use. In the 80's it had been used to ameloriate the Third World debt crisis. In the 90's, the U.S. budget deficit was now to be used to ameliorate the First World debt crisis; the deficit was allowed to increase in order to bail out the savings and loans, and the additional federal debt provided long term high interest government debt in which the commerical banks could place their low interest short term deposits. Like the Reagan administration, the Bush administration faced a number of difficult and complex crises. However, the Bush administration had far less economic and political room to maneuver than did the Reagan administration. The rapid debt led growth experienced during the Reagan years was becoming increasingly unsustainable, all the more so as the fall of communism and German reunification had put upward pressure on global interest rates. The Latin debtor countries, although they had undergone a widespread and substantive democratization, had also undergone a draconian economic crisis during the 80's, poverty had grown by leaps and bounds. In addition, Latin American debt was still growing, and steps had to be taken to reduce it directly rather than rely on an American led recovery ala the "Baker plan". Under the circumstances, the U.S. simply could not grow at a rate that put upward pressure on interest rates. It had to be guided to "a soft landing". Unlike Reagan, Bush could not count on a strong domestic economy to bolster his support. To be sure, Bush could count on the U.S. "victory" in the cold war to generate political support, but the fall of communism had also led to some very thorny and dangerous crises. One of these was the Iraqi invasion of Kuwait. Another was the fall of Likud/Labor alliance in Israel and the subsequent drive of the Likud government to build settlements until the West Bank was completely colonized or until the Likud government fell. The fact the Bush administration was able to deal with all these crises simultaneously was a triumph of tactical virtuosity. Bush, whatever one might think of his beliefs, goals, policies or methods, was anything but a "do nothing president". In fact, by early 1992, Bush and Baker were suffering from physical and mental exhaustion caused by all the things they were doing simultaneously. By the time of the Republican convention, many observers were getting the impression that Bush was keeping himself going by shear force of will. He seemed far more interested in locking in Middle East peace negotiations and foreign trade agreements than in getting re-elected. As New York

Magazine reporter, John Taylor, was to write after the election:

". . . the look on his face was a patrician version of one I had seen before in my old neigborhood in Staten Island: the Lomanesque look of a man who keeps working long after a job has lost all its excitement, because there are two years left until the pension or because there's still a kid in school."

In short the problems that Bush was forced to address were the problems caused by the fall of communism and the problems caused by the Reagan debt-led model of growth. The belief that Bush was a "do nothing president" stems from mistaken belief that these crises were somehow of less immediate importance than other problems, such as health care, national competitiveness, deficit reduction, and global warming, etc. In fact, the problems Bush dealt with were the problems in which U.S. interest was immediately involved, and in which "the clock was ticking". He tended to let other problems slide, not even subjecting them to "spin control". He went along with a Democratic tax rise, social spending increase and civil rights bill in order to placate Congress, thus alienating the Republican right. and then, at the Republican convention, he went alone with the Republican right, thus, alienating the Republican moderates, (and leaving the impression that he was too besieged by too many opponents to govern effectively).

The New World Order

At the beginning of this chapter, we promised to show that North/South relations were the driving force of global history from the Reagan revolution to the present. There was a bit of hyperbole in this promise. The fact is that the fall of communism and the end of the cold war cannot be reduced to North/South issues. The communist economic system collapsed under its own weight for reasons that were internal to the communist economic system.

What we will show, however, is that the impact of this collapse on the West cannot be understood apart from an understanding of North/South relations. For the past 500 years, two seminal forces have shaped the evolution of the world capitalist system; (1) scientific and technological advance in the West, and (2) the colonization by the West of, what is today, the Third World. The West and the Third World share with eachother a 500 year "historical relationship", to which the Eastern bloc was, to some extent, "external". In other words, the West + the Third World, on the one hand, and the "Eastern bloc", on the other hand, form two separate "world systems", whose "trajectories", over the past 1000 years, although intersecting at some times, have had very different equations of motion".

The widespread failure to appreciate this fact was to have enormous political and economic repercussions in the early 90's.

To explain this in more detail let's go back to Chater 4 of this book. In Chapter 4, we described the concept of rational expectations. Rational expectations is the way in which consumers, producers, and investors, change their future economic behavior in response, not to their perfect foreknowledge of future political changes, which is impossible, but to their "rational expectation" of future political changes, to their "acturial estimate" of the future impact of governmental and political changes. An important concept in understanding the political and economic crises of the early 90's is the concept of plausible but ahistorical expections. Plausible but ahistorical expectations (expectations precipitated by the fall of communism but shaped by North/South relations) lay behind the political and economic crises of the early 90's, the European monetary crises, the Gulf war, and the U.S./Israeli conflict over settlements. The most important of these plausible but ahistorical expectations was a belief, called by the Japanese white centrism, that the "white areas" of post-communist world, America, East and West Europe and Russia, constitute an economic bloc with enough people and resources to marginalize the Third World (and possibly Japan as well).

Let's give a brief overview of white centrist beliefs. According to left wing white centrism (ala Gorbachev and the western liberals), a massive "Marshall plan" from West to East can generate an economic boom in Europe, lift the Russian standard of living toward European levels, and provide an engine of growth for the developed world. According to right wing white centrism (ala Yeltsin and the western neocons), a high level of education, technology and "Western culture" will enable the newly liberated Eastern bloc to replace the Third World as a source of cheap labor and raw materials. The fallacy of left wing white centrism was demonstrated by the financial debacle of German re-unification. The fallacy of right wing white centrism was demonstrated by the political consequences of IMF shock therapy when applied to Russia.

Be that as it may, white centrism played a very important role in shaping world events. Indeed, it played an important role in the collapse of communism itself. Observers in the Eastern bloc, at all levels of society, had seen the success of Third World countries in attracting western capital and in capturing western markets. It was a sort step from this to the conviction that a non-communist Eastern bloc, being educated, technologically skilled and culturally European, would be at least as successful as the Third World in both endeavors, and would attract more direct western aid as well. For example, in early 1990, a Polish Solidarity member expressed a sentiment that was widespread in the post-communist Eastern bloc, when he said:

". . . a failure of democratic renewal in the heart of the Old Continent would be much more detrimental to the fundamental interests of the West than the perpetuation of gross social and political injustice in the Third World . . . Major economic interests will also be involved. Central European countries offer Third World advantages to investors; a cheap and eager labor force, a liberal tax and profit policy, an insatiable internal market. This comes without the inherent Third World dangers of political destabilization, while the technological and social infrastructure of Central Europe is more developed. The Third World will probably lose not only some of (its), but some of the private investment as well. There seems, of course, to be some sort of scandal attached to this. Central Europe's most serious basket case, is in better shape than, say, Bangladesh."

Givi Taktakashvili, Chairman of the Georgian Parliament's Committee on Economic Reform under the Gamsakhurdia regime, put the case even more bluntly:

"We helped the West during the crusades. When the Mongols were descending on Europe, we formed a barrier. The West will help. Gentlemen never forget to pay their debts."

Russian disappointment over the failure of this aid and capital investment to materialize in the amounts that were expected was one of the reasons for the coup attempt in 1991 and the rebellion of the Khasbulatov Parliament in 1993. In both cases, the insurrectionists thought anti-western hostility caused by failed expectations would enable them to muster military and popular support.

It is a truism to say that the fall of communism had a tremendous impact on American politics. This impact has been the subject of an enormous amount of discussion. What has been completely overlooked in this dicussion—to our knowledge—is the impact of the fall of communism on American race relations. Of course—you might be thinking—the fall of communism had an impact on everything and, therefore, also had an impact on race relations, but that's not what we mean. To see what we mean, let's go back to our concept of white centrism. By "white", in this context, we mean, not "Caucasoid", but "Anglo-European", as opposed to, say, East Indian, Arab, Persian, Turkish, Afghan, Berber, Hispanic, and so on. We mean "politically white" from the point of view of American racial politics. Prior to the fall of communism. an American observer looking at the world capitalist system would see a system in which "whites" were dominant from an economic point of view, but in which "non-whites" were overwhelmingly dominant from a demographic point of view. From a demographic point of view, non-whites were an "order of magnitude" superior to whites; billions as opposed to hundreds of millions. Unless one believed in endless economic expansion on a fixed population, it didn't take much imagination to see that continued capitalist expansion would eventually require the participation of the "non-whites". It was this perception, in the late 80's, that gave American black politics an overtone of "global social democracy", an overtone that showed up in Jesse Jackson's Rainbow Coalition. One of the messages of the Jackson moverment was that that American blacks could act as an economic and politicial bridge between American and the "non-white" world. Indeed, in the 1980's, Jackson was the only American politician with a broad base of popular support in American domestic politics who also had a broad base of popular support in the Third World. He was certainly the only presidential candidate who could meet with Yassir Arafat without being hooted out of the race. In other words, the Rainbow coalition and the Jackson movement gave American blacks what seemed at the time to be a potentially important role on the world stage.

After the fall of communism, however, this perception changed. Now it seemed that 400 million whites had been suddenly and instantanously thrown into the world capitalist system. The demographic balance did not now seem overwhelmingly unfavorable for whites. It was possible to imagine a global "white bloc" sufficiently populous to permit self-sustaining global economic growth without the need for the "non-whites". Many observers declared the Third World "irrelevant". Africa, in particular, with its famines, droughts, civil wars and plagues, having lost it's cold war importance, seemed to be headed for total isolation from the rest of the world. As the development economist, A. Frank (1993), put it:

"There is a decreasing market . . . for Africa's natural and human resources. Having been squeezed dry like a lemon . . . much of Africa may now be abandoned to its fate."

That such a perception would have an enormous impact on American race relations goes without saying. How could it not? The "global social democracy" of Jackson's rainbow coalition was replaced by a defensive black centrism, a militant American black particularism which said, "You might be able to ignore them, but you won't be able to ignore us so easily. We're here", a sentiment which was summed up in the phrase "no justice, no peace".

White centrism also had an enormous effect on politics within the Third World. We've already mentioned how Salinas of Mexico, nervous about the possibility of competition from the eastern bloc, began to seek admittance into the U.S.-Canadian free trade zone, and how Saddam, worried about becoming "another Ceaucescu", invaded Kuwait. In addition, there was a pervasive feeling in the Third World that—just at a time when the West, recovering from its euphoria over the fall of OPEC, and sensing the limits of the Western market, was beginning to attach renewed importance to Third World development—the Third World was suddenly marginalized yet again, this time by a newly capitalist Eastern bloc. In other words, to use a forced and rather flippant analogy (considering the seriousness of the issues involved), if we were to compare the world economy to a senior prom, we could say that, just as the West was about to "ask the Third World to dance", the Eastern bloc "cut in".

"Both (Latin America and Africa) . . . now fear they will be the losers as the West takes new interest in Eastern Europe . . . At the same time the majority from the developing world sees its influence at the United Nations diminishing as real power passes to the United States and the Soviet Union . . . The result is a growing Third World resentment." Paul Lewis, New York Times, 9/23/90.

The Palestinians, in particular, after having made concession after concession to Israel and its American sponsor, felt that they were now about to be overwhelmed by surge of Russian Jewish immigration into the West Bank. There's no doubt in our mind, that the resentment in the Third World over the West's sudden rapture at a newly capitalist Eastern bloc was one of the reasons why Saddam thought he would get popular support for his invasion of Kuwait. According to a New York Times editorial of 2/6/91, Saddam won the support of millions of people in the Third World:

"That they cheer such a loathsome tyrant sends Washington an important message, one that must be addressed if the war is to be followed by a durable peace. Pro-Iraqi sentiment is particularly strong in countries with pro-Western governments, including some that have sent troops to the Persian gulf . . . most countries in the Third World were once exploited colonies of Europe. Ordinary people in these lands do not consider themselves beneficiaries of the present world order, and doubt the promise of a new one.

And probably the only useful way to respond . . . is for Washington and its allies to show that the new world order is not going to become a rich man's club"

Perhaps this resentment was felt by Saddam personally. Certainly many people, such as Mubarak, who observed Saddam's regrets, anxieties and second thoughts after his invasion of Iran, were flabbergasted that he would provoke a war with the United States and its allies.

To summarize, at the end of 1989 and the beginning of 1990, the collapse of communism in the Eastern Bloc swept aside environmental concerns and produced a burst of euphoria in America at the prospect of hundreds of millions of white, Europeans entering the world capitalist system. It was assumed that because these people were white, European, skilled and educated, they would rapidly provide the West with economic stimulus as they "privatized". Comparisons were made to Western Europe after World War II. There were calls for a new "Marshall Plan" and predictions that the underdeveloped world was now "irrelevant". The Japanese called this sentiment "White Centrism". This "White Centrist" euphoria strengthened President Bush and the Republicans and thus tended to keep protectionist sentiment in check. However, in the latter half of 1991, the severe structural difficulties to privatization in the Eastern bloc began to become apparent. The Germans were shocked at the cost of absorbing the "Neue Laender" and the world was shocked at the extent of the economic collapse in the Eastern bloc. The American mood of "White Centrist" euphoria evaporated. The fact that even some of the "banana republics" in Latin America were having more success with their economic stabilization programs than the

313

white, European Eastern bloc, was seen as a humiliation by many middle class Americans. In addition, as the primitive nature of the Russian economy became apparent, many Americans began to see Russia as simply another Third World economic competitor, rather than as an economic ally against the Third World. This played an important role in the souring of the American mood, and the drop in consumer confidence. It also played a role in the disaffection with President Bush, in early 92, whose boasts of "victory over communism" fell flat.

One group that was genuinely emboldened by the events in the Eastern bloc was the Israeli right. The feeling of Third World irrelevance, the prospect of new trading partners among the cash hungry former Soviet republics, the flood of Russian Jews into Israel, all seemed like a "sign from God" to the Israeli right. In the spring of 1990, Rabbi Menachem Schneerson of Crown Heights in Brooklyn, N.Y., the spiritual mentor of the Israel's Agudath Israel party, (a small religious party in Israel) had a vision that the coming of the Messiah was at hand. He announced that there was now a religious necessity to annex the West Bank. The Agudath Israel party then formed a coalition with Likud which enabled the Israeli right to set up a narrow coalition government without the help of Labor. Ariel Sharon was made Minister of Housing and settlement activity in all the occupied territories increased exponentially. In the fall of 1991, Israel's supporters in congress were on the verge of pushing through 10 billion dollars in loan guarantees to finance these activities. A week before the legislation was due to be introduced to congress, Bush did the one thing that every American president dreaded, he confronted the Israeli lobby. In doing so, he had to make concessions to the liberal Democrats that alienated many of his conservative supporters (the support of the civil rights bill). He further split the "Reagan coalition", which had already been frayed by his breaking of his "no new taxes pledge", by alienating the pro-Israel neoconservatives. By early 1992, Bush was being besieged on so many fronts that there were serious doubts about his ability to govern. The only thing that was holding up his standing in the polls, was the fact (which, to our knowledge has never been touched upon) that the Israeli loan guarantee issue was scaring the big name Democrats away from entering the Presidential primaries. This, in turn, left the field open for an unknown candidate, the Governor of Arkansas, Bill Clinton, whose candidacy was initiated by a breakaway faction of AIPAC. Clinton supported unconditional loan guarantees to Israel and maintained that an Israeli settlements freeze was not necessary as a pre-condition of peace talks or Arab recognition of Israel. This position, so obviously politically motivated, and so at variance with American interest in the Middle East, led to a widespread distrust of Clinton and kept his rating in the polls at a low level. It was only after the election of Rabin ended the U.S./Shamir fight over settlements that Clinton's standing in the polls shot from third place to first place. All of this shows how two "North/South issues", namely the Israeli/Palestinian conflict, and fear of economic competition from Third World countries (Ala NAFTA) were the "driving forces" of the 1992 Presidential elections.

SINCE THE REAGAN REVOLUTION

[1]It is also necessary to emphasize that we are considering here only trends which are invariant to a wide range of environmental and technological assumptions. We are looking for a "stable platform" from which to project, among other things, the practical consequences of various environmental and technological assumptions. This "stable platform" cannot itself depend on environmental assumptions, which, while not necessarily implausible, are still only assumptions.

By "liberalism" we mean, not free trade and free market economics, but New Deal and Great Society liberalism. Sometimes, the Reagan/Bush approach to global development is called neoliberalism.

See B. Ginsberg, 1993.

Events in the Arab/Israeli conflict (a North/South issue and a paradigm for the North/South question as a whole) had tremendous repercussions in the U.S. political arena, a point we will be returning to again and again.

The fact that three ex-Presidents came to Washington to shake hands with Arafat and then immediately put in a plug for NAFTA only served to emphasize the "North/ South" symbolism of the NAFTA debate and add to the intensity of it.

This Japan-bashing of early 1994 was, in fact, Clinton's response to the large U.S. trade deficit of 1993. He was anxious to placate an economic nativism which had surged during the NAFTA debate, but, which, had, in fact, dissipated in early 1994, after the passage of NAFTA was followed by an upsurge in employment.

Particularly Intel's placing the entire central processing unit of a computer on a single chip in November of 1971. See G. Gilder (1989) for a readable account of the electronic advances of the last 30 years and their impact on the global economy.

Those who have a background in college economics, see Modern Macroeconomics, Geoffrey Woglom, (1988),

[2]In our books and newsletters, we referred to these two political tendencies as nativist and globalist.

A "wish-dream" which, in our opinion, was of the reasons for the popularity of the "new growth theories" if not an actual motivation for their creation.

The then Secretary of Agriculture, Bill Brock, expressed this when he said, "There's a lot of Third World out there and we are just beginning to realize how much we need eachother."

Later on in this chapter we will analyze the extent to which these policies are actually solutions to the problems they purport to address. which is one of the reasons why it was less popular than the Reagan administration.

This approach was symbolized at the economic summit in 1983 when Reagan had the other participants meet him in an elaborate ceremony at Williamsburg, Virginia and kept the press confined to a separate quarters several miles away. By these means, he symbolically "Americanized" the economic summits and put a halt to the anxiety producing public squabbling between America and its Trilateral partners.

A confusing point. The term "liberal" here is used in the 19th century sense of "free trade and free markets", not in the more customary sense of New Deal or Great Society liberalism. We would have chosen the term "global free market conservatism".

See J. G. Castaneda, 1993.

In the early 90's, the Reagan Democrats were to defect because of trade anxieties, the secular Republicans to be alienated by the abortion issue, and the neoconservatives to be alienated by Bush's fight with Shamir over the settlements. It is striking though how long the juggling act was kept up. Helpful in this was the euphoria over the fall of communism and the U.S. performance in the Gulf war.

Many economists claim population increase is not needed for long-term economic growth. See chapter 2 of this book.

The "hard landing scenario" for the U.S. dollar was formulated by Steven Marris of the International Institute of Economics.

And in what manner.

Another period when the Third World was growing faster than the West.

As a crisis to the world financial system. It was still a crisis to the debtor countries.

The confluence of these two crises in the summer of 1990 led to some genuinely hair raising possibilities, an upheaval in Jordan, another Arab/Israeli war, another exodus of Palestinians, a "greater Israel", a "Somalia-ization" the Middle East with its enormous arsenal of weapons.

2 [2]

New York Magazine, 11/30/92.

Prior to that the historical development of the West, the East, and (what is today) the Third World differed in the ways described in Chapter 3 of this book.

For purposes of this discussion, the "Eastern bloc" refers to the former Soviet Union plus Eastern Europe minus the central European countries of Poland, East Germany, Czechoslovakia, and Hungary.

See Chapter 3 of this book.

If Central America had gotten billions of dollars and trade concessions to be anti-communist, what would Russia get for being anti-communist?

Was a "new growth theorist" or had gotten totally carried away with the Reagan recovery.

After the breakup of the Soviet Union, Byelorus negotiated an economic cooperation treaty with Iraq. Bush's fear was that a coup in the Soviet Union could end its support for the anti-Iraq coalition or that a cash hungry former Soviet republic could break the arms embargo.

He was afraid, incorrectly as it turns out, that Western investment and aid would be siphoned away from the developing countries and towards the newly capitalist eastern bloc countries.

The Israeli labor party generally favored a "territorial compromise" in the occupied territories in return for peace. The Likud generally favored holding onto the territories and incorporating them into Israel by means of massive Jewish settlements. The argument given by Labor for its viewpoint was usually a demographic one; the Arab population was increasing faster than the Jewish one, and holding onto the territories would lead to an Arab majority and create a situation similar to that of apartheid. As we shall discuss later in this chapter, economics and not demographics underlay the pressure towards a settlement of the Arab/ Israeli dispute, but nonetheless the flood of Russian Jews into Israel weakened Labor's argument, and seemed like a "sign from God" to the Israeli hardliners that their policy was the right one. In the spring of 1990, Rabbi Menachem Schneerson of Brooklyn, N.Y., the spiritual mentor of the Israel's Agudath Israel party, (a small religious party in Israel) had a vision that the coming of the Messiah was at hand. He announced that there was now a religious necessity to annex the West Bank. The Agudath Israel party then formed a coalition with Likud which enabled the Israeli right to set up a narrow coalition government without the help of Labor. Ariel Sharon was made Minister of Housing and settlement activity in all the occupied territories increased exponentially. In the fall of 1991, Israel's supporters in congress were on the verge of pushing through 10 billion dollars in loan guarantees to finance these activities. A week before the legislation was due to be introduced to congress, Bush was forced to do the one thing that every American president since Eisenhower has dreaded, he got into a fight with the Israeli lobby during an election year.

It is truly striking how both Bush's approval rating and consumer confidence plunged vertically downward shortly after Bush's fight with Congress over unconditional loan guarantees to Israel. We'll elaborate on this connection later on in this chapter.

Nativism often finds its way into economic analyses. Here is one such analysis by D. Landes (1992):

"A few countries especially in East Asia, are clearly forging ahead and catching up; others seem to move in fits and starts . . . others do well in some regions and languish elsewhere—a pattern that we may call mottled development . . .—we are witnessing a selection process. The best prepared for development have moved or are moving in that direction. The least prepared will likely never enter the process . . . In the meantime economies, like love, laugh at locksmiths; if a society cannot export merchandise, it can, and will export people, or, in extreme cases, get them to sell their body parts. This too is not a basis for sustainable growth."

There are many terms (dualistic, disarticulated, dependent, hollow) that can be used to describe the type of development that Landes refers to as "mottled". The use of the term "mottled" projects an image of a leper colony. The use of the term "selection process" reminds one of the "selectzia" in a concentration camp. One doesn't have to be a mind reader, to say that the use of these terms in this way, together with the imagery of selling body parts, projects a morbid imagery which suggests an attitude of antagonism and revulsion towards the Third World and its problems.

After the fall of the Likud government and the election of Clinton, "America/Mexico" replaced "Israel/Palestine" as the paradigm of the North/South question. NAFTA replaced Arafat as the focus of anti-Third World anxieties. Fears of the low-wage Mexicans "stealing all our jobs" (fears as far-fetched as the fears of the "destruction of Israel by the PLO") began to manifest themselves. So even as Israeli Prime Minister Rabin shook hands with Arafat and admitted that there was no way in hell the PLO could pose a threat to Israel, Clinton and most of the country's economists were trying to convince a sceptical American public that Mexico would not bring the U.S. economy to its knees. Mexico, after all, is the only Third World country that is physically contiguous with the United States. Thus, Mexico became the target for the whole range of pent up anxieties about economic competition from the Third World.

New York Times, November 17, 1991.

The fracas between Bush and Congress left Bush in the position of "putting pressure on Israel", in what politically was the worst possible way. By denying Israel the loan guarantees to house the Russian Jewish immigrants, he was "holding the lives of a million harried and worried people (the Russian Jews) hostage to his demand that Israel surrender its most cherished possession (the West Bank) beforehand." (W. Safire, New York times, 10/9/91). Furthermore, he was doing this to help the Palestinians, the "Quislings" of the Gulf war, "the turncoats" who, after having obtained U.S. recognition in 1988, had sided with Saddam, a man Bush himself called the "new Hitler". All this was a public relations nightmare from hell, and the Bush administration knew it (even if Bush's chronic "foot in mouth disease" had, in fact, contributed to it). But Bush had no choice. As Shamir admitted after he lost to Rabin, if he had won the election he would have turned the Middle East peace talks into what the Japanese call an Odowara Hyojo, while he colonized the West Bank. (See Israeli newspaper, Maariv, 6/26/92.) No American President could be in the situation where the U.S. went to war in the Gulf to make the region safe for a "greater Israel". The relations between the U.S. and the Muslim world have irretrevably poisoned. In other words, in the "New World Order", the Third World was not simply to be ordered around, but actually had some rights, rights which could take precedence over the most sensitive of domestic political issues, rights which could force a sitting American President to knowingly shoot himself in the political foot, one year before the election. This was one of the reasons why Americans went into a funk in late 1991, a funk from which they have yet to recover.

New York Times, November 17, 1991

Some more disclaimers. We are not defining nativism as some sort of global prejudice which must be exposed and corrected. We are not saying that nativist anxieties are necessarily unrealistic, although, in many cases, (as witness the hysteria in the early 90's over the North American Free Trade Agreement) they are. Nor are we saying that opinions or criticisms based on nativist anxieties are necessarily wrong. We are not praising the benefits of global economic integration as a model of development as opposed to some sort of "delinking strategy". We stress again that this book is not about advocacy. We are saying nothing at all about what should happen, what should have happened in the past, or what should happen in the future. We leave those questions entirely up to you. We only analyzing what did happen, what is happening now and what will happen in the future.

There were several others factors at the time that contributed to the decline of nativist sentiment. The spectacle, in the Irangate scandal, of Reagan selling arms to Khomeini tended to "de-demonize" the Third World as a whole. Reagan's "teflon" rubbed off onto the Third World. In addition, the Palestinian Intifada, and the PLO's recognition of Israel gained public sympathy for the Palestinians, and this tended to extend to sympathy for the Third World as a whole. The proposed arms reduction treaty with the Soviet Union tended to improve the American attitude towards the outside world as a whole. As we put it in our talk at the Symposium on Global Change at the MITI in early 1990: "By presenting a threat which is in some sense 'external' to global society, a 'greenhouse crisis', should such a crisis

324

arise, would bring about the feeling that 'we're all in the same boat' together with a diminution of global 'rich/poor' antagonisms. In fact, the greenhouse issue has already had this effect on American politics. For a long time, Americans have been very loath to discuss North/South issues. In fact, since the Iranian hostage crisis in 1979, the popular American media has produced a steady diet of 'Third World' bashing articles, 'The OPEC threat', 'the import threat', 'the drug threat', 'illegal aliens', etc. There was always some threat from the LDC's. And, indeed, this was the attitude that the American media at first took towards the greenhouse issue. For example, in early 88, there was an articlue in Time magazine which presented the AIDS epidemic as nature's way of dealing with overpopulation in the underdeveloped world. To take another example, there was an eidtorial peace by Senator Albert Gore in the New York Times in which he compared the ecological threat caused by the burgeoning populations of the Third World to the 'Nazi threat to Western civilization' . . . As the potential gravity of a global ecological crisis began to sink in, however, the coverage of it in the popular media began to take a very different tone. The articles began to show far more sophistication about the links between the environment and Third World development. The whole range of North/South issues began to receive far more coverage in the American media than it ever had before. Ideas for 'North/South capital transfer' which had generally been portrayed as 'far out', 'utopian', by mainstream American political commentators, began to receive far more mainstream support. To take an example, at the end of 1988, rather than publish its usual 'man of the year' edition, Time magazine published a 'planet of the year' edition. (The only possible candidate for 'man of the year' at that point was Yassir Arafat because of the PLO recognition of Israel and it was probably to avoid him that Time created the 'planet of the year' idea. This shows that a global environmental crisis is a far safer way to introduce North/South issues into American political discourse than are touchy political issues such as the Palestinian issue). The striking thing about the Time magazine 'planet of the year' edition was the extent to which it addressed North/South economic and political issues. For example, an article entitled 'Hands Accross the Sea' and subtitled 'Rich and Poort, North and South Must Get it Together or Face Common Disaster,' called for a 'global bargain' in which the rich agreed to cut back their defense spending in order to provide funds for 'sustainable development' in the Third World."

As former Chairman of the Federal Reserve, Paul Volcker, puts it: "The world didn't come apart. Currencies had floated for several months. The changes in exchange rates that were ultimately agreed on were larger than most countries anticipated. During the protracted negotiations, trade restrictions were threatened, and considerable antagonism arose among governments. Yet stock and bond markets performed well, trade continued to expand, and business in general prospered in the ensuing year. While there were inevitable distortions and uncertainties, neither the world economy nor its trading system seemed so sensitive to monetary disturbances as had been feared by those of us raised in the Bretton Woods system." P. Volcker, 1993.

Keynesian economists explain unemployment by saying that the labor market "doesn't clear". Rational expectations economists maintain that "market clearing" assumptions together with probability theory can account for unemployment, recessions and business cycles, and, in addition, can also describe the ways in which government policies can cause structural changes in the economy which are not captured by the standard economic forecasting models. For a description of rational expectations see Modern Macroeconomics, Geoffrey Woglom, 1988.

We didn't mean to imply here that pro-business = pro-Third World and pro-labor = anti-Third World, although when trade issues are in the limelight, they might, at times, seem to be the case. We were predicting (correctly) that in the 80's, these would be the two tendencies that prevailed. "Blue collar" in the quoted passages refers primarily to the "Reagan Democrats". In the 80's, the U.S. labor movement, aside from some protectionism, largely didn't concern itself with issues of global development. In the 90's, that is likely to change, and we are likely to see advocacy, in at least some parts of the labor movement, of Third World development as a way of raising the wage rate in Third World countries to remove downward pressure on U.S. wages, and of providing exports markets for American manufactured products, a sort of "social democracy on a world scale".

These statements are not, in themselves, wrong, but to confine discussions of long term economic growth solely statements like these to the total exclusion of global econmic and trade issues is misleading.

Which, according to Lucas, would be limited by "human capital" shortages in the underdeveloped world.

These were also important causes of the "Asian economic miracle" since they opened up markets in commodity producing LDC's for exports of Asian manufactured goods.

Not the least of these was Saudi insistence that the PLO be given observer status at the IMF.

According to the New York Times, June 23, 1980, the strongest support for such talks came from Chancellor Helmut Schmidt of Germany, President Valery Giscard D'Estaing of France, Prime Minister Elliot Trudeau of Canada, and Prime Minister Francisco Cossiga of Italy. President Carter refrained from endorsing the idea of a global summit meeting, but he called for cooperation between the industrialized countries and moderate oil producing countries (who, after all, owned the bulk of the world's oil reserves).

"The (Israeli) . . . hope is that the stricken PLO, lacking a logistic and territorial base, will return to its earlier terrorism . . . In this way, the PLO will lose part of the political legitimacy, that it has gained and will mobilize the large majority of the Israeli nation in hatred and disgust against it, undercutting the danger that . . . the Palestinians . . . might become a legitimate negotiating partne for future political accomodations." Yehoshua Porath, *Ha'aretz* 6/25/82, quote taken from The Passionate Attachment, George W. Ball and Douglas B. Ball, W. W. Norton and Company, 1992.

Oral communication.
L. Cannon, 1991.

After which it was supplemented by the G5 agreements to force down the value of the dollar in 1985 and later, in the late 1980's, by European and Japanese economic stimulus programs in response to U.S. pressure, and still later by the 'Brady plan' for LDC debt and promises to trade past with the LDC in return for structural reforms all of which reversed the flow of flight capital and sucked in western exports.

Although many of them found the U.S. policy of using massive deficit spending as a "Keynesian' stimulus for the world economy hair raising.

Although, prior to the Mexican debt crisis, there was very little talk of 'the recession'. Instead the popular and business press was talking about 'the segmented economy' and 'the age of information'.

And very quickly producing an anxiety, from 1984 onwards, about the flood of cheap Third World imports.

The first of these was to be the biggest economic headache for the Reagan, the Bush, and now the Clinton administrations. The fourth became part of the Democratic political critique of Reaganomics. The rest did not materialize to any great in the period under discussion.

The original function of the IMF was to enable member states to maintain a fixed exchange rate versus the dollar, by providing financing, if necessary, to cover a current account deficit. The IMF also had a resonsibility to see that a member state making use of IMF financing "behaved responsibly". This led to the concept of conditionality. Conditionality is defined as, "the policies the Fund expects a member state to follow in order to be able to use the

Fund's general resources." After the collapse of the fixed exchange rate international monetary system in 1973, the IMF branched out into lending to countries that were in deficit because of an "external shock", an oil price rise, an interest rate rise, a drop in global export prices, or were in deficit because of "irresponsible policies", generally too much demand stimulation or too much monetary creation. The borrowers included poor countries (from a special fund generated by gold sales) and Third World debtor countries. The lending was subject to conditions specifying the measures a country had to take in order to "adjust" to a current account deficit. These measures would include demand reductions, restrictions on public and private credit, abolition of multiple exchange rates and devaluation. Measures to reduce demand might include wage freezes, dropping of price controls or subsidies, improvement in tax administration, and reductions in government spending. Measures to restrict credit might include abolishing interest rate controls, and increasing the amount of liquid reserves banks had to hold. The goal of the conditions was to bring the country out of deficit. In many cases, the "IMF stabilizations" as they were called led to a drastic reduction in economic growth for the borrowing country. In the 1980's, the IMF became heavily involved in the management of the Third World debt crisis. Under IMF tutelage, the Latin debtors underwent a draconian economic adjustment, their aggregate current acount deficit dropping from $51 billion in 1982 to nothing in 1985. But their economies were not growing and the debt crisis had not been resolved. The deficits had been decreased, not by export promotion, but by falls in imports and and falls in investment. In the 1980's, the IMF adopted the slogan of "adjustment with growth". In line with this strategy, IMF doctrine usually assumed the economic efficiency of market forces, and the desirability of export promotion, such as, for example, the dropping of price controls on tradable goods. During this period of time, the World Bank's role had also been undergoing changes. Historically, this role was the raising of money in the international capital markets and the issuing of loans to finance projects, such as dams, power stations, roads and other transport investments in Third World countries. In the 1970's, because of the oil prices rises, and for other reasons, the Bank noticed that more of its projects were failing. The Bank began to make some of its loans conditional on overall changes in the economic policies of the borrowing country. These types of loans were called Structural Adjustment Loans (SALS). To take an example, in the 1991 World Development Report the Bank examined 1200 projects and plotted the rates of return on these projects against a variety of measures of the economic policies of the countries in which the projects were financed. It found that a high rate of return on projects was correlated with a low level of trade restrictions, a low fiscal deficit, a "realistic" exchange rate (a small difference between the official and black market exchange rate), and an inflation rate lower than interest rate. In the 1980's, the Bank began making an increasing number of Structural Adjustment Loans (SALS), loans to finance economic reforms of the type described above. Structural adjustment stressed "free market reforms"; i.e., the privatization of state run enterprises, and the freeing up of restrictions on the movement of goods and capital, both within the country, and across the border. These policy changes could include, for example, the abolition of industrial licensing requirements, the changing of import quotas to import tariffs, the lifting of price controls and interest rate controls, the ending of subsidies, and the pitching of the official foreign exchange rate to correspond to the black market rate, the deregulation of foreign investments, and so on. Since use of domestic government measures to stimulate internal demand were, in general, inconsistent with these free market reforms, exports became the preferred source of final demand increases. For example, according to the World Bank Development Report of 1981, of those countries relying on structural adjustment policies to respond to an "external shock", during the 1970's, the most successful were countries following an "outward-oriented approach" leading to an expansion of exports. By and large, countries, including both semi-industrial countries and primary commodity producing countries which followed an export oriented strategy, maintained their growth rates in the face of an external shock, while the others had reduced growth rates. Thus, developing countries with economic problems were urged by the IMF and World Bank to follow the example of the "Asian tigers" and to seek export markets. However, given the unequal distribution of global wealth, many of these export markets would naturally have to be in the developed countries, at least initially. This, of course, imposed a corresponding obliglation on the developed countries to accept LDC imports. Bush, for all his negativity on what are usually called "North/South" issues, tried his hardest to meet this obligation (one of the reasons of his political demise). The concepts of IMF conditionality and World Bank structural adjustment played a very big role in Reagan and Bush thinking about global development in the 80's, and, in the early 90's, came to form a "global development consensus" among the world's elites both North and South, a consensus, which, in turn, led to the upsurge of populist economic nativist hysteria in the U.S. in the early 90's.

For a description of World Bank structural adjustment programs, see E. Stern (1983). For a succinct overview of IMF conditionality, see D. Avramovic (1989). For a critical (some would say hostile) analysis of World Bank programs, see C. Payer (1982). For a succinct history of the IMF and the World Bank, which stresses their roles in the Third World debt crisis, see the insert Sisters in the Wood: A Survey of the IMF and the World Bank in the October 12, 1991, issue of the *Economist* magazine.

M. Ghilan (1992) even says that these books were inspired by the Bush administration and the CIA to put pressure on Shamir.

Although, it obviously saw Israel itself as a strategic asset under different government. The "bedtime for Begin scenario".

It is important to mention, in this regard, the domestic role and international outlook of the very influential American Jewish community. When the Iranian revolution in 79 was followed by the oil price rises, a 12% inflation, fears of another depression, and the Iranian hostage taking (which threw America's domestic politics into a turmoil), Americans wondered how a "medieval" political revolution in a small country, half way around the world, could come to have such an impact on their own lives. They couldn't have been more astonished if the planet had cracked open like an enormous egg and a giant green bird had flown out. However, this graphic lesson in global economic interdependence was completely lost on most Americans. They were simply too flabbergasted to absorb it. All they felt instead was an anxious hostility towards the Third World as a whole. And when the giant green bird began to shout anti-Semitic slogans, American Jews, many of whom might have been sympathic to Third World economic aspirations, (liberal Jews were traditionally sympathetic to the "underdog" and conservative Jews saw Third World commercial success as weakening Soviet influence) were completely turned in the other direction.

"The 1980's have already begun. They began with the takeover of the American embassy in Tehran earlier this month and with the subsequent confrontation between the United States and a virulently anti-Western Iranian regime. This episode is, as it were, the shocking proloque to an equally tense drama that stands poised to unfold in the decade ahead. It promises to be an abolutely ghastly period. As the post-World War II international order falls apart—not only in the Middle East, but probably in Latin America as well—all thinking about American foreign policy from that era assumes an air of irrelevance. SALT becomes irrelevant. The United Nations becomes irrelevant. Foreign aid becomes irrelevant. Sermons on human rights become irrelevant. NATO itself may soon become irrelevant, as our European allies decide that, in the face of American weakness, sauve qui peut is the sensible flag to fly. What will be relevant is American foreign policy in which power and the readiness to use it boldly, will play a far more central role than have ever been the case in our history." Irving Kristol, WSJ, 11/18/79.

One knows exactly what was on Irving Kristol's mind when he wrote his hyperbolic editorial in the Wall Street Journal. He had obviously seen the pictures of hostage Barry Rubin blindfolded before a jeering Iranian mob and was thinking what every Jewish person in America was thinking, "Oh God! He's Jewish! It's starting again!". Israel's hardline goverment was able to make use of these Jewish anxieties to vastly increase its influence over the American Jewish community. All of which had a decisive impact on the domestic American political climate, when the administration was confronted with the Israeli invasion of Lebanon and the LDC debt crisis. American Jews, including many influential Jews in the Reagan administration, were hostile to any American policies, even Reagan administration policies, which were in conflict with the goals of Israel's hardline government (this tension within the Reagan administration was one of the reasons for Reagan's incoherent policies in the Middle East), and Americans, as a whole, were pretty much fed up with the entire Third World and its problems. The upshot was that the administration could not even begin to address these problems from any other vantage point than a non-inflationary, non-OPEC strengthening American recovery which had to be brought about by any means necessary.

As Reagan himself was to say in a 1984 speech to the IMF:

"Expansion here in the world's largest single market has meant increased trading opportunities for other nations. Total U.S. imports rose 32 percent in the first half of this year, and for the full year our imports are expected to exceed 1983 imports by over 25 percent. U.S. imports from non-oil developing countries rose about 14 percent in

1983, and they're up by nearly 30 per cent for the first half of 1984. Not enough mention is made of . . . the benefits developing countries receive from . . . open-market policies in the United States". (See R. Reagan, 1985)

Saudi Arabia, which had financial reserves of $120 billion dollars in the early 80's, was reported to be in deficit in 1993.

NYT Times Sunday Magazine.

It is interesting to note that these articles put more emphasis on social reform than did the 1991 World Bank Development Report, which is much more technocratic in nature, the result of the influence of the "new growth theories" (See Chapter 2) and, of course, the collapse of communism and the resulting discrediting of anything which smacked of "leftism".

For example, after pressuring Israel in late 1983 to allow Arafat to escape from Tripoli by sea, the administration attempted to "compensate" for this "pro-Third World" action, by withdrawing from UNESCO and taking protectionist measures against Third World steel. Even so, Americans were surprised at the spectacle of a conservative President like Reagan intervening to assist a "left-wing terrorist" like Arafat. It is somewhat ironic that in the fall of 1993 when Israel and the U.S. finally recognized the PLO and Clinton was able to shake hands with Arafat with no domestic political backlash whatsoever, Clinton was having just as much image problems with his necessity to support NAFTA as Reagan had with his necessity to get Arafat out of Tripoli. Americans were surprised at the spectacle of a left-wing Democrat like Clinton supporting a "union busting" trade agreement with Mexico. In the early 90's, the primary American nativist anxiety was not Arafat/OPEC/Khomeini, but U.S. economic integration with low wage LDC's ala NAFTA. There were many Americans who would have been made far more nervous by the sight of Clinton shaking hands with Salinas of Mexico than by the sight of Clinton shaking hands with Arafat.

An example of the use of political distractions was the Reagan visit to the Bitberg cemetery in Germany (in which storm troopers were buried) during the 1985, G7 economic summit, which started a raucous debate with the American Jewish community, a debate which Reagan well knew would get economic and trade issues off the front pages of the American press.

According to one report, during 1985 alone four hundred bills were introduced in Congress to protect American products, including an import surcharge proposed by leading Democrats. (See P. Volcker and T. Gyohten, 1992). In fact, during the 1984 elections, Reagan was quite vulnerable to a Ross Perot type economic nationalist attack. However, fortunately for Reagan (and the world economy) Mondale was too responsible (the "wimp factor") to make one.

[i]. This historical summary of the GATT negotiations was taken from the Statement on the Uruguay Round, adapted by the South Commission, at its third meeting in Cocoyoc, Mexico, 5-8 August, 1988.

See K. Mahbubani (1992).

Like the IMF and the World Bank, the GATT (General Agreement of Trade and Tariffs) was designed in the small New Hampshire town of Bretton Woods in 1944. Formalized in 1948, the GATT has undergone a lot of negotiated changes since then. These negotiating changes are called rounds. The eighth of these rounds, the Uruguay round was started in 1986. The Uruguay round was proposed by the former chairman of American Express, James Robinson, however one can be sure that the basic ideas behind the Uruguay round emerged from Reagan administration thinking about North/South development problems. In fact, one could say that the Uruguay round of GATT takes the World Bank concept of structural adjustment and blows it up into a global trade and development strategy. At first, the GATT dealt mainly with tariffs. Later rounds dealt with non-tariff barriers to trade, the set of rules and regulations that countries apply to traded products. For example, Canada has charged the U.S. with non-fair trade for requiring the use of recycled paper in newsprint. The Uruguay round goes much further than previously in attempting to develop rules to deregulate non-tariff barriers. There are four main issues addressed by the Uruguay round. They are (1) Liberalization of trade in services such as transport, education, health care, banking and insurance, (2) Strengthening of trade related intellectual property rights (TRIPS) such as patents and copyrights, including patents on seeds, software or new forms of ariticial DNA. Some critics of GATT maintain that this would lock developing countries into technologicial backwardness, (3) Reduction of trade related investment measure (TRIMS) which are performance requirements on foreign capital investment, such as, for example, limits on profit repatriation, minimum requirements for the use of local materials in production ("local content"), the requirement to use a use a national bank, etc.,(4) elimination of discriminatory trade measures directed against exports in which the developing countries have a comparative advantage, such as tropical and agricultural products, textiles and other forms of labor intensive manufacture. In many important sectors where developing countries have emerged as major exporters over the past decade or so, reductions in visible protection have been accompanied by a proliferation of "grey area" measures and non-tariff barriers by developed countries such as sector specific quantitative restrictions in steel, leather goods, foorwear and consumer electronics. Essentially, the Uruguay Round of GATT offers the following "grand bargain" to the Third World: the developed countries will agree to (4) above, if the developing countries agree to measures (1),(2),(3) above. In fact, in the early 1990's, alarmed by the specter of competition from the newly capitalist countries of the eastern bloc many developing countries became more willing to do this. It was at this point that free trade, free markets and unrestrained capitalism began to lose some of their appeal to the American voters, making free trade as touchy an issue in the early 1990's as talking to Arafat was in the early 1980's. Thus, right before the 1992 elections, Bush mused, "Over the past four years, we have seen a change of almost biblical proportions. But here's the irony. At the very moment in which the rest of the world is moving my way, my opponent wants us to move the old way. (i.s. away from free trade and free markets)" (NY Times 10/31/92). And it seems that the electorate felt the same way. To some extent, the reason for this was nativism.

For a succinct description of the issues under negotiation in the Uruguay round of the GATT negotiations see H. B. Junz (1991).

Such as criticism of the U.S. role in Vietnam, of the U.S. role in the Central American civils wars, of the U.S. role in the overthrow of Mossadegh by Khomeini, or of former episodes of U.S. "gunboat diplomacy".

At the 1984 Republican convention, one of the theme songs was a country and western song, entitled, "I'm proud to be an American". The point of the song was that "even if I had to start over again with nothing but my children and my wife, I would still be free and still be an American". In other words, one could be proud to be an American and could feel "special" even in the abscence of an American standard of living. This message was to lose its appeal to many of the Reagan Democrats and to many of the "Perotista" Republicans after the end of the cold war and in the recession of the early 90's. Many of the people in these groups were to feel that they had been "suckered" by having been bought off with American pride, while America's "industrial base" was handed over to the rest of the world. Hence Perot's "sucking sound". Or as Pat Buchanan said in a September 1992, New York Post editorial, "What, then is NAFTA (the North American Free Trade Agreement) really about? . . . It is about losing America, where the first duty of the government is to look out for Americans, not just those with the 'skills . . . to prosper in the new (global) economy'. Behind the rising spirit of rebellion in this land is a gathering consnsus that the nation's elites do not give a damn about the old Republic."

Thus, the Jewish neocons in the Reagan coalition feared Arab financial power, not because they feared Third World commercial success per se, but because they saw Arab financial power as a "threat to Israel". In fact, many Jewish neocons and even some Jewish liberals, were very distrustful of any discussion of Third World needs, fearing that it would draw attention to the Palestinians. For example, after the overthrow of Marcos in the Phillipines, the columnist Max Lerner expressed nervousness at the Reagan administration's willingness to cooperate in the overthrow of Marcos. He stressed the fact that Americans preside over an "imperfect imperium" in which it would be foolish to insist on civil and social progress in all cases. The unspoken anxiety here was, "If the Phillipinos have rights, then what about the Palestinians?"

Which it would if inflation was contained and liberal calls to broaden Third World markets via increased aid were resisted.

An approach to North/South issues which stresses structural adjustments and market access can be portrayed as "free trade", "supply side economics on a world scale", as opposed a to more elaborate global economic polity such as global Keysnesianism, global monetary creation, or North/South "grand bargains", etc. which could be seen as a "satanic world government" by the Christian right. However, if trade agreements become loaded down with environmental and labor standards/ and or middle class job loss becomes sufficiently severe. one could certainly see the Christian right turning against regional or global trade agreements. As far as the Jewish right is concerned, the desire to keep Israel's access to the American market openned certainly would predispose them towards free trade. However, one could see them supporting trade sanctions for political reasons such as "lack of religious tolerance", "lack of democracy" and so on.

In other words, the banks were making new loans, but, because of the high dollar interest rates, in amounts less than the interest payments they were receiving from the debtor countries.

According to the 1986 Inter-American Development Bank Report, Economic and Social Programs in Latin America, the net resource transfer from the debtor countries since 1982 was more than $95 billion dollars.

Thus, in the late 80's almost every country in the world was rooting for the Republicans (who were seen as much better customers than the Democrats) and doing what they could to make them look good. For example, Taiwan bought U.S. gold to reduce its trade surplus with the U.S. and Japan stimulated its economy.

In other words, the debt-led model of Western growth kept the Western import market at a level in which the fallacy of composition arising from all the poor countries adapting a strategy of export led growth to the rich countries was postponed to an indeterminate future. As R. Lucas (1992) puts it:

"The main engine of growth is the accumulation of human capital—of knowledge—and the main source of differences in living standards among nations is differences in human capital . . . Learning on the job seems to be by far the most central (engine for accumulation of human capital). For such learning to occur on a sustained basis, it is necessary that workers and managers continue to take on tasks that are new to them, to continue to move up what Grossman and Helpman call the 'quality ladder'. For this to be done on a large scale the economy must be a large scale exporter. This picture has the virtue of being consistent with the recent experience of both the Philippines and Korea. It would be equally consistent with post-1960 history with the roles of these two economies switched. It is a picture that is consistent with any individual small economy following the East Asian example producing a different mix of goods from the mix it consumes. It does not appear to be consistent with the third world as a whole beginning to grow at East Asian rates: There is a zero-sum aspect, with inevitatable mercantilist overtones, to productivity growth fueled by learning-by-doing." (R. Lucas 1992).

The Western debt-led model of growth postponed Luca's, "zero-sum aspect with inevitable mercantilist overtones" from the early 80's to the early 90's.

The Economist 10/24-10/30 1992.

NYT, January 15, 1992.

The Bush administration's strategy for reducing Third World Debt was the so-called Brady plan initiated in 1989. Negotiations between the Third World debtor countries, the Western governments, the creditor banks and the official lending insitutions were very complicated. They spawned a voluminous literature on Third World debt. Two important concepts associated with the Brady plan were the debt Laffer curve and the free rider problem. To explain them, recall the Laffer curve of supply side economics in the 1970's. The Laffer curve expressed the relationship between the income tax rate and the total tax revenues received. At a tax rate of zero, there are no tax revenues. As the tax rate increases, so do total tax revenues. Eventually, however, when the tax rate gets high enough, total tax revenues begin to drop because the high tax rate has suppressed economic activity and reduced the total amount of income subject to taxation. Thus, the Laffer curve rises at first, as the tax rate grows, but then falls, as the tax rate continues to increase. The Laffer curve for Third World debt expresses the relationship between the total face value of a country's external debt and its total market value on the secondary market. If investors anticipate that the debt will not be repaid in full, then the value of the debt on the secondary market is less than the face value. Up to a certain point, a growth in the face value of a country's debt will cause a growth in the value of the debt in the secondary market. Beyond that point, however, a continued growth in the face value of the debt will cause its value in the secondary market to drop. This is because, at a certain point, the debt service requirements will become so onerous that they will suppress economic activity in the debtor country and lead to a drop in the percentage of debt repaid which will more than counterbalance the increase in total face value. The economist Paul Krugman, using a "scatter diagram" of debtor countries to plot the Laffer curve for Third World debt. This graph showed that, for many heavily indebted countries, it make economic sense for the creditors to get together and write off a portion of the debt (or sell it back to the debtor country at a heavy discount). This is because the subsequent rise in the market value of the remaining debt would more than compensate the creditor banks for the reduction in the face value. Nonetheless, the creditor banks were reluctant to collaborate in this manner. The reason for this reluctance was the so-called free rider problem. According to the free rider problem, it was in the interest of any creditor bank, acting separately, to wait for the others to collaborate in a combinded debt reduction, and then not participate. It would then get the benefit of the rise in the secondary market value while avoiding any of the cost. This would put the free rider bank at a competitive advantage to the others. International banking, after all, is a very competitive business. To make a long story short, the Brady plan for Third World debt reduction consisted of a wide variety of extremely intricate, Rube Goldberg devices, using IMF, World Bank and Japanese funding, to induce the creditor banks to collaborate in concerted reductions of Third World debt.

"As cramming for the match-ups (debates) proceeded, however, Bush seemed disengaged, several aids said, and the image carried into the debates themselves. Except in the final debate, where he performed well, he sat passively as Clinton wooed the audience and Perot rattled on." NY Times, 11/29/92

The West, together with the Third World, forms a single "system", the world capitalist system and the Eastern bloc wants to join this system. Left wing white centrism maintained that the West can be expanded via a "Marshall plan" to absorb the East. Right wing white centrism maintained that the East would, if it submitted to IMF shock therapy, be able to successfully compete with the Third World for Western markets and capital.

It has to be emphasized here that the IMF could not treat the Eastern bloc countries differently than the Third World countries, however structurally different their economies were. It certainly could not be harsher on a poor non-white country than on a "middle income" white country. Also, the main reason for the economic collapse in the Eastern bloc was the collapse of the communist economic system. The effect of later reforms on this collapse is hard to determine at best. The reason for the political backlash to the IMF reforms is that they were treated as a panacea at the outset.

Konstanty Gebert, one of the founders of Solidarity, writing in *Peace and Democracy News,* Fall, 1990.

The Nation, 3/2/93.

In July of 1990, on the night that King Hussein of Jordan predicted a Middle east war on *Nightline*, but before Saddam invaded Kuwait, in telephone conversation with Palestinians in Jordan, the sentiment that we observed was, "The West has abandoned us. Saddam is a son of a bitch, but maybe he can give the West a kick in the ass!. What other hope is there?"

CAMBRIDGE FORECAST GROUP:

AMERICA'S TRAP OF INFORMATION CONTROL OVER JAPAN

http://www.cambridgeforecast.org/review.jpg
(Translation of Review from *Asahi Shinbun* 5/6)

AUTHORS:

Noboru Fujii, Lawrence Feiner, Richard Melson,
Muhammad Alwan

This book provides a new perspective on the dynamics of the world economy. I would recommend this book especially to teachers of social science at this time when the Japanese economy cannot be discussed without a global context. I agree with the book's assertion that we live in a time when we should think of economic growth in global terms, and that the narrow mindset of pursuing only Japanese economic growth must be avoided.

Despite the impression of the book's sensational title, if the theme dealt with in the book were to be summarized, it might be "The Reagan administration and the world economic crisis—its strategies for practical responses."

The book points out that seemingly independent events such as the accumulation of debt in the Third World, situations in the Middle East, U.S.-Soviet relations, and domestic American political activities are indeed structurally interrelated. Although the world view that emerges from this perspective is different from the so-called "common sense" interpretation of international relations, it is logical and consistent in its own way.

The themes discussed in this book center on the changes in the world economy since 1979 to this day and the responses to them by the Reagan administration. FRB chairman Volcker contained the inflation in the late 70's by controlling the money supply, and this policy led to higher interest rates which resulted in the very rapid accumulation of debt by third world countries. In order to solve this, the United States increased its own external debt, while opening its domestic market to third world countries, giving rise to the protectionism which exists today. The book doesn't lay blame on conspiracies of media control as the title suggests, but instead points out that, in the huge waves of structural change in world economy, the Reagan administration attempted to respond unilaterally, without coordination with industrial, OPEC and developing countries. The observation that the nature of the Reagan administration changed from grass roots conservatism to multi-national globalism is also interesting. This book severely criticizes some Japanese perspectives on world economy and U.S. policy which have become normative, and I found this very persuasive in its own right.

As in their previous work, World Economy/Big Prediction (Kappa publishing 1984), the authors base their long term view on the assumption that modernization of the developing world will be the engine of world economic growth in the future.

Even to a reader who doesn't agree with this prediction, this book should be stimulating. For example, it sees a connection between the invasion of Lebanon by the Israeli army in the spring of 1982 and the default by Mexico in the summer of the same year. A "hypothesis" like this is well worth our notice. It is this kind of strategic thinking that views and understands international situations as an organic whole, without being fooled by the flood of information from the mass media, that the Japanese need today, and with which the book wanted to provide readers.

Review from *Asahi Shinbun* in 5/86

Translated by *Columbia University Tutoring and Translation Agency* in 9/94.

ECONOMICS

CAMBRIDGE FORECAST GROUP:

AMERICA'S TRAP OF INFORMATION CONTROL OVER JAPAN

http://www.camJapanese
bridgeforecast.org/review.jpg
(Translation of Review from Asahi Shinbun 5/6)

AUTHORS:

Noboru Fujii, Lawrence Feiner, Richard Melson,
Muhammad Alwan

PUBLISHER: Hamano Publishing, Tokyo, Japan

COPYRIGHT: Cambridge Forecast Group, 1985

This book provides a new perspective on the dynamics of the world economy. I would recommend this book especially to teachers of social science at this time when the Japanese economy cannot be discussed without a global context. I agree with the book's assertion that we live in a time when we should think of economic growth in global terms, and that the narrow mindset of pursuing only Japanese economic growth must be avoided.

Despite the impression of the book's sensational title, if the theme dealt with in the book were to be summarized, it might be "The Reagan administration and the world economic crisis—its strategies for practical responses."

The book points out that seemingly independent events such as the accumulation of debt in the Third World, situations in the Middle East, U.S.-Soviet relations, and domestic American political activities are indeed structurally interrelated. Although the world view that emerges from this perspective is different from the so-called "common sense" interpretation of international relations, it is logical and consistent in its own way.

The themes discussed in this book center on the changes in the world economy since 1979 to this day and the responses to them by the Reagan administration. FRB chairman Volcker contained the inflation in the late 70's by controlling the money supply, and this policy led to higher interest rates which resulted in the very rapid accumulation of debt by third world countries. In order to solve this, the United States increased its own external debt, while opening its domestic market to third world countries, giving rise to the protectionism which exists today. The book doesn't lay blame on conspiracies of media control as the title suggests, but instead points out that, in the huge waves of structural change in world economy, the Reagan administration attempted to respond unilaterally, without coordination with industrial, OPEC and developing countries. The observation that the nature of the Reagan administration changed from grass roots conservatism to multi-national globalism is also interesting. This book severely criticizes some Japanese perspectives on world economy and U.S. policy which have become normative, and I found this very persuasive in its own right.

As in their previous work, World Economy/Big Prediction (Kappa publishing 1984), the authors base their longterm view on the assumption that modernization of the developing world will be the engine of world economic growth in the future.

Even to a reader who doesn't agree with this prediction, this book should be stimulating. For example, it sees a connection between the invasion of Lebanon by the Israeli army in the spring of 1982 and the default by Mexico in the summer of the same year. A "hypothesis" like this is well worth our notice. It is this kind of strategic thinking that views and understands international situations as an organic whole, without being fooled by the flood of information from the mass media, that the Japanese need today, and with which the book wanted to provide readers.

Review from Asahi Shinbun in 5/86

Translated by Columbia University Tutoring and Translation Agency in 9/94.

See extract below: